The Bhagavad Gita
in the Light of Kriya Yoga

Book Two

PARAMAHAMSA HARIHARANANDA

Based on Babaji, Lahiri Mahasaya and Shriyukteshwarji's original and authentic teachings of Kriya Yoga

Compiled and organized by
Swami Prajñanananda Giri

THAT IS THE PATH WHICH IS DIRECTED BY THE REALIZED

क्षणमिह सज्जन सङ्गतिरेका भवति भवार्णव तरणे नौका

Acknowledgments

We would like to offer our deepest love and thanks for the many volunteers who have participated in the production of this book. Their love and service to God and gurus has been exemplary.

Typing and correcting: Margot Borden, Ana McGroarty, Ruud Wierdsma, Jan Teegardin
Editing: Peter Bumpus and Little Ma
Cover design: Chip Weston
Original art: Karen Johnson
Introduction for Book One: Michael Winn

The cover illustration is a classical style of hand painting from Orissa, India. The scene from the Mahabharata depicts Lord Krishna addressing Arjuna regarding the entire realm of the manifestation of the human spirit. The dialogue between Arjuna and the Lord on the battle field is the Bhagavad Gita.

Edited, designed and produced by
Kriya Yoga Institute
P.O. Box 924615
Homestead, FL 33092-4615
U.S.A.

Dedication

I dedicate this book to all true seekers

Paramahamsa Hariharananda

Library of Congress Catalog Card Number:
ISBN 0-9639107-1-X
Printed in the United States of America

Introduction

The Bhagavad Gita, popularly called the Gita, is a divine message from the great master to an able disciple. The master, well-tuned to the core of spiritual life, leads the disciple in a slow, steady, continuous search toward the highest attainment of spiritual experience. In the beginning, the disciple is reluctant and hesitant to follow the spiritual path of self-discipline and self-mastery, but to succeed, the disciple must endeavor to eliminate his ego and proceed in the holy company of the divine master, his guru and preceptor.

The Bhagavad Gita is a spiritual, philosophical, and moral masterpiece, a handbook that true seekers can read, follow, and practice, irrespective of their religious beliefs or way of life. Like the vital air, the breath, the Bhagavad Gita is for everyone.

The Bhagavad Gita expresses the essence of the Vedas as well as the spiritual doctrines incorporated in the Upanishads. In fact, the prayer at the beginning of the Bhagavad Gita is a famous verse quoted from the Vaishnaviya Tantrasara:

sarvopaniṣado gāvo dogdhā gopālanandanaḥ
pārtho vatsaḥ sudhīr bhoktā dugdham gītāmṛtam mahat

which means, "The Upanishads are the cows and Shri Krishna is the milker; Arjuna is the calf and the Bhagavad Gita is the milk of the cows. People with a pure intellect drink this milk of immortality." All people who have the desire to grow, to be nourished, and to become stronger can enjoy the health-giving milk of the Bhagavad Gita.

The essence of the Upanishads is contained in four great pronouncements, which in Sanskrit are called the *mahavakyas*:

1. *Prajñanam brahma*: "Wisdom is Brahman (the Absolute God)." (Aitareya Upanishad 3:1:3, Rig Veda)
2. *Aham brahmasmi*: "I am Brahman." (Brihadaranyaka Upanishad 1:4:10, Yajur Veda)
3. *Tattvamasi*: "That thou art." (Chhandogya Upanishad 6:8:7, Sama Veda)
4. *Ayamatma brahma*: "This soul is Brahman." (Mandukya Upanishad 2, Atharva Veda)

Although short, the *mahavakyas* are profound. Among these four Vedic dictums, the third is called *upadesha vakya*—the instruction pronouncement; the other three are called *anubhavavakyas*—the pronouncements after experience or realization. The instruction pronouncement is the divine instruction of the great master to the able and worthy disciple.

The *upadesha vakya* is only three words: *tat* (That), *tvam* (thou), *asi* (art), which mean, "You are That." The meaning of these three words is explained and elaborated upon nicely in the Bhagavad Gita in the form of *upadesha* (instruction) from the Lord to His disciple Arjuna. This instruction imparts three levels of spiritual upliftment; each level contains six steps, which become six chapters. Through each one of the three levels, one is to ascend to the peak of spiritual experience; therefore, the Bhagavad Gita is usually divided into *tri-satakas*—three sections of six chapters each.

This *upadesha vakya* contains the same three fundamental concepts that are addressed in the three sections of the Bhagavad Gita:

1. Chapters 1 to 6: "Who are you?" (*tvam* = you) "You" means every individual self, considered by most people to be a separate entity.
2. Chapters 7 to 12: "Who am I?" (*tat* = That) Here, "I" represents, the Lord, the supreme. What is the relation between the individual self and the cosmic Self, God?
3. Chapters 13 to 18: "I and You are one." (*asi* = are). Discovering unity in diversity—the eternal relationship between creation and creator.

Each individual thinks of himself as a body endowed with attributes such as gender, age, color, caste, language, intelligence, and so on. But one is not the body; one is beyond all the limitations that cause bondage and suffering. The spiritual journey is from darkness to light, from falsehood to truth, from death to immortality.

In the first six chapters, the Lord explained to Arjuna the perishable nature of the body and imperishable nature of the soul, and how one can turn one's attention inward towards God by the practice of meditation. It also explains karma, right action, which brings awareness of one's own state. This section of the Bhagavad Gita starts with Arjuna's grief and ends with instructions about meditation. In essence, this section teaches: "O Arjuna, You are not the body, the mind, the intellect, or the ego, you are not male or female, young or old. You are the imperishable soul." This answers the question posed by the middle word of *tattvamasi—tvam*: "Who are you?"

In the second part of the Bhagavad Gita, through his discourse with Arjuna, the Lord answers the second question, "Who am I?" which means, "Who is God, the Lord?" Thus, Chapters 7 through 12 reveal the meaning behind the first word of the *upadesha vakya—tat* (That). Starting with a chapter entitled "The Yoga of Knowledge and Applied Knowledge" and ending with the "Yoga of Divine Love," the Lord explains His own divine glories, and through His love and grace, the Lord also ultimately reveals His universal cosmic form and His unique compassion and care to Arjuna.

Remember, Arjuna had doubts that were expressed and addressed in Chapter 4 of the Bhagavad Gita, Verse 4. Just as it requires two legs to enable us to walk, the knowledge of the self, which is knowledge of the Lord, is possible only through a two-step process. The first step is self-endeavor, the second is divine grace. Effort is first—to receive the grace of God, one must make oneself ready and worthy. Divine grace, which is available equally to all, in all abundance, follows.

Spiritual truth is not a matter for debate or discussion.

It remains only within the domain of practice and experience. Practice brings perfection. People read and analyze a lot. But self-analysis, self-discipline, and self-mastery are necessary for a spiritual life.

In this section God states, "Arjuna! Do not view Me as a man with all his inherent limitations. I am the Lord endowed with all divine glories, which you can perceive thanks to your sincere desire and My grace."

The third part of the Bhagavad Gita explains the third word of the *upadesha vakya—asi* (are). It reveals the relationship between the individual self and the cosmic spirit—the eternal unity, which in Sanskrit is *so-ham* or *aham-sah.* For example, imagine that God is gold and each of His creations is a gold ornament. Gold appears more beautiful when it bears the name and form of ornaments because ego, ignorance, and arrogance distract one from seeing the eternal beauty of formless gold. In the same way, if one looks beyond the beauty of God's creations, the unity of the individual self and the formless God can be perceived. Within the experience of this unity, all suffering and unhappiness disappear as darkness disappears with the rising of the shining sun. In conclusion, the Lord says, "O Arjuna! Through your action, knowledge and love, realize the eternal unity which is the path to peace, bliss and joy."

The three divisions of the Bhagavad Gita are also made on the basis of content that describes three types of yoga: *karma* (action), *jñana* (knowledge), and *bhakti* (divine love). Furthermore, the threefold division can be classified as *yoga, yogamaya,* and Yogeshwar. *Yoga* means self-discipline through right action and meditation. *Yogamaya* means that through meditation one has many experiences and may even develop *siddhis* (powers); this is called *vibhuti*—beholding the divine glory and many holy visions. But, one should never forget the supreme goal of self-realization—merging into Yogeshwar (the Lord of yoga), God, the indwelling spirit. Don't be satisfied with a little experience; true happiness requires the state of Yogeshwar—merging with the cosmic spirit. The three aspects of yoga and of divine life are nicely explained in the Bhagavad Gita in three phases, which are the *tri-sataka*: Chapters 1 to 6, Chapters 7 to 12, and Chapters 13 to 18.

Always remember that each chapter of the Bhagavad Gita is a step in one's spiritual journey. One must be very careful and enterprising on this pilgrimage until the goal of the journey is reached—the freedom from all doubt and confusion, a flood of love and devotion.

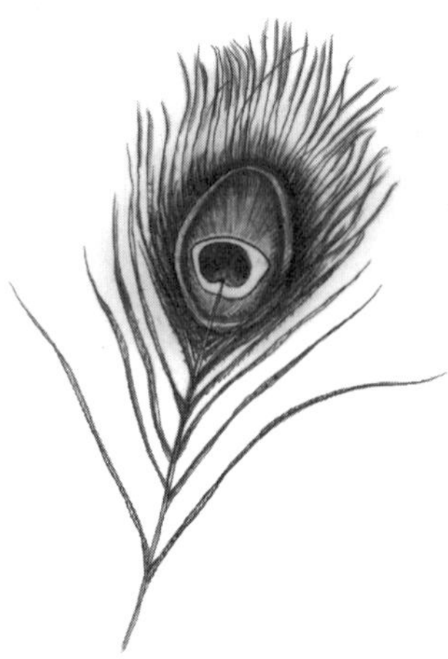

Chapter 7

Jñana vijñana yoga

The Yoga of Knowledge & Applied Knowledge

Introduction

Madgata chitta: "Blessed are they, whose minds are always devoted and dedicated to Me," spoke the Lord in his conclusive remarks explaining meditation and self-mastery in the Bhagavad Gita 6:47. Thus, the Lord ignited the flame of knowledge, self-inquiry, and self-discovery in Arjuna, the seeker. Every spiritual seeker is like a lamp ready to be lit by the illuminated master's divine fire of spiritual knowledge.

All people want to know more and more. No one wants to be ignorant. Inquisitiveness and the desire to know and learn are easily detected even in children—in their constant questioning and searching. Ultimately, everybody wants continuous peace, bliss, and joy—the end of all knowledge. This is the real quest of every person, but it remains unidentified.

During growth and evolution, a child gathers a lot of information. Most of the information comes from those whose faculty of intellect is more developed are able to acquire more information. In the scriptural view, this kind of information is called *paroksha jñana*—indirect knowledge. For such knowledge, one needs the help of the mind (*manas*), intellect (*buddhi*), memory (*chitta*), and the sense organs (*indriyas*). These are called the inner instruments. Whatever one learns in this world through the senses is called *aparavidya*—indirect information. Information is the first step, transformation is the next.

In spiritual life, indirect knowledge of the self is available through *shastra vakyas*, the instruction of the scriptures, and *guru vakya*, the instruction of the masters that is based on their experiences. Each disciple must undergo self-study in the first stage of spiritual life, using the scriptures and discourses heard from his own guru preceptor. This process creates a thirst for one's own unfolding (*anubhava*).

Borrowed wealth is not an asset, it is a liability. When borrowed wealth is used in a productive manner, it can become an asset in the sense that it can contribute to one's wealth. This principle applies in both material and spiritual life. The peak of achievement in material activities is reached by great scientists or other successful people whose constant endeavor and enterprise "dis–covers" their desired object. This is called *vijñana,* applied knowledge. For example, a medical student collects knowledge through education, but the application of his knowledge as a qualified doctor in practice makes him more efficient. This is the difference between *jñana* (knowledge) and *vijñana* (applied knowledge).

Knowledge is the first step, and wisdom is the last. In Sanskrit, knowledge is *jñana*, but wisdom is *prajñana*, the ultimate experience. Knowledge is information due to inquiry, and *prajñana* (wisdom) is the end of every inquiry—establishing the truth. In between these two there is the bridge called *vijñana* (applied knowledge). *Jñana* means collected information; *vijñana*, the journey according to the available or acquired knowledge, and *prajñana* is the end of the journey, reaching the goal, the end of all efforts and trials. So, on the path of realization, one proceeds from *jñana* to *vijñana*, and then becomes established in *prajñana*.

In this chapter, the Lord begins to explain "Who am I?" This chapter is called *jñana-vijñana yoga*, the "Yoga of Knowledge and Applied Knowledge."

Verse 1

śrībhagavān uvāca
mayy āsaktamanāḥ pārtha
yogam yuñjan madāśrayaḥ
asamśayam samagram mām
yathā jñāsyasi tac chṛṇu

Translation

The Lord said:
O Partha! (Arjuna) Please listen to Me with careful attention. If a person practices yoga with deep concentration, with his mind attached to Me, and with absolute dependence on Me, he will be able to know My real nature without any shadow of a doubt.

Metaphorical Interpretation

The Lord is explaining that the ordinary human mind is always absorbed in sense objects; it is never idle and cannot remain idle. But if someone wants soul culture and quick spiritual evolution, the mind must be detached from the five lower spinal centers and the associated sense-objects. The seeker must attach his mind to the Lord, who is the soul inside the cranium. This is the meaning of *mayy asakta manah*, the mind attached to Me, the indwelling self.

The Lord addresses Arjuna as Partha, a name for someone who has the strength to control the mind. Partha has the ability to see the two as One, which is the state of yoga. Previously (in Chapter 6), the Lord spoke in detail about how to practice meditation, where to sit, how to sit, how to concentrate, and so forth. Now, the Lord describes the next stage of spiritual life, *yoga-yuñjan,* which means to continue the practice of yoga and to meditate. Now, He explains that yoga is a constant perception of unity, during every breath and in every moment.

As a result of yoga practice one attains the state of *madashraya*. *Madashraya* means to love God and to take refuge in Him. God is all-pervading. He is holding everything together like the string inside the beads of a rosary. Only by the power of God, does the breath go in and out. Without breath, there is no life; without Him, there is nothing. When one practices yoga, one becomes attached to the Lord, perceives the presence of God, and can feel the protecting power of God in every breath.

Darkness and light cannot remain together—where there is light, there is no darkness. Through the practice of Kriya meditation, one gradually becomes merged in God consciousness. The intelligent practice of yoga with love and God consciousness dispels doubt, confusion, and chaos; it is the root of enlightenment. Meditation is the cause of spiritual wisdom. But there are different stages of perception, divinity, and light. Informative knowledge is indirect perception, but after some practice, consciousness, then super consciousness, cosmic consciousness, and wisdom will provide direct perception of the oneness with the supreme almighty father.

Therefore, the Lord is saying to Arjuna, "O Arjuna! You are pure and divine. You are not entangled with evils; rather, you have the ability to fight all the negative qualities of life. Keep your mind always in the pituitary and in the fontanel and be inwardly detached from the lower centers; this will make you free from all doubts and the knots of ignorance will be opened. Practice Kriya with love and faith; then you will perceive the divine glory. This is *upasana*, to sit near the soul."

Verse 2

jñānam te 'ham savijñānam
idam vakṣyāmy aśeṣataḥ
yaj jñātvā ne 'ha bhūyo 'nyaj
jñātavyam avaśiṣyate

Translation

I shall reveal this knowledge to you completely, with intimate and inner experience. Knowing this, nothing else remains to be known.

Metaphorical Interpretation

This verse is extremely beautiful. The Lord Himself has assumed the role of the divine master, the guru. When a seeker sincerely seeks the truth, God manifests Himself to this person. The guru is the personification of the unmanifest God. In the Guru Gita it is said, *mantra-mulam gurur vakyam*: "The words of the master are the *mantra*, the holy scripture."

The Lord is telling Arjuna, "O Arjuna! You are my loving student. Most people in the world are extrovert; their minds chase after the material world; they pursue many things, and they do not know the Truth. But you, Arjuna, have a deep desire for soul culture and self-realization."

The Mundaka Upanishad (1:1:3) asks, *kasmin nu bhagavo vijñāte sarvam idam vijñātam bhavati iti:* "Through what being known, does all become known?" The answer is that knowledge of the self is supreme. If gold is known, then all gold ornaments are known. If the soul is known, then everything is revealed. The Bhagavad Gita (6:22) highlights this divine state. *Jñana* (knowledge) is the first step, and *vijñana* (spiritual experience) is the second step. *Jñana* is indirect information. *Vijñana*—the super-conscious and cosmic-conscious states—is direct perception.

For self-realization, formal education is not so important. Although Shri Ramakrishna Paramahamsa did not read any scripture in his life, it is clearly seen that the essence of all holy books was on his tongue. God, having created everything, remains everywhere in the atom form. If one can realize this atom through deep meditation, one can know everything. Omniscience is achieved through deep meditation.

Shri Krishna, the manifestation of God, is speaking from the state of cosmic consciousness: "O Arjuna! I am telling not only you, but all people, if one remains in the north of the body, in the fontanel and even above it, he will reach the divine state of super consciousness and cosmic consciousness. He will become free from all bondage and negative qualities. He will achieve constant liberation."

Verse 3

manuṣyāṇām sahasreṣu
kaścid yatati siddhaye
yatatām api siddhānām
kaścin mām vetti tattvataḥ

Translation

Among thousands of people, rarely does one carefully try to attain perfection or realization; among those striving and succeeding, rarely does one know Me in reality.

Metaphorical Interpretation

Self knowledge and God-realization are the birthright of every human being, but as a result of wrong heredity and environment, and due to delusion, illusion, and error, people are extremely extrovert and sense-oriented. Their minds are always running after sense objects. They are not at peace. Their lives are tortured. They think that only sense objects can bring happiness. Sense attraction and attachment hide their divine nature.

Thus, so engrossed in the material world, there is no time for self-inquiry. It is forgotten that the soul is the sole doer and is constantly creating the breath, day and night. Love and thanks are not offered to the indwelling soul or to God.

Most people are like this—they look like people, but in reality, they are subhuman.

Among thousands of people, only a few fortunate ones have the desire to know the indwelling self. How does one know the indwelling self? What is the way? Yoga is the real way for soul culture and God perception, and real yoga is perceiving God's presence in every moment. Thus, yoga is the achievement of perfection already existing in man.

Often, those fortunate people who have the desire to perceive the divine self go to different teachers and try to practice different techniques. They meditate with the five sense organs, with emotion, hallucination, singing, and chanting. But in this verse, the Lord speaks of the real way, *yatati siddhaye*, which means to achieve perfection by striving for self-discipline. Human life is very short and everything passes quickly. Those who strive sincerely, who try to become more sincere by constantly fixing their attention on the top, who try to be free from doubts and who try to kindle the light of God's existence, slowly, they will reach perfection. Such sincere and fortunate seekers are rare.

The Lord speaks of two stages of spiritual practice. The first is *yatati siddhaye,* meditation through self-discipline, which is action. Action is the seed of knowledge. But what is true action? It is *prana karma*, the practice of Kriya. When one practices Kriya sincerely, one prepares for the second stage. Those who can reach *paravastha*, the formless meditation, and who can enter the second stage are very rare.

The second stage is *mam vetti tattvatah,* to know God in reality, in His essence. This is not knowledge (*jñana*), it is *vijñana* and *prajñana*. This is the state of wisdom. Wisdom cannot be perceived by the five sense organs, but it can be perceived by entering into the atom point. In this stage, the rarest of the rare seekers perceives *vasudeva sarvam iti*, everything pervaded by formless God. God is perceived everywhere—in the ether, air, fire, water, earth, plants, trees, insects, animals, and man, in friends as well as in enemies.

This state is also called *isha vasyam idam sarvam*, God's presence everywhere (Isha Upanishad, Mantra 1). Such a person is called *mahatma*, a great soul. He is free from delusion, illusion, and error. He is not only rare, but also fortunate.

Verse 4

bhūmir āpo 'nalo vāyuḥ
kham mano buddhir eva ca
ahamkāra itī 'yam me
bhinnā prakṛtir aṣṭadhā

Translation

Earth, water, fire, air, ether (vacuum), mind, intellect, and ego are the eightfold divisions of My nature.

Metaphorical Interpretation

Man searching for God is like ice searching for water. Ice does not realize that it is entirely comprised of water. Similarly, man does not realize that God is all-pervading. The universe and God are one. Everything manifest in the universe is mother nature, *prakriti*. The body is also the manifestation of mother nature. Every human body is a little universe, a microcosm. In every part of the body, there is a play of the indwelling self, the presence of God's power.

Whatever is seen or perceived in the universe, in mother nature, or even in the body nature, all belong to the eightfold principles. Nature is earth, water, fire, air, ether, mind, intellect, and ego. To understand this eightfold nature, it is helpful to consider the description of creation in the Taittiriya Upanishad (2:1:1): *etasmād ātmana ākāśas sambhūtaḥ . . .*: "Creation started with the manifestation of nature. It is a descent: ego, intellect, mind, ether, air, fire, water, and earth."

(Also see the Katha Upanishad, 1:3:10–11).

Every human body consists of the five elements, and each human life is regulated by the eightfold nature. This eightfold nature is represented by the six centers in the spine and the brain:

1. The *muladhara* chakra (coccygeal center) is the earth element. The earth element contains the characteristics of smell, which are present in the nose, the power of smell. The anus, *payn,* is also activated by the earth element.
2. The *svadhisthana* chakra (sacral center) represents the water element. Three fourths of each human body is water. Water also dominates the tongue, taste, and the sex organ (*upastha*).
3. In the *manipura* chakra (lumbar center), the fire element presides. The fire element is in the eyes, the power of vision, as well as in *vak*, the power of speech.
4. The element of air is in the *anahata* chakra (dorsal center), which regulates the touch sensation and the hands.
5. In the *visuddha* chakra (cervical center) is the vacuum, ether, which predominates in the ears, the power to hear, and the legs.

Apart from these five elements in the five lower centers, there are three present in the *ajña* chakra (pituitary): *manas* (6) *buddhi* (7), and *ahamkara* (8). *Manas* is mind, *buddhi*, the intellect, and *ahamkara*, the ego. In the yogic scriptures it is said that the mind is associated with the moon, the intellect with the sun, and the ego with darkness. When one concentrates in the *ajña* chakra, one perceives the light of the moon, the light of the sun, and darkness. These three perceptions are associated with these three natures.

To understand the eightfold nature, one must constantly perceive that the power of God, *purusha*, the indwelling self, is the cause of all activities in nature, *prakriti*.

Verse 5

apare 'yam itas tv anyām
prakṛtim viddhi me parām
jīvabhūtām mahābāho
yaye 'dam dhāryate jagat

Translation

O Mahabahu! (mighty-armed Arjuna) This is My lower, material nature. Apart from this, I have My higher, spiritual nature, which is the soul, by which the whole universe is sustained.

Metaphorical Interpretation

The Lord addresses Arjuna as Mahabahu, which simply means "mighty-armed." Arjuna has extreme strength. The arms and hands are the organs of action and are dominated by the air element. One who has thorough control over breathing, who has mastered the art of breath control, is Mahabahu.

The Lord explains the two aspects of nature: *para* and *apara*. *Para* is the spiritual and higher qualities. *Apara* is the lower and material. *Apara prakriti* or material nature is extrovert, restless, and kinetic. *Para* is introvert, silent, and static. Material nature is the cause of all extrovert activities and ultimately of bondage, while the *para* nature enables liberation.

In the scriptures it is said that although the five centers and the five gross elements, mind, intellect, and ego (the eightfold nature) are very dominant—all this is *jagat*, the material universe. The meaning of *jagat* is *gamyate gachhate iti,* that which is constantly changing. This *jagat* or material universe is sustained by *para prakriti*, the spiritual nature. What is this *para prakriti*? How does it sustain, uphold, and maintain the universe?

In the yogic scriptures it is said: *prāṇena dhāryate lokaḥ sarvam prāṇayam jagat. Prana*, the vital breath, sustains the universe and is the manifestation of the whole universe. This will be extremely clear if one thinks of his own life and activities. Remember, each human body is *jagat*, a little universe. The body, cells, atoms, tissues, and so forth change continuously. *Prana* is the spiritual qualities in this constantly changing body.

Every human body can be divided into two parts. From the *ajña* chakra down, the eightfold nature predominates, namely *apara prakriti*. From the *ajña* chakra to the fontanel is *para prakriti* or the spiritual nature, which is superior. *Apara prakriti*, material nature, is *maya*: delusion, illusion, and error. *Para prakriti*, spiritual nature, is disillusion. Each gross breath goes into the body and is transformed and merged into the vital breath, *prana*. The gross breath goes to the lungs, the subtle breath circulates in the whole body, and the finest or causal breath merges with the inner vital breath. This is called *sthira prana*, tranquil vital breath.

Our material nature is the cause of restlessness, bondage, and attachment, while the spiritual nature is the way to realization and liberation. Through this spiritual nature, one can enter the stage of *samadhi*. This duality of nature is explained in the Mundaka Upanishad (3:1:1–2) with the allegory of two birds in the tree. One bird is eating the fruit of the tree, sweet and sour, happy and unhappy. The other bird is not eating; he is remaining constantly detached.

When a person practices the Kriya Yoga technique and rises above the propensities of the lower natures, he becomes free from mind, thought, intellect, and ego. He is pure. He is merged in God consciousness. His breath is so feeble that warm breath does not come out of the nostrils. In this state, the true nature of reality is revealed.

Verse 6

etadyonīni bhūtāni
sarvāṇī 'ty upadhāraya
aham kṛtsnasya jagataḥ
prabhavaḥ pralayas tathā

Translation

Know clearly that all living beings are born from these sources, the twofold nature. I am the source of origin of this entire world as well as its dissolution.

Metaphorical Interpretation

When the wind blows, there are waves and ripples in the lake. The lake and the wind are the external cause of all waves. Waves are born in water, live in water, and merge back into water. The union of these two—*vari,* water and *vayu*, air—creates waves, ripples, and bubbles. Similarly, the *para prakriti* spiritual nature and the *apara prakriti* material nature are called the *yoni*, the place of origin. This *yoni* or place of origin is a beautiful concept. Many things are born in the external universe, including the human body; many thoughts are born in the mind; different perceptions are generated in the sense organs. Sight is born in the eyes, sound is born in the ears, smell in the nose, taste in the mouth, and the touch sensation is born on the skin. Speech is also born in the tongue; the sex sensation is born in the sexual organs. Every part of the body is like a *yoni*, which literally means "womb"—the place of creation—from which many perceptions, thoughts, and feelings are born. Not only are they born there, but they remain alive for a time, and then they are dissolved. The Lord is telling us that the union of two natures, spiritual and material, are the source of these many births.

The gross body, made of five elements, and the mental body, made from mind, thought, and ego, make up the eightfold material nature. The breath is the spiritual nature. The joining of these two natures, body and breath, is the place of creation: nature is the place of creation. Without the body, the breath cannot create anything. Similarly, while breathing out, the body is dead, no creation is possible. The spiritual source, *spiritus*, the breath, is masculine; nature is feminine. Creation requires the presence of both feminine and masculine.

The Lord is saying, "O Arjuna! I am the real cause, the seed of all creation. Without Me, the breath will not flow through the nostrils. Without the breath, the material natures of the gross and mental body—the six centers from *muladhara* to *ajña*—cannot be activated. Nature is the field and I am the seed of all creation. Everything, including every living being comes from Me, lives in Me, and ultimately dissolves in Me. Parameshvara, the supreme Lord, is the cause of *prakriti*, the two natures, procreation—everything."

Verse 7

mattaḥ parataram nā 'nyat
kimcid asti dhanamjaya
mayi sarvam idam protam
sūtre maṇigaṇā iva

Translation

Nothing exists which is superior to Me, O Dhanamjaya (Arjuna)! Everything clusters together like pearls on the thread that is in Me.

Metaphorical Interpretation

The Vedas, the Upanishads, the Holy Bible, and the Koran declare that there is only one God. *Ekam eva advitiya brahma*: "When nature is unmanifest, God is known as Brahman, but when nature develops, He is Parameshvara, the supreme Lord." His divine nature *prakriti* is also called *maya*, and His nature is spiritual as well as material. Nature also has triple qualities. Everything is created, preserved, and dissolved from this nature and from God Himself.

"O Arjuna! There is nothing superior to Me. I am the supreme Self, the supreme person. I am the sole doer of everything. I am both positive and negative. I am the conductor of *maya—prakriti*."

People are extrovert. They are attracted by external beauty. They cannot easily penetrate into the veil of nature's splendor. So, the Lord addresses Arjuna as Dhanamjaya, which means the conqueror of wealth. What is the real wealth of a person? Ordinary people consider money, gold, land, houses, cars, bank balances (properties of the *muladhara* chakra), physical beauty (*svadhisthana*), food and strength (*manipura*), and so forth—the qualities of the lower five centers—to be their wealth. But they do not know that the real treasure is the breath. Breath is our true wealth. The spiritual treasure of a person resides inside the cranium. Without the soul and the breath, man has nothing. One who has thorough control over the breath, who can easily go into the pituitary, is called Dhanamjaya.

The Lord gives the example of a rosary of pearls to explain the secret doctrine of spirituality. It is undoubtedly beautiful. People look at some attractive pearls and they are attracted and enchanted, but they do not see the hidden thread that keeps the pearls together. Without the thread, the pearls cannot be assembled into a beautiful rosary. Pearls are *prakriti*. The hidden thread, *sutra*, is not an ordinary thread; it is *brahma sutra*, the thread of the divine. The breath is the thread of God that keeps life joined to the body, along with a rosary of thoughts and activities.

In the rosary, there is a distinction between the thread and the pearls; yet in reality, everything is God. God is hidden in every thing and in every being. This thread is also called *prana sutra*, the link of breath. When a person becomes conscious of his breath, night and day and in every activity, he will be conscious of God and ultimately will get liberation. This is the supreme teaching of Kriya Yoga.

Verse 8

raso 'ham apsu kaunteya
prabhā 'smi śaśisūryayoḥ

praṇavaḥ sarvavedeṣu
śabdaḥ khe pauruṣam nṛṣu

Translation

O Son of Kunti (Arjuna)! I am the taste of water. I am the brilliance in the moon and sun. I am the *aum* sound, *pranava* in all the Vedas. I am the sound in the ether. I am the vitality of all human beings.

Metaphorical Interpretation

God is omnipresent, omniscient, and omnipotent. The entire universe is God's creation. God has created *prakriti*, nature. From nature, by God's power, we can see different things. It is possible to find the glory of God everywhere, God is present in everything, in every being, even in every gold ornament. *Isha vasyam idam sarvam yat kim cha jagatyam jagat*: "God is in everything, no matter how insignificant a thing may seem." (Isha Upanishad, Mantra 1). But as a result of ignorance, many people cannot perceive the presence of God.

In this verse and in the next four, the Lord explains the subtle presence of God in everything, that He is the shelter of everything, that every object exists only in Him. The Lord also explains that man can perceive God's presence and glory in every past and current thought, word, and action if he can meditate according to the guidance the realized master and achieve divine vision.

In these five verses, the Lord speaks of His sixteen glories:

1. *Rasah aham apsu*: "I am the taste of the water."

   I am the water principle, the taste of water, the principle in the tongue. I am present in the *svadhisthana* chakra.

2. *Prabhasmi shashisuryayoh*: "I am the brilliance in the moon and the sun."

I am the light that illumines the sun and the moon. Without Me, the sun and moon cannot shine. Inside the human body, the *ida nadi* is the sun and the *pingala nadi* is the moon. Their activities are done by the power of God. When one comes up to the pituitary, one perceives divine illumination. That illumination is also from Me.

3. *Pranavah sarva vedeshu*: "I am *pranava* in all the Vedas."

   I am *aum*, in every sense perception, in the knowledge of man, and even in every speech coming from the mouth of a human being. "A" is the formless power of God. If someone perceives hunger, this is in the astral plane, which is "U." If this person communicates to others that he is hungry by the gross body, this is "M." The three bodies together are AUM. Veda is from the root *vid*, which means to know. All knowledge and perception is *aum*, which is possible by the three bodies: causal, astral, and physical.

4. *Shabdah khe*: "I am the sound in the ether."

   Sound comes from the ether. If there is no ether, there is no sound. Every sound that man hears comes from God. When one rises above the vacuum center and enters the ethereal plane, one is able to hear the divine sound.

5. *Paurusham nrishu*: "I am the glory or manliness of human beings."

   A person who is run by the ego thinks that it is he who is doing everything, but the vitality or the capability to work in each human being is the power of God. If God does not breathe, man cannot work.

Verse 9

puṇyo gandhaḥ pṛthivyām ca
tejaś cā 'smi vibhāvasau

jīvanam sarvabhūteṣu
tapaś cā 'smi tapasviṣu

Translation

I am the pure fragrance of the earth, I am the brightness in fire, I am the life in all being, I am the penance of the ascetics.

Metaphorical Interpretation

6. *Punyo gandhah prithivyam*: "I am the pure or holy fragrance of the earth."

The *muladhara* chakra is the earth center. The perfume one smells from the flower is perceived by the nose, where the element of earth is active. Everyone knows that there are odors from other centers as well. There is odor in the coccyx or anus, the smell of urine, and so forth in the sex center; and the smell of food and drink in the food center. Smell is transmitted by the air. There are fifty types of air representing different propensities in man. There is the smell of anger, ego, pride, or cruelty in the heart center. There is an odor in the cervical area, the religion center. All smells are perceived through the faculty of breath from the pituitary and the fontanel. All smells are the smell of God—that is why they are holy and pure.

7. *Tejash cha asmi vibhavasau*: "I am the brilliance of the sun."

Here "the sun" is not the sun of our planetary system, rather, it is the soul sun, *atmasurya*. We get our strength from this soul sun. If the soul sun does not inhale, then we have no strength, vitality, or vigor. In the *Gayatri* mantra, people pray to the sun. This is the sun that gives illumination even to the stars, the planets, and our planetary sun. This is the Sun that gives brilliance to the body through the seven centers.

8. *Jivanam sarva bhuteshu*: "I am the life of all beings."

God is the life breath of all living beings. Air is life. This air enters the body by the living power of God. Plants, animals, and humans are all breathing beings. Their breath is the breath of God. Only rational spiritual people can realize this. Those who meditate and practice Kriya Yoga know how this *prana* or vital breath holds life in the body.

9. *Tapash cha asmi tapasvishu*: "I am the penance of the ascetics.

   The real meaning of *tapas* is not to undertake strenuous austerities, but simply to perceive the power of God. God maintains life in the body so that the body temperature, *tapas*, is there. This is the soul fire. Every breath is an oblation to the soul fire. Body heat is maintained due to the combustion of oxygen with other substances. *Tapas* means to offer love with every breath. This is meditation—the technique for going beyond the mind. If one searches the power of God with a very slow and feeble breath, he is performing the real *tapasya*, the real penance.

Verse 10

bījam mām sarvabhūtānām
viddhi pārtha sanātanam
buddhir buddhimatām asmi
tejas tejasvinām aham

Translation

O Partha (Arjuna, son of Pritha), know that I am the eternal seed of all beings. I am the intelligence of the intelligent. I am the luster (glory) of the glorious.

Metaphorical Interpretation

10. *Bijam mam sarvabhutanam...sanatanam*: "I am the eternal seed of all beings."

Seed in Sanskrit is *bija* or *vija*. If this is reversed it becomes *jiva*, which means living being. God is the eternal seed of all living beings. *Vija* and *jiva* are one. The seed and the tree are one. A seed has the power to create a tree and ultimately to create numerous seeds, so it is eternal. To say that God is the seed of all beings means that God is the cause of all creation.

Without a seed, there can be no plant, animal, or human being. The seed is the essence of creation and life. God gives the power of procreation. Everything, copulation, conception, and creation are possible only through breath. If there is no breath, creation is not possible. (See the Bhagavad Gita 14:3–4)

11. *Buddhir buddhimatam asmi*: "I am the intelligence of the intelligent."

The play of the mind is below the *ajña* chakra, and a little above the *ajña* chakra is the place of *buddhi*. Ordinarily, people are engrossed in the lower centers. They remain ignorant; they are far away from Truth. But those who know how to control the breath, who can bring their awareness up into the pituitary and above, and who can remain in *paravastha*, they are truly intelligent. God is the source of divine intelligence.

12. *Tejas tejasvinam-aham*: "I am the luster of the lustrous."

What is the luster, the glory, of man? Strength of mind, courage, and the power of yoga and meditation are *tejas*—glory. This type of enthusiasm is unshakable. This is a divine quality. This strength, this glory, truly belongs to the soul. Without the power of God, the human body becomes dead and lifeless. "O, son of Kunti," says the Lord, "with your divine intelligence, please understand My glory."

Verse 11

balam balavatām cā 'ham
kāmarāgavivarjitam

dharmāviruddho bhūteṣu
kāmo 'smi bharatarṣabha

Translation

O best of the Bharatas, I am the strength of the strong, devoid of passion and attachment. I am the desire in all beings that does not conflict with law and morality.

Metaphorical Interpretation

"O Arjuna! You are the best of the Kauravas and the Pandavas because you are truly intelligent. You chose to sit near Me (the soul) in this body chariot, and you have the strength to fight the negative. Arjuna, you must clearly know that I am the strength of the strong, free from passion and attachment."

In this verse, there are four words which must be clearly understood: *bala, kama, raga,* and *dharma.*

Bala is strength. People have a lot of ego related to the strength in the body such as physical strength (animal strength), the strength of their sexual capacity, strength of digestive power, strength of monetary possession, strength of mind, and so forth. But the real strength, *bala*, is the power of the soul, which is spiritual strength. This strength, vitality, energy, agility, activity can be truly divine if it is free from *kama* (passion) and *raga* (attachment).

What is *kama*? Here, the word *kama* is used in two ways. First, "I am the strength devoid of *kama*", where *kama* means the passion to get and to possess that which a man does not have. This is a lower propensity of the human mind. This passion is endless. Second, "I am also man's *kama* for morality and principle"; in this context, *kama* is the desire of the divine will.

Kama means to acquire that which one does not have, but *raga* means to possess and to be attached to the things one already has in hand. The lower five centers are full of these ambitions, but the higher centers in the pituitary and the fontanel are free from such human propensities. Strength devoid of passion and attachment increases with meditation and spiritual practice. If a person practices techniques like Kriya Yoga, then great inner strength and spiritual power develop.

Dharma ordinarily means "righteousness", but in reality it refers to "that which upholds." Breath upholds life in the body. To love breath is *dharma*.

13. *Balam balavatam chaham*: "I am the strength of the strong."

"O Arjuna! I am the spiritual strength, which is pure and free from passion and attachment. This is called yogic power and the strength of the indwelling self."

14. *Kamaragavivarjitam:* "I am devoid of passion and attachment." *Dharma aviruddho bhuteshu kamo asmi:* "I am the desire in all beings that does not conflict with law and morality."

Shri Krishna is saying, "I am the desire in all beings that does not conflict with law and morality. I am *kama* in the spiritual person. I am the holy man's desire to meditate and to be liberated, giving a strong will for pursuit of soul culture and spiritual evolution." This *kama* (desire) brings liberation, while, *kama* (passion) is the cause of suffering and bondage. In this verse, there is also the phrase, *dharma aviruddho bhuta,* which describes a person who is always seeking truth through breath control. Breath is the *dharma* that holds life in the body. The spiritual person does not misuse or abuse his breath.

Verse 12

ye cai 'va sāttvikā bhāvā
rājasās tāmasāś ca ye
matta eve 'ti tān viddhi
na tv aham teṣu te mayi

Translation

I am the creative source of qualities such as *sattva* (spiritual goodness), *rajas* (passionate activity), and *tamas* (idleness or slothfulness). Those qualities are under My control, but I am not under theirs.

Metaphorical Interpretation

15. *Ye caiva sattvika bhava rajasas tamasashcha ye matta evetti tan viddhi*: "I am the cause of the three qualities of nature."

There are three qualities in nature: *sattva, rajas,* and *tamas*. The spiritual, sattvic qualities are ordinarily six in number: *shama* (control of the senses), *dama* (control of the mind), *uparati* (the desire to remain above, in the top), *titiksha* (tolerance), *shraddha* (devotion and love for God and guru), and *samadhana* (equanimity, the state of continuous God consciousness). These spiritual dispositions are located from the cervical center in the neck up to the pituitary.

Passionate rajasic dispositions are also six in number: *harsa* (laughter), *darpa* (vanity), *krodha* (anger), *raga* (attachment), *lobha* (greed), and *pravritti* (involvement). *Raja*sic qualities are dominant from above the navel to below the neck.

The six tamasic, slothful and idle qualities, are *aprakash* (veiling), *apravritti* (without determination, insincerity), *pramada* (doubt), *alasya* (idleness), *nidra* (sleep), and *moha* (infatuation and delusion). The lower three centers are predominated by tamasic qualities.

These three qualities are born of nature and ultimately, the power of God. If God does not inhale, then there is no activity of the body and no play of nature. Each individual possesses more or less all of these dispositions.

16. *Na tv aham teshu te mayi*: "I am not under them, they are under Me."

Although God is the cause of nature and her three qualities, God remains compassionately detached. (See the Bhagavad Gita 9:10 and the Shvetashvatara Upanishad 6:11.) The sun is the cause of all illumination, but it is not attached to anything. Similarly, all the natural qualities are under the soul, but the soul is not under the three qualities of nature. The presence of soul is in the waking state, in all dreams, in deep sleep, even in deep meditation, but the soul is ever detached, pure, perfect, and free. It is the cause of everything, but it has no cause. The soul center is above the six centers and above the three qualities.

Verse 13

tribhir guṇamayair bhāvair
ebhiḥ sarvam idam jagat
mohitam nā bhijānāti
mām ebhyaḥ param avyayam

Translation

People are deluded by the three qualities of nature. Therefore, the whole world does not recognize Me. I am above all these qualities, I am imperishable.

Metaphorical Interpretation

Many waves and bubbles rise up in the ocean of consciousness as names and forms. Human beings are extremely attracted and attached to these bubbles. Immersed in them, they are happy, but when the bubbles disappear, they are unhappy and sad. This is the cosmic drama of delusion. No one realizes that these waves and bubbles are transitory and ever changing. Engrossed in the delusive play of nature and overpowered by her triple qualities, no one tries to penetrate the restless waves and perceive the ocean.

People with sattvic qualities are busy with religious play. They spend a lot of time and energy chanting, singing, and trying to worship with the five sense organs—but they do not realize that God is beyond the reach of the senses. Rajasic people are buried in material activity—but they are so full of ego that they cannot really understand the Truth. Tamasic people are full of idleness and sleep.

"Nature is My creation, but people do not perceive My presence," says the Lord. People are absorbed in the delusive veil of nature's splendor. People play in the lower five centers. They do not have the desire to come up to the pituitary and fontanel. People constantly deviate from the vision of the changeless ocean; their eyes are so preoccupied with the waves: "Although, I am the cause of the triple qualities of nature, I am also beyond them (*gunatita*), and I am taintless and pure (*nirañjana*). Nature is changeable and perishable, but I am imperishable and changeless."

Sunlight is visible when it shines onto objects, but sunlight in space is invisible. Until people become introvert and go beyond the worldly senses, they cannot perceive God. Therefore, practice Kriya Yoga, follow the footsteps of a realized master, go above the body, mind, thought, intellect, and ego—attain the state of realization.

Verse 14

daivī hy eṣā guṇamayī
mama māyā duratyayā
mām eva ye prapadyante
māyām etām taranti te

Translation

This divine *maya* (delusion) of Mine consists of the three qualities of nature. It is extremely difficult to overcome, except by

those who constantly keep their attention on Me (meditate).

Metaphorical Interpretation

The Lord is explaining what *maya* is and how we can be free from *maya*.

Maya (delusion) is divine and extremely powerful because it is created by God. *Maya* is *prakriti* or nature of both the material and the spiritual. *Maya* is mother nature. *Maya* is God's creation (see the Bhagavad Gita 7:4–5).

Maya is *gunamayi*. Mother nature has three qualities: *sattva* (spiritual), *rajas* (passionate), and *tamas* (slothful). The play of *maya* is below the pituitary in all the lower centers.

Maya is *duratyaya*. It is extremely difficult to cross the ocean of *maya*. Delusion is so tempting and overpowering, it seems to be impossible to overcome its temptation. The Shvetashvatara Upanishad 4:10 says, *māyām tu prakṛtim viddhi, māyinam tu maheśvaram*: "Know *maya* to be true nature, but the supreme God is the Lord of *maya*."

Maya is tempting and alluring. Although it is extremely difficult, it is not impossible to free ourselves from temptation; in the second half of this verse, the Lord explains how. To human beings, this wonderful *maya* has three extremely sweet, pleasing, and alluring qualities. Constantly engrossed in *maya*, people remain in the lower five centers of the spine with an endless desire for money, sex, variety of food, anger, ego, pride, amusement, cinema, television, evil propensities, immoral activities, superiority and inferiority complexes, ans well as different types of religious formalities, *japa* (chanting the Lord's names) and prayer, to name a few.

The Lord tells us, however, "Those who become attached to Me alone can overcome the tempting pull of *maya*." If one sincerely follows the directions of the master with discrimination and detachment, lives in good company, and follows the prescription of the scriptures, then his mind becomes pure. By the practice of regular meditation, the breath becomes extremely fine. Restless breath is the cause of the play of *maya*. Slow breath or calmness causes *maya* to dissolve.

The marvelous power of God is hiding in the pituitary and fontanel. If, by the grace of God and the realized master, people practice breath control, they can be free from delusion, illusion, and error. They will become constantly aware of the indwelling self in every breath, and they can be free from the play of the triple qualities of *maya.*

Verse 15

na mām duṣkṛtino mūḍhāḥ
prapadyante narādhamāḥ
māyayā 'paḥrtajñānā
āsuram bhāvam āśritāḥ

Translation

People who pursue evil activity, who are foolish, who are sub-men or of lower human nature, and whose intellect and knowledge are carried away by delusion and demonic nature do not really seek Me.

Metaphorical Interpretation

In the previous verse, the Lord said that those who seek their own immortal self and love God can easily cross the ocean of delusion. In the verse, He says that there are four types of people having no desire for meditation and spiritual practice. They are the foolish, those of lower nature, those who are carried away by intellectual delusion, and people of demonic nature. These people thrive on evil activities.

The Foolish (*mudha*): Ordinary human beings engrossed in sense objects all have four common motivations: food, sleep, fear, and sexuality. Such people are animal in nature. They have no desire for God-realization.

The Sub-Men (*naradham*): Animals are not rational; they are always conditioned by their environment and instinct. But man is said to be a rational animal. A man should have discrimination, and constantly strive for evolution and progress. A person whose mind is always occupied by the qualities of the lower centers, who is not pursuing soul culture and not fulfilling the higher purpose of life is of a lower human nature.

Overpowered by Delusion (*mayayapahritajñana*): These people have a desire for self-unfoldment and progress. They seek out holy men, saints, and sages. They hear many things. Instead of undertaking good practices, however, they search for defects in the teachings. Their minds are not pure. They are deluded.

People of Demonic Nature (*asura*): Full of ego and vanity, these people are consciously devilish. They know what is good and bad, but they are unable to avoid bad and are unable to practice good. They love falsehood and hypocrisy. We can even find such people in the spiritual field—outwardly very saintly, but inwardly devilish. They are always doing evil deeds. They cannot really perceive the divinity within them. (See the Bible, Matthew, Chapter 7, and the Bhagavad Gita 16:4–20.)

Verse 16

caturvidhā bhajante mām
janāḥ sukṛtino 'rjuna
ārto jijñāsur arthārthī
jñānī ca bharatarṣabha

Translation

O Arjuna! O Bharatarshabha (lord of the Bharatas)! There are four types of devotees who are noble in deed and who meditate upon Me: the man in distress, the seeker of knowledge, the person with desire for material possession, and the man of knowledge and wisdom.

Metaphorical Interpretation

In the previous verse, the Lord discussed people of evil deeds (*dushkritanah*), and they were characterized as four types. In this verse, the Lord explains four types of devotees who are noble in deed (*sukritinah*). People whose deeds are evil are not after God, but people whose deeds are noble are always God-conscious. They are true lovers of God and they embody the four stages of devotion and realization.

The Distressed (*arta*): Who is distressed? The ordinary meaning of distress is the person who is troubled with disease, discomforts, poverty, and difficulties. People who are in extreme trouble pray to God to overcome it. They are also devotees of God. The spiritual meaning of *arta* is to be seeking God because everything without God is painful.

The Seeker of Knowledge (*jijñasu*): These lovers of God seek the company of the realized master with the desire to know. They read holy scriptures and inquire constantly. They practice different techniques. *Jijñasa* means to question, to ask, and to know (See the Bhagavad Gita 6:44).

The Person with the Desire to Have (*artharthi*): Some people pray and meditate for enjoyment and prosperity. They have strong faith in God. They want to fulfill their desire by worshiping God and working in the world. For them, every job done in God consciousness will give them more prosperity and comfort. The spiritual meaning of *artha* is God's glory or divine power. Those who try to possess divine power and God's grace are *artharthi*.

The Man of Knowledge (*jñani*): Three types of devotees love God with motive and objective, but those of this fourth type are the true devotees who love God without ambition. Everything they do is only for God. All their actions, thoughts, and words are for God. They follow the realized master very closely. They are engrossed in knowledge, consciousness, and super consciousness. They are *bharata*, engrossed in divine illumination.

Verse 17

teṣam jñānī nityayukta
ekabhaktir viśiṣyate
priyo hi jñānino 'tyartham
aham sa ca mama priyaḥ

Translation

Among them, the man of wisdom is the best, because he perceives constant union with the divine. He has single-minded devotion, which is meditation. I am extremely dear to him and he is extremely dear to Me.

Metaphorical Interpretation

A man of divine knowledge has two real qualities: *nitya yukta*, the ability to be constantly united with God, and *ekabhakti*, single-minded devotion.

In the previous verse, the Lord explained that three types of devotees love God with motive and ambition, but the last type, the man of wisdom, loves God for God alone. Now the Lord explains the two special qualities of the man of wisdom:

Nitya yukta (constantly united): The devotee remains in the super-conscious, cosmic-conscious, and even wisdom stages. Day and night, he remembers and loves God. In every breath, he offers his gratitude to God. He never forgets God even for a single moment. God is his life. He always keeps his mind in the north, the fontanel, where he tries to perceive the divine presence.

Ekabhakti (single-minded devotion): The human mind is restless, and man has divided love. Even when one sits for meditation and prayer, the mind roams here and there (See the Bhagavad Gita 8:10). But the single-minded devotee loves God extremely. In every activity—sleeping, sitting, eating, standing, and waking—he loves God. He is free from *maya*, the delusive force of nature. In his practical life, if any thoughts are coming, he feels, "O Lord! You have given me this thought. I am not doing this work. You are working through this body." He perceives God as his own and as his beloved. He is free from evils, debauchery, and immorality. He has one hundred percent concentration and love for God alone. He has nothing dear in the world except God. God is his nearest of the near and his dearest of the dear. So the Lord is saying, "The man of wisdom is truly dear to God." God loves this devotee extremely.

The man of wisdom perceives God everywhere, loving and seeing everything as the manifestation of God. The perception of such a devotee is always true. Perceiving himself as dear to God, he becomes pure and divine in all his work. He forgets himself, his own identity; his identity is God's identity; he and God are always one. This is real unity. This is real yoga. Those who practice the technique of Kriya Yoga sincerely, with love, reach this state.

Verse 18

udārāḥ sarva evai 'te
jñānī tv ātmai 'va me matam
āsthitaḥ sa hi yuktātmā
mām evā 'nuttamām gatim

Translation

No doubt, these are all noble (great, soul, divine, sage, and compassionate), but the man of wisdom is really My own Self because such a person is always united with Me. To him, being established in Me is the highest goal.

Metaphorical Interpretation

Without a doubt, all four types of devotees are spiritual; they are God-oriented; their minds are not going downward. Among the four however, the man of knowledge is the highest. This man of wisdom is free from ego. A man free from ego is always merged in the divine stage, in the super-conscious and cosmic-conscious states. So, the man of wisdom is the perfect image of God. He does not see anything different from God. He is always established in the state of yoga. His mind is extremely still, and tranquility of mind is divinity.

The Lord is saying, "All four types of devotees try to perceive Me and they are all great, but the man of wisdom is merged in Me. He has achieved the supreme stage of realization and liberation." By regular practice of Kriya Yoga, one can reach such a divine stage—to be a true lover of God.

Verse 19

bahūnām janmanām ante
jñānavān mām prapadyate

vāsudevaḥ sarvam iti
sa mahātmā sudurlabhaḥ

Translation

At the end of many lifetimes, the man of wisdom takes refuge in Me. He realizes that Vasudeva, the all-pervading God, is in everything and is everywhere. Such a great soul is extremely rare.

Metaphorical Interpretation

The Lord is noting the rarity of the highest spiritual attainment. It takes time and sincere effort to attain the highest state of perfection, but every person should try for perfection. *Bahunam janmanam ante*: After striving for many lifetimes, people will head towards perfection. This has a deep spiritual meaning. Just as there are four categories of devotees, there are also four stages of spiritual progress. To understand this verse, one must understand the real meaning of *janma* (birth or life), and *bahu* (several). The ordinary translation of *bahu janma* is "after many lives," that is, births and rebirths. But *janma* here really means "breath."

From the time of birth, there is breath. That breath is inhaled and exhaled by the power of God. Every inhalation brings new life, and every exhalation is a death. Each breath is a symbolic birth and death. Those who practice Kriya (those who are aware of the breath[1]) and can perceive the living presence of God make every breath a beautiful birth. This requires a long practice of Kriya Yoga with awareness constantly remaining in the fontanel. Then one becomes *jñanavan*, a man of divine wisdom. In this state, people are constantly aware of the divine. In the words of Shri Krishna, *vasudevah sarvam*: "Everything is God, the formless, the absolute, the all-pervading."

---

[1] The special Kriya breath can only be learned directly from the teacher.

In the Vedas it is said, *dve vava brahmano rupe*, which means God is manifested or realized in two ways. One way is withdrawing from all the senses and remaining compassionately detached in the fontanel. This is the state of inner realization. The other way is *sarva khalvidam brahma,* by realizing that everything is God. Similarly, the Isha Upanishad declares, *Ishavasyam idam sarvam*, "God abides everywhere." In the Mundaka Upanishad (2:2–12), it is also expressed, *brahmaivedam amṛtam purastād brahma, paścād brahma dakṣinataś cottareṇa adhaścordhvam prasṛtam brahmaivedam viśvam idam variṣṭham*: "The Brahman (one supreme God) alone is immortal: Brahman in the front, in the back, in the right and left, above and below. The Brahman alone is manifested everywhere in the universe."

A true spiritual person is a *mahatma*, a great soul, in the word of the Lord. He is free from all ambition, desires, and expectations. A being of this type is extremely rare.

Verse 20

kāmais tais-tair hṛtajñānāḥ
prapadyante 'nyadevatāḥ
tam-tam niyamam āsthāya
prakṛtyā niyatāḥ svayā

Translation

There are people whose knowledge is carried away by desires that are too varied. They worship other gods, observing various rites and rituals as prompted by their own nature.

Metaphorical Interpretation

Not everyone can be a man of wisdom. Among many thousands, only a few try to achieve a state where they perceive the universe as the manifested form of Vasudeva, the all-pervading father, where they are devoid of all differentiation and discrimination. Others, engrossed in the lower five centers, pursue only needs, passions, and possessions.

The soul is fulfilling all wishes. God is really a wish-fulfilling tree. Any desire satisfied with any object, possession, or achievement is nothing but a manifestation of God in the name and form in which it occurs. There is nothing without Him, but the mind clouded by desires and ambition forgets this truth. Then, with deluded and impure knowledge, people will worship God in different names and forms and with numerous rituals. They will follow various rigid teachings and modes of worship. They worship Ganesh for prosperity, Sasthi for children, Shitala from fear of diseases, Saraswati for knowledge, Lakshmi for wealth, and Manasha to be free from snakebites. These human beings are overpowered by the triple qualities of nature. Some people may be more spiritual, some more religious, and some more materialistic, but they all forget that all gods or goddesses are getting their power from the one supreme almighty father who illuminates and empowers everything.

Whenever one worships, ultimately God the almighty fulfills their ambition and expectation. Without God, there is nothing according to the Taittiriya Upanishad (2:5), *ekam eva advitiya brahma*: "God is one and without equal; He is the Brahman," and *vijñānam devaḥ sarve brahma jyeṣṭham upāsate:* "All gods glorify the one, Brahman, the eldest."

Verse 21

yo-yo yām-yām tanum bhaktaḥ
śraddhayā 'rcitum icchati
tasya-tasyā 'calām śraddhām
tām eva vidadhāmy aham

Translation

Whatever form a devotee wishes to worship, if he does it with love and reverence, I strengthen the faith of that particular devotee in that very form.

Metaphorical Interpretation

"O Arjuna," the Lord says, "Many have love, faith, devotion, and determination that is not directed toward emancipation, realization, or liberation. Their love and devotion are full of ambition and expectation. Their devotion is constantly changing. Their love is motivated only by a desire to gain in the material world, not absolutely in Me, the formless, the absolute, and the supreme. Their devotion is centered on a very small aspect of Me; however, their love is My love."

Human behavior is mostly overpowered by people's inner personalities and *samskaras* (impressions of previous thoughts and actions), which direct them towards different gods and goddesses, in an attempt to fulfill their desires. A devotee's chosen form of worship depends upon his inner nature, ambitions, and expectations—following different forms and formalities of fasting, charity, worship, and so forth. But faith and love are behind this formal worship, and through this worship, faith and love are strengthened. With the passage of time, as the needs and expectations of a person change, so will his worship and devotion. In any activity, success depends upon the quality of faith and love.

In this verse the Lord is saying, "O Arjuna! I am all pervading. I am in everything. I am in all these rituals and even in religious play. I am in the different names and forms of deities. Whomever one may worship, with love and faith, I am ultimately worshiped. I increase their faith and love in order that they may achieve some success in their worldly life."

As all the rivers flow and merge with the ocean, similarly, all worship is directed toward the one God. God is present in all the deities and rituals. Ultimately, God is pleased by all these activities.

Verse 22

sa tayā śraddhayā yuktas
tasyā 'rādhanam īhate
labhate ca tataḥ kāmān
mayai 'va vihitān hi tān

Translation

Endowed with such faith, he worships a particular form[2] and obtains his desired enjoyments from him as ordained by Me.

Metaphorical Interpretation

Faith is the pillar of success for material or spiritual accomplishment. Without faith, progress is impossible. Faith is the first step, and effort is the next. Faith and effort follow each other and must alternate. Faith is a divine quality that comes from God, and the harder a person strives, the stronger his faith becomes.

"O Arjuna!" the Lord is saying, "All worship is ultimately worship of Me. Even for those who do not know that I am the supreme being, I breathe into them. When devoted people work hard to fulfill of their needs, I fulfill their expectations according to their faith, even if they do not seek Me. No effort is in vain. Work brings success according to faith. I give light to the sun and moon. I give energy and vitality to all. When faithful devotees worship and love anyone, ultimately I am pleased. I have faith in them."

In the scriptures it is said, *yādṛṣi bhāvanār yasya siddhi bhavatir tādṛṣi*: "Perfection or achievement depends upon the intensity of the expectation and effort." Most people, engrossed in the lower centers, are trying to fulfill the lower desires; their worship of the deities may be motivated by this.

---

[2] People worship different forms of deities in order to fulfill their desire.

As one thinks, so one becomes. Thought is primary, success is secondary.

Verse 23

antavat tu phalam teṣām
tad bhavaty alpamedhasām
devān devayajo yānti
madbhaktā yānti mām api

Translation

The fruit (results) gained by these people of little understanding is temporary and perishable. The worshipers of the gods go to the gods, but My devotees come unto Me.

Metaphorical Interpretation

Lord Krishna is saying, "Only I am infinite, endless, formless, and absolute. Everything in this universe is created by Me and is dissolved in Me. Even the deities emanate from Me and are finite. They too will meet their end in the course of time. Only I have no beginning or end."

Those who worship gods or deities will have limited achievements. Whatever they expect, pray for, and achieve will be finite and perishable. Their vision and ambition is narrow and small. Those who do not train their mind to go to the state of formlessness are people of less intelligence and understanding. Their prayers to the gods give finite enjoyment. After rigorous prayer, they get something that is transitory. Those of limited understanding cannot see that by trying to fulfill material ambitions, they are snared in the clutches of *maya*. They are not after bad things, but neither are they after the infinite.

With the help of the realized master, those who are truly intelligent will meditate on the one God and become merged in

Him. Their life becomes fulfilled. All people should try to achieve the supreme state. When they reach it, they will not want anything else (See the Bhagavad Gita 6:22).

Verse 24

avyaktam vyaktim āpannam
manyante mām abuddhayaḥ
param bhāvam ajānanto
mamā 'vyayam anuttamam

Translation

Men of no understanding, ignorant people, think of Me as the manifested One who has form. They do not know that I am the unmanifest, unsurpassable, and undecaying supreme and eternal spirit.

Metaphorical Interpretation

The supreme and absolute cannot be perceived by those in a state of body consciousness. People with body consciousness are encumbered with virtues and vices. Their sense perception is limited and perishable; their understanding is narrow. The supreme self is beyond all limitation: eternal, formless, and absolute.

Those who go to the supreme state of *paravastha* through deep meditation get a taste of the formless. They may enter the state of *samadhi*, which is complete union with the unmanifest. After this achievement, they reach the state of perception called *vasudeva sarvam*, the all-pervading and all-manifesting God. This is the state of *advaita*, the non-dual realization of the One. To achieve such a state of cosmic consciousness and wisdom is extremely rare.

People with little understanding and intelligence cannot comprehend *avyakta*—the unmanifest. Their mind is manifest, engrossed with the senses, and therefore they perceive God as manifest and incarnate. This vision is extremely narrow and limited. Ignorant people see the waves rather than the ocean. They think the waves are the real essence. So, these people with little intelligence are busy with the worship of forms and rituals. They do not understand that God is the transcendental, formless ocean that makes the waves. They do not know the absolute and supreme reality of God.

Verse 25

nā 'ham prakāśaḥ sarvasya
yogamāyāsamāvṛtaḥ
mūḍho 'yam nā bhijānāti
loko mām ajam avyayam

Translation

Veiled by My *yoga-maya* (the divine creative potency), I am not revealed to all. Ignorant people fail to recognize Me, the unborn, unchanging One.

Metaphorical Interpretation

Here, the beautiful word *yoga-maya,* meaning "the divine power that deludes," is used by the Lord. The Lord himself is called Yogeshwara, the Lord of yoga (See the Bhagavad Gita 18:78). God can be realized by yoga, that is by meditation alone, but people are not after yoga or Yogeshwara, they are after *yoga-maya*. People are attached to the material world, engrossed in divine *maya*.

Here the Lord speaks of ignorant people as *mudha* (See the Bhagavad Gita 9:11). *Mudha,* "the ignorant," refers to the people who are extremely extrovert. By avoiding this state of restlessness and going toward complete union, one proceeds slowly from *mudha* to the state of *niruddha,* or "realized" (See the Yoga Sutras of Patañjali).

Maya, the delusive drama of the divine *yoga-maya,* is played out in the *ida, pingala,* and *sushumna,* the three channels of life force present in the spine. These three channels correspond to the three qualities of nature: *tamas, rajas,* and *sattva.* By the grace of the realized master, when one practices scientific techniques like Kriya Yoga with constant God awareness, one penetrates into the veil of nature's splendor and the delusive forces of nature are overcome. God communion is achieved. The vision is no longer extrovert or restless; within every form, the presence of the formless is perceived.

There is butter in milk, but the butter is invisible. People see milk, not butter. When the milk is churned and properly processed, then the butter can be perceived.

Verse 26

vedā 'ham samatītāni
vartamānān cā 'rjuna
bhaviṣyāni ca bhūtāni
mām tu veda na kaśცana

Translation

O Arjuna! I know all the beings of the past, present, and even those who are yet to come, but no one knows Me.

Metaphorical Interpretation

People consider material skills to be their intelligence, but this is not true intelligence. True intelligence is the discrimination that enables a person to distinguish the real from the unreal. People's minds are deluded by the play of nature; they are extremely restless, always busy with "me" and "mine." Thus, they cannot enter the state of yoga. Arjuna, however, is truly intelligent. He is constantly trying to sit near the soul, Krishna, and hear the inner voice. To one such as this, the Lord reveals His divine nature of all intelligence.

Time in Sanskrit is *kala*, but the real spontaneity of time is Mahakala, God Himself. In truth, time is absolute, but when time is perceived in a limited perspective, it seems to be divided into three aspects: past, present, and future. It appears to be changing—the present becomes the past, the future becomes the present—but absolute time is changeless.

The breath is also called *kala*. Exhalation is the past, and inhalation is the present. One who watches the incoming and outgoing breath in every moment, perceives the presence of divinity. Day and night, one sees only divinity and that it is He who knows the past, present, and future of everything. The veiling power of *yoga-maya* disappears. He becomes one with God. Only through deep meditation, practical spiritual life, and divine love can one reach this state of cosmic consciousness and divine wisdom.

In Verse 19, Vasudeva, the omnipresence of God, was explained. In this verse, the Lord speaks of His omniscience. God knows the past, present, and future. The wave does not know its own true nature, that it is part and parcel of the ocean. A wave is within the ocean, but this is beyond the perception of the wave. The ocean knows the past, present, and future of the wave. The ego of man is delusion and is devoid of divine intelligence. The mind and intellect are narrow and limited, but through meditation the mind becomes clear, vision becomes vast, and man becomes aware of his inner reality.

Verse 27

icchādveṣasamutthena
dvandvamohena bhārata

sarvabhūtāni sammoham
sarge yānti paramtapa

Translation

O Bharata! O Paramtapa! Because of delusion, after a person is born he is overpowered by the dualities which arise from desire and hatred.

Metaphorical Interpretation

In this verse, the Lord addresses Arjuna as Bharata and Paramtapa. When a person meditates and remains inside the cranium, divine illumination is perceived. He becomes Bharata, the lover of illumination. Arjuna is constantly sitting near the pituitary, behind the soul, behind Krishna. In this position, he is free from all negative qualities and inner enemies. Every spiritual seeker must try, through constant self-effort and meditation, to achieve the state of Bharata, who is Paramtapa, the conqueror of inner enemies.

The external world is nature's play of duality. Pleasure and pain, heat and cold, summer and winter, gain and loss, friend and enemy, birth and death are all examples. People divide their experience and understand the world in this way. People are attached to the favorable, their wishes and desires, and they want to avoid the unfavorable, which is their hatred. Desire and hatred are always associated with duality and cause people to become overpowered with delusion.

Those who are extremely materialistic, extrovert, and body-conscious are always overpowered by desire, ambition, hatred, repulsion, delusion, and duality. *Dvandva* or duality means two things existing together, each trying to exhibit their superiority. Those busy with this duality, busy in the lower centers, engrossed in delusive power, and diverging from reality are truly ignorant. They cannot perceive unity. They are restless, and their life is full of suffering. Duality is death.

A truly spiritual person, who meditates and follows the footprints of the master, perceives the presence of God in everything. Unity is life.

Verse 28

yeṣām tv antagatam pāpam
janānām puṇyakarmaṇām
te dvandvamohanirmuktā
bhajante mām ḍṛḍhavratāḥ

Translation

Those people whose deeds are virtuous, free from all sins, free from delusion in the form of dualities, meditate upon Me and worship Me with strong determination.

Metaphorical Interpretation

It is important to understand four points the Lord is making in this verse: freedom from all sins, performance of virtuous deeds, freedom from duality and delusion, and meditation with strong determination.

What is sin? People are truly afraid of sin, but they do not really understand what it is. They do not understand its cause: sin is impurity of body and mind, attachment to the senses, forgetting the indwelling self, and restlessness.

God has created everything and remains in everything. All breath is the breath of God, but people are not aware of this. They are extremely attached to the body and the material world. They are so engrossed in the body and the material world that they think they are the body, not the soul. They forget that they are the living power of God, the image of God. This is sin. Just as dirt is cleansed away by water and detergent, sins are cleansed by the virtuous deed—*punya karma.*

People who perform charitable deeds, speak the truth, do good to others, read good books, seek the company of good people, and so forth are *punya karma* or virtuous in deed. *Prana karma* is also the virtuous deed. All impurities of body, mind, thought, intellect, and action can be cleansed by *prana karma* (Kriya breath). The power of God is breathing day and night. One who watches this breath sincerely, practices Kriya, and loves the power of God is truly performing the virtuous deed. To perform this virtuous deed, breath control is the path to releasing oneself from duality and delusion. When a person practices breath control, he purifies his mind, thoughts, intellect, and ego. His body becomes still and pure. Attractions and attachments disappear. Restlessness disappears and inner tranquility is perceived. At this point, there is no longer any doubt, delusion, or duality; rather, there is constant unity and God consciousness. To achieve this pure, sinless state requires daily, regular, and sincere meditation with strong determination.

Devotion and determination are the two legs used to walk on the path of spirituality. Meditation and maintaining the effects of meditation during daily life are essential.

Verse 29

jarāmaraṇamokṣāya
mām āśritya yatanti ye
te brahma tad viduḥ kṛtsnam
adhyātmam karma cā 'khilam

Translation

Those who take refuge in Me, who strive to be free from old age and death, and who try to attain liberation through self-control know the Brahman (the supreme, the absolute) and know spirituality completely in every action.

Metaphorical Interpretation

In this verse, the Lord speaks of human nature and how to achieve the supreme goal of self-realization. People in the world are depressed by two major things: old age and death. Every person is afraid of old age and death even though it is the law of nature that the body will meet them. People are afraid of that which is natural and inevitable because they think they are their body and because they consider the death of their body to be the death of themselves.

Who am I? This is the fundamental question, and the solution to this question brings eternal peace. Although ordinary people think that they are the body, that they are male or female and so forth, they are really the soul. The soul is eternally young. The body is born and grows old, but the soul is the real self, the perfect image of God, the changeless eternal being.

Can people be free from old age? The Lord says it is possible, so there is no doubt. Old age is a state of mind. The fear of old age can be eradicated by practicing a scientific technique like Kriya Yoga. One can enjoy perfect health and a youthful life if one practices meditation daily with sincerity.

Man's second fear is death, but the soul is deathless. Every moment millions of cells die in the body; no one is afraid of this. Every exhalation is a death; no one knows this. Every moment is a moment of death; no one is aware of this. Death is a psychological fear. If one perceives that he is not the body, but is the indwelling self, then he is ever new, eternal, and deathless. Then, where is the fear of death? (See the Bhagavad Gita 2:11–30) "O death! Where is thy sting? O grave, where is thy victory?" (Bible, 1 Corinthians 15:55)

One should take refuge in God and have self-control. But how can one take refuge in God? Breath is the link between all living beings and God. If one loves God and perceives His presence in every breath, then he is always associated with and united with God. "As the body without the spirit (breath or soul) is dead, so faith without deed is dead." (Bible, James 2:26)

Self-control is the spice of spiritual life. Breath control is self-control. An average man breathes 21,600 breaths every twenty-four hours. When a person practices Kriya meditation, faithfully following his teacher, he will achieve a well-regulated breath and a self-disciplined life. As a result of meditation, he is able to know Brahman, true spirituality, and the spiritual principle in every action.

Verse 30

sādhibhūtādhidaivam mām
sādhiyajñam ca ye viduḥ
prayāṇakāle 'pi ca mām
te vidur yuktacetasah

Translation

Those who know Me as the integration of *adhibhuta* (perishable existence related to material objects), *adhidaiva* (the indweller from which living beings derive their sense power), and *adhiyajña* (all actions undertaken in a spirit of sacrifice) with their balanced and harmonized mind, have the knowledge of Me and even at the time of death are united with Me.

Metaphorical Interpretation

God is all-pervading, inside and outside of everything. He is in every human being and even in the material world. *Vasudeva sarva,* everything is permeated by God alone. This is the *adhibhuta* stage (See the Isha Upanishad, Mantra 1).

For those who practice Kriya Yoga, wherever their eye may go, they perceive the presence of God. They can even use the five sense organs for God perception. This is Kriya Yoga in practical life. People who remain in the material world can lead a spiritual life as Shri Lahiri Mahasaya and Shri Sanyal Mahasaya did: While living with their families, these men remained compassionately detached.

The indwelling self in every human being is the imperishable power of God (*akshara brahma*). He is constantly breathing from the fontanel through the nostrils of all living beings. He is the Lord of *maya* (delusion). If one can enter into the cave of the cranium and discover this self, then constant liberation is achieved. This is *adhidaiva*.

The almighty father, although present in everything, is still detached. He is Purushottama. To perceive Him is *adhiyajña*.

Through these three types of supreme knowledge, people will achieve the state of *samadhi*, the stage of divine wisdom. Thus, completely engrossed and merged in God consciousness, they will enjoy liberation—constantly and forever united with God—in life and in death.

Summary

This chapter is called *jñana vijñana yoga*—the "Yoga of Knowledge and Applied Knowledge." The five sense organs (the instruments of knowledge which are the eyes, ears, nose, skin, and tongue) and the four internal instruments (mind, intellect, ego, and memory) help a person acquire knowledge, but this knowledge is indirect in nature. These instruments enable a person to get the knowledge of the material world, *apara-prakriti.* The material world is the domain of observation and experiment, of the scientist in the laboratory. But God the creator is manifested and permeates the entire creation. This can be perceived only through deep meditation and realization. This is *aparoksha jñana*, direct realization.

Most people are extrovert and restless; attracted, enchanted, and even deluded by the elusive force of material nature. There are only a fortunate few who introvert their minds and senses to merge in the ocean of cosmic consciousness.

This chapter is one of the smallest, consisting of only thirty verses. Another remarkable feature is that there are no questions from Arjuna. All the verses herein are divine gospels of the Lord; in His own words, the Lord is explaining His divine nature and play.

The entire chapter can be divided as follows:

Verses 1 to 3: Explain the divine nature of the Lord and the rarity of the true seeker.

Verses 4 to 7: *Para* and *apara prakriti* (divine and material nature) are narrated. *Apara prakriti* consists of eight elements, and *para* (the divine) is the manifestation of life.

Verses 8 to 12: God's presence is everywhere.

Verses 13 to 15: Nature's three qualities are described.

Verses 16 to 19: Describe the four types of devotees, among which the *jñani* is the best.

Verses 20 to 23: Describe how people love God and pray to Him for the purpose of attaining comfort and pleasure.

Verses 24 to 30: Extol the path to self-realization in spite of all difficulties.

In general, people think that yoga is a difficult and hard spiritual path to tread. They forget that every breath is the effect of the union of body and soul, which is yoga. To love God in every breath and perceive God's presence everywhere is as easy as inhalation and exhalation—but this perception is possible only by following the teaching of a realized master and practicing spiritual discipline with strong determination.

"One who loves breath (*dharma*) is dear to Me, and one who is not taking care of breath, missing breath, the real spiritual treasure, is away from Me," this is the essence of the Lord's instruction in this chapter. The real lover of God, through his breath, is always united in God, (*nitya yukta*) and is a single-minded devotee.

Each person should divert and channel his ambition into God, so that he will be free from all dualities and restlessness. Then he will perceive eternal peace and bliss.

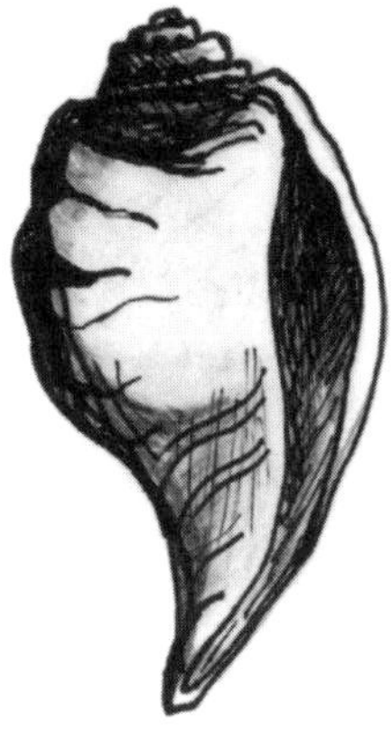

Chapter 8

Akshara brahma yoga

The Yoga of the Imperishable Brahman

Introduction

The entire universe, the manifestation of the unmanifest, which is perceived through the senses and the mind, is in a state of constant change. Everything changes. Change is the nature of the visible universe.

Each human body is a little universe, and this body universe also changes continuously. This change is in one direction only, which cannot be reversed. Infancy, childhood, adolescence, maturity, and old age are the visible changes of the body.

Everyone loves the body. Everyone is attached to it and engrossed in it. Everyone is body-conscious, thinking that the body is who they are. When a body conscious person realizes that his body, so dear and near, is aging, he faces its imaginary death and becomes unhappy and frightened. But inevitably, both the universe and the body universe are always changing. This is *kshara bhava*, perishable nature.

Behind every change, there is something changeless. But people don't realize this. In the cinema, before the beginning of a movie, one can see a big white screen, and at the end of the movie, one sees the same screen. But during the movie, people forget the screen because they are attracted, allured, amazed, and amused by the colorful dance of light and shadow on the screen. The universe is *kshara* (mutable), the body universe is perishable, but behind all these changes is the imperishable Brahman, the imperishable soul, the *akshara brahma*.

At the end of the last chapter, while explaining the ever-chang ing and dancing nature of *prakriti*, the Lord also wanted to describe the imperishable, immutable, and changeless soul—Brahman. So, he told Arjuna: "Someone who knows *adhibhuta* and *adhiyajña* is free from suffering and the fear of death. His mind is always on Me. He is *yukta chetasa*, in constant communion with the center of soul awareness and God consciousness." Thus, with His marvelous teaching in the last verse of the previous chapter, the Lord increases Arjuna's thirst for self-inquiry.

This chapter is called *akshara brahma* yoga—the way to constantly unite with the imperishable soul, Brahman, in all activities, even at the time of death.

Verses 1-2

arjuna uvāca
kim tad brahma kim adhyātmam
kim karma puruṣottama
adhibhūtam ca kim proktam
adhidaivam kim ucyate

adhiyajñaḥ katham ko 'tra
dehe 'smin madhusūdana
prayāṇakāle ca katham
jñeyo 'si niyatātmabhiḥ

Translation

Arjuna asked:

O Purushottama (Krishna)! What is Brahman (the absolute)? What is the self and spirituality? What is action? What is said about *adhibhuta*? What is divinity?

O Madhusudana (Krishna)! Where is the place of *adhiyajña*, the spiritual sacrifice, in the body? What is it? How may self-controlled people realize You at the moment of death?

Metaphorical Interpretation

In the first two verses of the eighth chapter, Arjuna questions Shri Krishna, his divine master, friend, philosopher, and guide. In the subsequent Verses 3, 4, and 5, the Lord answers Arjuna's eight fundamental questions about human life and spirituality.

In the first verse, Arjuna addresses Shri Krishna as Purushottama. Purushottama consists of two words, *purusha*, the indwelling spirit, and *uttama*, the supreme or the best; Purushottama therefore means the supreme self, cosmic person, or universal spirit. Another meaning of Purushottama is found in the Bhagavad Gita 15:18: It is *prana-krishna*, He who is beyond perishable and imperishable qualities.

Madhusudana, the name Arjuna uses for Shri Krishna in the second verse, also has deep spiritual meaning. Madhu means *maya* (delusion). The Lord of *maya* is Madhusudana—Madhu was a mythological demon, and *sudana* means destroyer. In the spiritual tradition of India, it is said that at the time of danger one must remember Madhusudana. In human life, death is the real danger. So, Arjuna addresses Shri Krishna as Madhusudana when he asks about the human predicament of death.

The name Brahman is used in the scripture in many ways, such as *saguna* Brahman (with attributes), *nirguna* Brahman (beyond qualities), *kshara* Brahman (perishable), *akshara* Brahman (imperishable), *shabda* Brahman (sound), and so on. A spiritual seeker may be confused about what Brahman really is, and this is the first question Arjuna asks his divine guide. His second question is about the nature of *adhyatma*, the soul, which exists with the support of the body and also supports the body. His third question is about what actions should a spiritual seeker undertake. *Adhiyajña* means the divine qualities or the presiding deities of the sense organs. What is *adhiyajña,* and how can a person perceive it during his life? What is the place of *adhiyajña*, the spiritual sacrifice, in the human body? Finally, Arjuna asks how a self-restraining yogi realizes God at the time of death—how do they leave the body in complete God consciousness.

Arjuna is a sincere seeker. His mind is always on Shri Krishna. He wants to know Truth. With an aptitude for self-development, he asks these beautiful questions. The thirst for spirituality is essential in every seeker.

Verse 3

śrībhagavān uvāca
akṣaram brahma paramam
svabhāvo 'dhyātmam ucyate
bhūtabhāvodbhavakaro
visargaḥ karmasamjñitaḥ

Translation

The Lord said:

The absolute Brahman is the imperishable (*akshara*) and the supreme. The essential nature of one's own self is called *adhyatma* or soul. The birth and growth of living beings, as well as their death, is karma or action.

Metaphorical Interpretation

In this verse, the Lord answers Arjuna's first three questions.

Aksharam brahma paramam: "Parambrahman, the absolute Brahman, is *aksharam*—indestructible, imperishable, and supreme." In the Vedas, it is said: "He is near, but He is very far; He is vast, yet He is very subtle; He is still, but He is dynamic." One can perceive this state by constantly remaining in the pituitary, i.e. the atom point of deep concentration. While concentrating in the pituitary, one perceives divine illumination, calmness, divine sound, and God consciousness. When a person practices *jyoti mudra* as taught by the master, he visualizes *kutastha akshara brahma*, the all-engulfing divine light which is formless and infinite. The Bhagavad Gita (15:15) says that *kutastha* (soul, the unchangeable principle in the changing body) is *akshara* Brahman, the imperishable power of God that exists in each human being as an atom.

Svabhava adhyatmam uchyate: The Lord answers the second question: What is *adhyatma*, soul or spirit? *Svabhava* consists of two parts: *sva* and *bhava*. *Sva* means one's self, and *bhava* is one's perception, expression, and manifestation. Each human being is essentially the living power of God, the perfect image of God. Although a person may identify with his body, each individual is really the soul, hiding in the body form. *Adhyatma* is the essential nature of one's self. *Adhyatma* is also split into two parts, a prefix *adhi*, which means the certainty of anything, and *atma* which refers to the soul. If one constantly perceives the living presence of God, lives in the presence of God, and works accordingly, then this is true spirituality, *adhyatma.* Spiritual life reveals one's real nature—the self.

Bhuta bhava udbhavakara visargah karma samjñitah: *Bhava* means creation. *Udbhava* means growth. *Visarga* has many meanings: sacrifice, surrender, destruction, and death. The birth, growth, and death of a living being is called action or karma. All action starts with birth, and the first action, *bhuta,* is breath. This action is also called *prana-karma,* the process of breathing. This action or karma continues through the living power of God until death. Breath is the foundation of life and all activity. To make the breath tranquil and still through meditation is real karma or action. In the Bhagavad Gita 3:15 it is said, *karma brahmodbhavam viddhi brahma akṣarat samudbhavam tasmāt sarva-gatam brahma nityam yajñe pratiṣṭhitam*:

Karma brahmodbhavam viddhi: Every action is done through the breath, which comes from the indwelling self. If there is no breath, there is no action. Through the action of the breath, all living beings are born, grow, and reach the ultimate state.

Brahma aksharat samudbhavam: This changeable and perishable action, the breath, is coming from imperishable *akshara brahma,* the *kutastha,* from the pituitary.

Tasmat sarva-gatam brahma: Know everything as the living power of God who is all-pervading. Thus, the Lord is explaining that God is formless, imperishable, and omnipresent.

Because of the breath, all the centers, the sense organs, and the entire body are full of activity. God is manifest in a more absolute form in *kutastha,* the indwelling self; therefore, the breath and actions, which are less absolute, can be offered as an oblation and a sacrifice to the almighty father. This is the state of breath control and realization of the absolute.

Verse 4

adhibhūtam kṣaro bhāvaḥ
puruṣaś cā 'dhidaivatam
adhiyajño 'ham evā 'tra
dehe dehabhṛtām vara

Translation

The basis of all created beings is perishable in nature. The basis of all divine elements is the shining self, the cosmic spirit. O Best of all those in human form (Arjuna)! The basis of all sacrifices (fire ceremony) is I, Myself, in this body.

Metaphorical Interpretation

In the Bhagavad Gita 7:3, the Lord spoke of the rarity of truly spiritual people. Similarly, in Shri Shankaracharya's Viveka-chundamani, Verse 3, it says, "The three rarest things in the world are to be born into the form of a human, to have a strong desire for liberation, and to be in the company of the realized master (the great soul)." Arjuna has two additional spiritual qualities: He constantly tries to remain in the company of the soul that is Krishna, and he listens to the voice of the Lord in extreme silence.

Here, the Lord addresses Arjuna as *dehabhritam vara*, the best of all those in human form. Arjuna is the best of all humans and the fortunate one because he is after truth and spirituality. Without these qualities, people lead a life like animals—always engrossed in food, drink, procreation, enjoyment, and fear. The Lord is telling Arjuna: "When one meditates deeply in the pituitary, one perceives a milk-white light and varieties of divine sound."

In this verse, the Lord answers Arjuna's questions about *adhibhuta*, *adhidaiva*, and *adhiyajña*:

What is *adhibhuta*? In the Upanishads, it says that from the imperishable soul, first manifested the vacuum, then air, fire, water, and earth. Then from the earth and all other elements came life such as fungus, insects, weeds, plants, trees, animals, and human beings. *Bhuta* means the five elements as well as all living beings. All living beings have a body made of the five elements. All these five elements and all living beings are the living presence of God.

The Lord says, *adhibhuta kshara bhava*, "The material nature is perishable and changeable." In every moment, the body, the cells, the atoms, the tissues, all constituents down to the five gross elements are undergoing change. This is body nature. This change, *kshara,* is coming from the changeless *akshara* remaining at the top. Thus, the body nature is conducted by the father nature, Purusha. (For details, see the Bhagavad Gita 8:19)

What is *adhidaiva*, the true divinity? The Lord says that *adhidaiva* comes from Purusha, the indwelling spirit. What is Purusha? It is *puryam shete iti*, the one who is hiding in the city of the body. The living power of God is hiding in every being. As one sun shining in the sky gives light everywhere, similarly, one soul sun in the body illuminates all the centers and sense organs. God is Purusha and *adhidaiva*, the cause of all action and light.

Aham adhi-yajña: The Lord is saying, "I am *adhi-yajña*. I am the perishable body. I am the imperishable spirit. I am in everything, and I am beyond everything. I am the conductor of all living beings and the twenty-four principles. I am the knower of the past, present, and future. I cannot be realized by twenty-six or even fifty letters."

Aham atra dehe: "I am remaining in the body, from the pituitary to the fontanel." Those who practice Kriya Yoga may attain the true stage of *adhiyajña,* the fire ceremony or divine sacrifice in the soul fire. In *kshara* (perishable) and *akshara* (imperishable), every action is *yajña*, sacrifice and worship of the supreme father. If one goes beyond the perishable nature and the imperishable *kutastha*, one enters into the state of the supreme self.

Verse 5

antakāle ca mām eva
smaran muktvā kalevaram
yaḥ prayāti sa madbhāvam
yāti nā 'sty atra samśayaḥ

Translation

He, who is thinking of Me at the time of death, will certainly attain My state when he leaves the body.

Metaphorical Interpretation

Antakale means at the time of the end, the moment of death. Arjuna's last question is about people at the time of their death. This verse beautifully explains the ultimate achievement of mankind.

During every moment of life, the indwelling self is giving a person different thoughts and dispositions. Every thought brings transformation in the body. With each thought and disposition, the cells of the body change. When there is anger, the body is different, and so is the breath. During fear, emotion, or sleep, the entire human system changes. But when someone thinks of God as the indwelling self, every cell of his body is charged with divine energy. This person perceives that he is not the body and becomes constantly united with the soul. The life of such a person is beautiful. While living, he is aware of God. When the end of his life comes, he is also remembering God. Ordinary people are afraid of death, but a truly spiritual person constantly loves God and is aware of God, even at death. A rational human being should be extremely careful of negative thought and should cultivate positive and divine thought.

To think is to be. As one thinks, so one becomes. In this verse, the Lord says, *mam smaran:* "remember Me." People are engrossed in thoughts of money, sex, food, ego, and so forth, but how many people really remember Him in every activity? The Lord says that *mam smaran* is *kri* and *ya*, to remember the indwelling self in every action. In every thought, one must perceive the living presence of God. Practice makes a person perfect, divine. Divine thought at the end of any action will bring constant peace, bliss, and joy.

The Lord is saying, "O Arjuna! One who thinks of Me and perceives Me during every aspect of life, becomes one with Me. There is no doubt about it. Be completely confident of your spiritual practice. In every breath, you perceive the divine. This will give you eternal peace and liberation."

Verse 6

yam-yam vā 'pi smaran bhāvam
tyajaty ante kalevaram
tam-tam evai 'ti kaunteya
sadā tadbhāvabhāvitaḥ

Translation

O Son of Kunti (Arjuna)! If one leaves the body at the end (death) while thinking of a particular state of being, one attains that alone, being ever absorbed in that thought.

Metaphorical Interpretation

The Lord is saying, "O Arjuna! You are the son of Kunti. You have sharp intelligence and divine moods. You want to know and realize your own divine self. A true and sincere disciple is extremely rare."

Human beings can make their life beautiful. It depends upon their desire. If they do not want beauty in human life, then they can make their life devilish. Every person is the product of his own thoughts. This is the secret of human life.

In the Upanishads, as well as in the Bible and other holy scriptures, it says that the universe is the product of God's thought. *Sa akamayata*: "God thought and wanted to create." Each human being is the creation of God's thought. Furthermore, each human being can transform his life, his body, and his activities by his own thought processes. Thought is the activity of the astral body. The astral body regulates the physical body. A peaceful loving thought can make one's body and life full of peace and divinity. The thought of God can bring goodness to one's life. It is the duty of every person to perceive the power of God in every thought.

An average person breathes 21,600 times a day. The Lord causes this breathing day and night, and during every breath, the seeker must love Him. The person who is aware of the indwelling self in every breath is becoming the self. His body consciousness disappears. He is full of love and divinity. He is truly in a state of liberation.

"O Arjuna! If someone is fortunate and is practicing remembrance[1], then this person is constantly proceeding along the spiritual path. His present life becomes peaceful, and his death is beautiful. To most people, death is painful, but for those who perceive death in every exhalation, there is no fear of death. For them, the present and future life is God-oriented and divine." (See the Isha Upanishad 17.)

---

[1] *mam-smaram* — as mentioned in the previous verse, to love God in every breath.

Verse 7

tasmāt sarveṣu kāleṣu
mām anusmara yudhya ca
mayy arpitamanobuddhir
mām evai 'ṣyasy asamśayaḥ

Translation

Therefore O Arjuna! Remember Me at all times and fight. When your mind and understanding are directed toward Me, you will come to Me, there is no doubt.

Metaphorical Interpretation

Spiritual life is not an accident, temporary incident, or a dream. It is a life in eternity and God. God has created everything from Himself and is abiding in everything. But people do not perceive it; they are not aware of it. They are so engrossed in the material world that they forget the truth, and they suffer.

Some people have the wrong idea about spiritual life. They think that it is an easy going, smooth life, but this is not so. True spiritual life is a life of constant struggle and effort. All people should try sincerely to achieve success in spiritual life. In this verse, the Lord mentions two secrets for success: Remember God constantly throughout life, and fight all negativity. These two things are the foundation of spiritual life. We need both feet to tread the spiritual path.

One must remember God in every moment, every breath, every action, and every state of life. The easiest way to remember God is to watch the breath and to thank God because He is breathing day and night. If one is really adept at loving God during every moment, during so-called pleasure as well as pain, then one can easily remember to love God. If one thinks of God at the time of death, then it becomes a peaceful and loving experience.

Each person is a brave soldier on the battlefield of spiritual life. He should not fight with others. Enemies are not outside oneself. The real enemies are inside: enemies such as anger, ego, pride, hypocrisy, and so on. The spiritual soldier must be well-equipped and strong (See the Bhagavad Gita 4:42). He must fight ignorance, passion, and temptation that crop up from the heart. Ordinary people give their mind and intellect to the sense organs and sense objects, but a spiritual person always gives his mind and intellect to God, becoming engrossed in the higher centers. When mind and intellect are pure, the real beauty of God is perceived.

So the Lord is saying, "O Arjuna! Constantly fight all your negative qualities while remembering Me. I am always with you. I am inseparable from you. Give your mind to Me and follow Me. You are certain to attain success in your life. There is no doubt about it. I give you my complete assurance."

Verse 8

abhyāsayogayuktena
cetasā nā 'nyagāminā
paramam puruṣam divyam
yāti pārthā 'nucintayan

Translation

O Partha (Arjuna)! He who has disciplined his thoughts and mind, who meditates on the Supreme Person and is constantly practicing, his mind does not go anywhere and he reaches Him (the supreme being).

Metaphorical Interpretation

In the previous verse, the Lord spoke of giving one's mind to God. This is not so easy; the mind is ordinarily restless and fickle; it does not remain in one place for any considerable time. In this verse, the Lord explains the necessity for *abhyasa yoga*, the yoga of continuous practice. Continuous spiritual practice frees one from negative thoughts and emotions. It allows one to meditate constantly without disruption. A child learns to write the alphabet by repeated practice. Perfection in any field of activity is achieved by repeated practice, daily and regularly. There is no other way to be God-directed except by repeated practice with the mind.

Everyone should constantly try to be united with the indwelling self. To achieve this, the Lord implies that one must repeatedly practice Kriya Yoga, a unique, scientific breath learned directly from the teacher. This is the way to breath control. Through breath control, one gains control over the restless mind. The mind loses its fickleness and restlessness. Just as a placid lake reflects the moon, a calm mind reflects the beauty of God. A disciplined mind is the beauty of man.

The restless mind roams in the lower centers, wanting money, sex, food, and so forth, but with regular practice of meditation, the mind moves to the higher centers and becomes formless; then the mind is completely merged in God awareness. This is how to achieve the supreme being, Paramapurusha, the supreme self who is hiding in the body and in the universe. Deep meditation enables one to perceive God's formless state and to be one with the supreme.

"O Partha", the Lord is saying, "With your brilliant intelligence, perceive this truth and act accordingly. Act now. Do not waste your time."

Verse 9

kavim purāṇam anuśāsitāram
aṇor aṇīyāmsam anusmared yaḥ
sarvasya dhātāram acintyarūpam
ādityavarṇam tamasaḥ parastāt

Translation

He who meditates on the seer, the ancient (ageless being), the ruler of all, the subtler than the subtle, the universal sustainer, who poses a form (formless form) beyond human conception, and who is effulgent like the sun and beyond the darkness of ignorance;

Metaphorical Interpretation

In the previous two verses, the Lord discussed constant practice of meditation. He used two words, *anusmaran* and *anuchintayan,* which stress the importance of keeping the mind constantly on the supreme self. Through meditation, one rises from limited awareness to perceive the supreme state. This state cannot be achieved with the mind. In the Kena Upanishad (1:6) it says, *yanmanasā na manute yenāhur mano matam tad eva brahma twam viddhi nedam yad idam upāsate*: "That which mind cannot comprehend, but who cognizes the mind, know that to be God alone, and not any other form that people worship."

By meditating in the *ajña* and *sahasrara* centers, one can reach divine experience, one can perceive the divine illumination, the atom point. Penetrating into the pituitary and remaining there without distraction, one perceives the state of *kavi,* the seer. The indwelling self, *kavi,* is the knower of past, present, and future. The state cannot be explained by words, but the divine perception is described beautifully in this verse.

All creation comes from this indwelling self, the ancient father who is before creation and who remains after creation. He is the ancient, ageless being who rules the universe. He is the supreme Lord who makes the sun and moon shine. He disciplines and maintains everything. He is the cause of life. He is the one who is breathing inside every human body, maintaining every cell of the body with life energy. He is subtler than the subtle and cannot be perceived by the senses. He is transcendental. He is the universal sustainer, the Lord of the universe and the Lord of each human being. He is present everywhere, in space, air, fire, water, and earth. He gives light to the eyes to perceive, but His form cannot be visualized by human eyes. Eyes can see form, but He is the formless, beyond every form: He is the formless form. He is beyond human comprehension, but those of pure mind can perceive Him. He is beyond the measure of time, *kala*: He is *mahakala*, but through meditation, one can reach this timeless state.

In the Vedas it says, *Veda aham etam purusham mahantam aditya varnam tamasah parastat*: "Know Me as the supreme self; I am effulgent like the sun and beyond darkness." Those who meditate perceive the beauty of the soul sun inside the atom point. With eyes closed and concentrating on the proper place as directed by the teacher, they see that beyond all darkness, there is the brilliance of the Self.

Darkness is ignorance, light is knowledge. Ordinary people are not aware of the indwelling self. They cannot realize this indwelling self. But those who practice the technique as taught by the realized master, with deepest desire and love, will perceive the divine, self-effulgent being. This is the state of meditation.

Verse 10

prayāṇakāle manasā 'calena
bhaktyā yukto yogabalena cai 'va
bhruvor madhye prāṇam āveśya samyak
sa tam param puruṣam upaiti divyam

Translation

He who practices with a calm mind, devotion, and the power of yoga (meditation) and directs his life force in the center of the eyebrows, at the time of departure will attain this supreme, divine, indwelling self (*purusha*).

Metaphorical Interpretation

Here the Lord discusses the time of departure, *prayana kala*. This state may be called the time of death, the time of exit, the time of exhalation, or the moment of liberation from body consciousness. What should a person do at such a time?

There are four things to do: *manasa achalena*, concentration or steadiness of mind; *bhaktya yukta*, maintaining deep, divine love; *yoga yukta*, perception of constant unity; and *bhruvor madhye pranam aveshya samyak*, directing the life force to the center of the eyebrows.

To achieve the first, deep concentration of mind, one must regularly and sincerely practice the scientific breath of Kriya Yoga as directed by the master. Next, the practice of meditation must be done with love and devotion; it is not mechanical; the same action performed with love gives better results. Meditation helps an individual manifest the divinity already within. Yoga is not an exercise; rather it is the continuous and constant perception of unity with the supreme. The Lord is also telling us where to concentrate and penetrate—the midpoint between the two eyebrows, three to four inches inside the brain, near the pituitary gland.

People are generally extrovert. They are allured by natural phenomena and are full of delusion, illusion, and error. They are engrossed in money, sex, food, affection, attachment, anger, cruelty, and so on. Their vital breath, *prana,* flows downward; this is why they cannot realize the indwelling self. A spiritual seeker, however, practices breath control and directs his life force, the vital breath, into the cranium. His breath is so fine that it does not come out of the nostrils (See the Bhagavad Gita 5:27). Practicing meditation sincerely with love and following the guidance of the master faithfully, he becomes free from attachment. He does not remain below, but rather, goes above. This is the state of liberation. Such a state is achieved by *yogabala*, the strength of meditation.

While escaping from the clutches of body consciousness, one merges with the supreme indwelling self (*param-purush*) who is *divya,* which means vacuum and illuminating. This is the state of formless perception and emancipation. Each spiritual seeker must try to achieve this. When milk is churned, the cream comes to the top; when all the extrovert *prana* is churned by the scientific technique of Kriya *pranayama*, one gets super consciousness and cosmic consciousness. This is not death; it is freedom from death.

The person who forgets the indwelling self and egotistically thinks of himself as the doer is constantly facing death and all difficulties. Exhalation is also called the time of departure. In every exhalation, one must perceive divinity. In every breath, one must touch the imperishable soul, Krishna, who is Parama Krishna, Purushottama, the supreme indwelling spirit.

Verse 11

yad akṣaram vedavido vadanti
viśanti yad yatayo vītarāgāḥ
yad icchanto brahmacaryam caranti
tat te padam samgraheṇa pravakṣye

Translation

That supreme state (God) that the knowers of the Vedas (the realized ones) call the imperishable (*akshara* or *aum*), which people of inner detachment, who desire God and who

are free from passion, enter and lead a life of self-control, that I shall present to you in brief.

Metaphorical Interpretation

The Vedas are the scriptures of divine wisdom, the embodiment of the spiritual experiences of sages and seers. The word Veda comes from the Sanskrit root *vid*, which means to know. *vedavid* means man of wisdom, a state achieved by deep meditation and emancipation. From this state, God is perceived as *akshara,* the imperishable.

The word *akshara* is beautiful for its many different meanings, three in particular: *akshara*, the imperishable; *aum*, the eternal divine sound; and *kutastha*, the immutable one. Realized people perceive God as the imperishable, absolute one. They also perceive God as *aum*, the eternal divine sound. In the Bhagavad Gita 8:13 it says, *aum ity eka akshara brahma*: "*Aum* is the one, *akshara* Brahma." This will be explained in the following verses. As mentioned in the previous verse, those who meditate with concentration are able to penetrate between the eyebrows. This is called *kutastha*, which is synonymous with the *ajña* center. To perceive this divine state, they must follow the path of inner detachment, thoroughly controlling the mind and senses. They become truly free from the duality of the material world: pleasure and pain, heat and cold, and so forth.

In this verse, the word *brahmacharya* is used, which literally means celibacy. But, its real meaning is to roam in Brahma, to live in constant God-consciousness. This is the activity of the yogis, who follow the path of meditation. Through divine illumination and the eternal *om* sound, they perceive constant God-awareness and unity with Him.

Verse 12

sarvadvārāṇi samyamya
mano hṛdi nirudhya ca
mūrdhny ādhāyā 'tmanaḥ prāṇam
āsthito yogadhāraṇām

Translation

All the doors of the body are closed. The mind is firmly confined in the cavity of the soul. One's life is fixed in the head (cranium or fontanel). Then one is established in yoga.

Metaphorical Interpretation

This verse explains how to practice meditation and perceive the divine. Each human body is a city with nine gates—a house with nine doors. The soul is living in this body house that has nine open doors. These nine doors are the two eyes, the two ears, the two nostrils, the mouth, the anus, and the urinary-sexual organs. Because these doors are usually open, people become restless and active.

The Lord says,

> *Sarvadvarani samyamya,* which means regulating or closing the doors of the body. *Sarva* (all) here refers to the senses. *Sarva-dvarani* means the doors of the senses. The sense organs are the path of perception of sense objects. Man becomes restless because he does not know how to control, regulate, or close these doors. The Bible says it in a similar way: "And when you pray, you shall not be like hypocrites... When you pray, enter into your closet, and when you have shut the door, pray to your Father, which is in secret..." (See Matthew 6:5–6).
>
> It is easy to close all the doors except the nostrils, which are

used to breathe. By closing the doors of the eyes, one may perceive divine illumination. By closing the ears, one may hear the divine sound. But it is difficult to close the door of the nostrils. This door should be closed slowly. Closing this door implies learning the art of breath control. By controlling the breath, one will be able to control the restless mind. Without mind control, one cannot meditate. By slowly closing the door of the nostrils, one can reach the breathless state.

Mano hridi nirudhya ca: The mind should be captivated or confined in *hridaya*. Ordinarily, *hridaya* means heart. But the real meaning of *hridaya* is *hri*, to perceive or receive, *da*, to give or donate, and *ya*, motion or the power of God—it really means the cavity of the cranium or brain. The mind is to be controlled through regular practice of Kriya Yoga, in the brain, above the *ajña* chakra. That is the place of breath control and mind control.

Murdhny adhaya 'tmanah pranam: Through self-effort remain in the top of the head, the fontanel. This is *murdhani*, the place of real meditation. When one comes up to the fontanel, the state of *anor aniyan*, the atom soul, is perceived. (For more details, see the Shvetashvatara Upanishad 3:20). This is the real state of yoga. This state can be achieved by regulating all the doors of the senses, by learning breath control and by slowly coming up from the lower centers of the spine and becoming established in the fontanel.

Verse 13

aum ity ekākṣaram brahma
vyāharan mām anusmaran
yaḥ prayāti tyajan deham
sa yāti paramām gatim

Translation

Uttering *aum* (perceiving the one, indestructible Brahman), remembering Me, he who goes forth casting aside the body reaches the highest goal.

Metaphorical Interpretation

The Lord is explaining the essence of all spiritual practice. There is no simpler process than this. In the previous verse, the Lord spoke of controlling and closing the nine doors and concentrating in the fontanel. Now, the Lord explains the next step of practical spiritual practice, techniques such as Kriya Yoga.

The Lord says,

> *Aum ity ekaksharam brahma*: "*Aum (om)* is the one, indestructible, Brahman." But what is *AUM*? "A" is the causal body, the fontanel, the place of the almighty father, Purushottama. "U" is the astral body, the place of *akshara* Brahman, inside the brain where there is intellect, knowledge, super consciousness, and cosmic consciousness. "M" is the gross body, the place of *kshara* Brahman, the perishable one. The aggregation of these three is *aum,* a representation of the one, the absolute. *Aum* is also called His manifesting word: *tasya vachakah pranavah* (See Patanjali's Yoga Sutras 1:27). *Aum* is also called *nada brahma* (manifestation of the Absolute in the form of sound).
>
> *Aum* cannot really be chanted by the mouth. In the previous verse, the Lord explained how to close all the doors. When the doors of the senses are closed in meditation, one can perceive the marvelous power of God and the divine sound of *aum*.
>
> *Mam anusmaran*: "Remembering Me", comes from *anu*, the atom, plus *smaran*, remembering and merging. God is beyond the perception of mind, thought, and intellect. Here,

the Lord says that while meditating, one should close the doors of the senses, go to the fontanel, and merge the mind in God consciousness—this is true remembrance of God.

Yah prayati tyajan deham: "In this state, one truly casts off the body senses." When one is free from body-consciousness and wordly awareness, one enters into the stage of cosmic consciousness and wisdom, *samadhi.*

Those who truly have an extreme desire for God-realization, who through meditation go beyond the body sense and remain in the causal body and even beyond that, have entered into *sa*, leaving behind *ham.*

Sa yati paramam gatim: "Thus one goes to the highest state of God-realization." So, the Lord tells us how a person can enter the state of supreme bliss through meditation.

Verse 14

ananyacetāḥ satatam
yo mām smarati nityaśaḥ
tasyā 'ham sulabhaḥ pārtha
nityayuktasya yoginaḥ

Translation

O Partha (Arjuna)! He who constantly meditates on Me, absorbed in Me, thinking of nothing else, is the true yogi, and for him, I am easily attainable.

Metaphorical Interpretation

People think that self-realization is difficult, but in this verse, the Lord is telling Arjuna that self-realization and soul culture are simple, giving no discomfort and easily attainable. The Lord is saying, "O Arjuna! I constantly remain within and without you. I told you previously (See the Bhagavad Gita 6:46) to be a man of meditation—a yogi. For the yogi, I am always present."

The Lord describes the qualities of a yogi:

> *Ananyachetah satatam:* "Constantly meditate." The human mind is constantly restless. The easy way to regulate the mind is to practice the art of breath-control. The mind is always focusing on objects of the senses—this is obvious—but if someone practices perceiving God's presence in everything and in every living being, then his mind becomes calm and divine. Restlessness is animal and human, calmness is divine.
>
> Suppose there is a beautiful flower, very tender and full of fragrance. Instead of perceiving it with the eyes, nose, and hands, try to perceive the presence of God in the flower. Perceive the beauty of God, the smell of God, and the touch of God. In this way, it is possible in daily life to keep the mind constantly focused on the One and not on the many. To perceive the many is delusion. To perceive the One in the many is divine.
>
> *Yo mam smarati nityashah*: "Remember Me constantly." People who are absorbed in sense gratification with the ego, forget the Lord. But one who perceives *ham* (body or matter) and *sa* (soul or spirit) in everything and in every being is constantly perceiving His presence. He is constantly remembering God. As one thinks, so one becomes.
>
> *Tasya aham sulabhah partha*, "To them I am easily attainable." The Lord is saying, " O Partha! You are truly intelligent. You want my constant company. For those such as you, I am easily attainable. Please practice *kri* and *ya* (watching God in every action and every breath) constantly and perceive the eternal presence of God. God and you are one and have always been one."

Nityayuktasya yoginah: "He is the yogi, who is constantly united (attached)." Yoga means to perceive the constant union, unity, or copulation in every breath, in every moment, in every activity, and in every achievement. Those who practice Kriya Yoga regularly know how to maintain this state of divine perception. (See Patanjali's Yoga Sutras 1:14).

Verse 15

mām upetya punarjanma
duḥkhālayam aśāśvatam
nā 'pnuvanti mahātmānaḥ
samsiddhim paramām gatāḥ

Translation

Great souls, who have attained the state of highest perfection, having come to Me, are not reborn to the abode of sorrow and impermanence.

Metaphorical Interpretation

Mahatman means great soul. Who is a great soul? Soul is always greater than the greates t—*mahato mahiyan* (See the Katha Upanishad 1:2:20). Ordinary people, being body-conscious, consider themselves very small. Their ego is big, but their mind and thoughts are very narrow and as a result their life is miserable. Those who by the practice of meditation perceive the constant presence of God, become truly great. They are endowed with a broad mind and a vast outlook. Just as a river merged with the ocean becomes the ocean, *brahma veda brahmaiva bhavati*: The knower of God becomes God. One becomes a great soul by achieving the highest state of perfection. A rusty, insignificant wire, plugged into the electric socket becomes charged with marvelous current; a person whose mind is constantly absorbed in God consciousness becomes full of divine quality.

This world is perishable. It is full of pain and suffering, distress, and difficulties for those who are not able to perceive the presence of God everywhere. But how can this world be painful for one who can feel the living presence of God everywhere? This world is the temple of God.

One who practices Kriya Yoga, the scientific process of breath control, can attain the state of breath control, breathlessness, and *samadhi*. During every breath, there is one cycle of birth and death. Every exhalation is death. Every inhalation is birth. If a seeker practices the technique of breath control, reaches the state of meditation and is able to maintain *paravastha*—during and even after meditation—then this person will enjoy divine bliss. For this person, who is still living in the world, the world is completely different: There is no more threat of pain or ending; there is only the play of consciousness and the drama of the divine. This is the truly divine life.

Verse 16

ā brahmabhuvanāl lokāḥ
punarāvartino 'rjuna
mām upetya tu kaunteya
punarjanma na vidyate

Translation

O Arjuna! All the worlds from *brahmaloka* down are liable to appear and reappear. But O son of Kunti! On attaining Me, there is no rebirth.

Metaphorical Interpretation

In this verse, the Lord explains the rarity of *apunaravritti*, reaching complete liberation and not returning to the ordinary plane of life.

There are fourteen planes of consciousness which are represented in the human spine as seven ascending centers and seven descending centers. This world of creation is called *a brahma bhuvanal lokah,* which is divided into seven *lokas* called *bhuh, bhuvah, svah, mahah, janah, tapah,* and *satyam* (*brahma*). These *lokas* are associated respectively with the seven centers from the *muladhara* (coccyx) to the *sahasrara* (fontanel) and then back down from top to bottom.

When through meditation, someone ascends from the lower centers to the upper centers, immense calmness and godly qualities are perceived, but most people cannot remain there too long. The material world, *maya,* is extremely tempting and alluring, so they come down. Even after a great deal of spiritual practice, people will come back down, even into so-called ordinary planes of life. Those who are more fortunate, will try more vigorously. Even during their ordinary breath, they remain attached to the almighty Lord. They maintain constant alertness of the indwelling self and are therefore free from pitfalls, shortcomings, and negative tendencies. With deep meditation and sincere practice and with the compassion and grace of God and gurus, they will enter the state of *samadhi,* after which there is no possibility of downfall. In *samadhi,* there is no sense of the world, the body, or human existence; there is only liberation and complete, constant God communion.

The Lord addresses his disciple by two names in this verse: Arjuna and Kaunteya. He is saying, "O Arjuna! You are truly spiritual. Still, you are not free from delusion. Although you are constantly remaining with Me, you are still deluded and full of sorrows and anxiety. This is due to the play of *maya.* You are Kaunteya, the son of Kunti (a man of sharp intelligence). By virtue of your inner, pure conscience, you rise up and realize Me. This is *mam-upetya.* Be one with Me. Perceive the state of constant union, *nitya yukta,* and you will enjoy the state of liberation, the stage where there is no birth or death."

Verse 17

sahasrayugaparyantam
ahar yad brahmaṇo viduḥ
rātrim yugasahasrāntām
te 'horātravido janāḥ

Translation

The knower of day and night knows that the day of Brahman is a thousand *yugas* (ages) and that the night is also a thousand *yugas* long.

Metaphorical Interpretation

Ordinarily, people associate day and night with the rising and the setting of the sun. These are people with limited intelligence; they do not really know day and night. Without being a yogi, one cannot know day or night. When the breath is going through the right nostril, *pingala*, it is the day, when through the left, *ida*, it is the night. A man breathes all day and all night—an average of 21,600 times per 24-hour cycle.

In this verse, there is a word, *yuga*. The ordinary meaning of this word is "age" or "era", but the real meaning is "dual" or "two". Every breath consists of an inhalation and an exhalation; this is the dual state or *yuga*. Many propensities are created and dissolved with each breath. This is the activity of *yugas*. Those who practice ordinary methods of breath control hold the breath in an unscientific and uncomfortable way, but yogis who practice the scientific technique of Kriya Yoga know the easiest technique of breath control—without holding the breath. By the regular practice of Kriya Yoga, following the instructions of the teacher, the breathing system is regulated in such a nice way that the breath rate gradually slows down. *Sahasra yuga paryantam* means 1,000 breaths in the day, and *ratrim yuga sahasrantam* is 1,000 breaths in the night. This is approximately 2,000 breaths in a complete cycle of day and night. This state can be achieved by leading a life of moderation, regular practice of Kriya Yoga, maintaining love and loyalty for the guru, and devotion to God.

In this verse, the Lord is telling Arjuna: "If you really want to make spiritual progress, do not get confused. The easiest way to know Me is the way of breath. Day and night, there is a constant flow of breath, but you are not aware of this. Breath is your life. Your life is maintained by Me. If you love Me during every breath and lead a regulated life in all the centers, then through the practice of Kriya Yoga, you will achieve regulated breathing. Then you will be aware of spiritual truth, and you will attain liberation."

Verse 18

avyaktād vyaktayaḥ sarvāḥ
prabhavanty aharāgame
rātryāgame pralīyante
tatrai 'vā 'vyaktasamjñake

Translation

At the coming of the day, all embodied beings emanate from the unmanifest, and at the coming of night, they merge into the same subtle state, called the unmanifest.

Metaphorical Interpretation

In the previous verse, day and night were explained. When the breath flows in the right nostril, it is day. Day is the symbol of activity. Breath in the right nostril brings restlessness and lots of thoughts. Breath in the left nostril is the night, which is the cause of slothfulness and inertia. But, when the breath is flowing equally in both the nostrils, it is in the *sushumna*, the middle path. During this time, the mind is extremely calm. This is the best situation for meditation and spiritual practice. The junction point of night and day is dawn, and the junction point of day and night is dusk. In Sanskrit these two times are called *samdhya, samhak dhyana,* the time for perfect meditation.

Those who want to meditate and be free from all thoughts, worries, and anxieties must learn how to control the breath, and at the same time, must know how to get the breath to flow through the *sushumna. Avyakta* is called *sushumna. Avyakta* is the unmanifest. The *sushumna* passage is also the unmanifest. *Avyakta* and *sushumna* are the states of extreme tranquility, which can be achieved by making the breath extremely slow and fine. In this state, the breath does not come out of the nostrils. After *avyakta,* comes the *vyakta* state, the manifest. Then from *vyakta,* one can re-enter *avyakta.*

Let's look at this verse another way. Day means sunlight, which pervades everywhere. The meaning of day is the perception of divine illumination. If a person meditates very deeply, then he is engrossed in God consciousness; he is not in darkness. When a person forgets the indwelling self, then he is in darkness; he cannot perceive the divine presence; it is night, full of delusion, illusion, and error. In the Brihadaranyaka Upanishad 4:4:19 and Katha Upanishad 2:1:10 it says, *mṛtyuḥ sa mṛtyum āpnoti ya iha nāneva paśyati*: "The perception of multiplicity (not perceiving the unity of the soul) is the cause of destruction." When a person is not able to see the presence of God, that the soul sun is everything, this is *pralaya* or dissolution. When a person remains in the cerebral cortex and meditates, he perceives divine illumination of the soul sun. This is the day of the realized person.

Verse 19

bhūtagrāmaḥ sa evā 'yam
bhūtvā-bhūtvā pralīyate
rātryāgame 'vaśaḥ pārtha
prabhavaty aharāgame

Translation

O Partha (Arjuna)! This multitude of beings born again and again is dissolved under the compulsion of nature at the coming of the night and rises again at the coming of the day.

Metaphorical Interpretation

Bhuta means the gross elements. *Grama* means aggregation. Each human body is an aggregation of the five gross elements. *Grama* also means village. Each human body is a village of five gross elements, five sense organs, where the soul lives. This body undergoes constant change. The body is born, it grows, and then it starts to decay. Ultimately, it meets its death. This body passes through death and birth with different thoughts, emotions, and activities. When anger comes, the body is full of anger. Then it is a different body. When anger disappears, that body is dead. This is *bhutva bhutva praliyate*, again and again, the body is born and dissolved.

Most people obey the impulses of nature, but it is also possible to go beyond the pull of nature. Those who meditate and lead a strict, disciplined, spiritual life, practicing Kriya Yoga sincerely, are constantly in daytime and full of light. They shed the darkness of night. For them, there is no division of *kala* (time) into day and night, past and future—there is only one flow of time, *mahakala*. They are completely free from body consciousness and the influence of the five gross elements, *bhuta grama*, which are present in the lower five centers of the spine.

Verse 20

paras tasmāt tu bhāvo 'nyo
'vyakto 'vyaktāt sanātanaḥ
yaḥ sa sarveṣu bhūteṣu
naśyatsu na vinaśyati

Translation

Far beyond even the unmanifest, there is another unmanifest existence, which is a supreme divine person, who does not perish even though all beings (elements) perish.

Metaphorical Interpretation

Vyakta means the manifested, that is the *ida* and *pingala*. *Avyakta* means the unmanifest, which is the *sushumna*. Both *vyakta* and *avyakta*, the *ida*, the *pingala*, and the *sushumna*, are present inside the spine and pituitary. This is the whole world, the place of all activity, where all people are engrossed. This is the *ham* body, the *kshara* body—the perishable body. Then, near the *ajña* chakra, there is *akshara*, the imperishable and unmanifest. But far beyond even this unmanifest *avyakta*, which is also the *sushumna* and the feeble breath, there is the place of unmanifest existence—a supreme, divine person. One who meditates very deeply, who goes above the pituitary and penetrates into the cerebral cortex and even beyond that, perceives this supreme being. This state is called Purushottama, the supreme self, or *sanatana*, the eternal.

One who practices Kriya Yoga sincerely and enters into the state of *paravastha*, can easily experience the eternal, where there is neither attachment nor detachment, but where there is supreme peace, bliss, and joy. Although the sense organs are there, they are no longer a distraction.

In this verse, the Lord is telling his great devotee Arjuna: "I am *vyakta* (manifested). I am also *avyakta* (unmanifested). I am present everywhere. I am in *ida*, *pingala*, and *sushumna*. I am in the spine, the brain, and beyond. I activate all the gross elements, *sarveshu-bhuteshu*. Although I am in the gross elements, which are perishable, I am still beyond all. I am eternal. I am imperishable."

Verse 21

avyakto 'kṣara ity uktas
tam āhuḥ paramām gatim
yam prāpya na nivartante
tad dhāma paramam mama

Translation

The unmanifest is called the imperishable. He is also called the supreme goal. He, who attains that supreme abode of Mine, never goes back.

Metaphorical Interpretation

In this verse, the Lord explains that *avyakta* is *akshara,* that the unmanifest is imperishable. *Ida* and *pingala* are called *kshara*, perishable, because when the breath is here, there is destruction of the breath. But, when the breath flows through the *sushumna*, it is very fine and feeble. By bringing the breath into the *sushumna,* one can enter into the place of *kutastha,* which is also *akshara*. Remember, the Lord says (Bhagavad Gita 15:16) that *kutastha* is inside the brain, near the pituitary. Through sincere practice of meditation and Kriya Yoga, one enters into the divine kingdom, the cave of the cranium.

Most people are busy in the lower five centers, engrossed in money, sex, food, ego, and religious play. This is the domain of *kshara*, where people move downward. But those who are truly fortunate try to go to *akshara,* which is upward movement. This upward movement is also called the supreme movement. The man of meditation tries to go beyond *avyakta*, the unmanifest, and *akshara,* the imperishable.

With the help of a realized master and through sincere self-effort, one can move upward, leaving aside the temptations of the lower centers. On this upward journey, if one goes beyond the feeble breath, *avyakta,* up to the fontanel and even above it to the breathless *samadhi* state, one will find the supreme abode of the almighty—the divine kingdom and liberation. In this state, there is constant unity; there is no separation. Merged in God consciousness, one does not go on the downward journey any more.

Verse 22

puruṣaḥ sa paraḥ pārtha
bhaktyā labhyas tv ananyayā
yasyā 'ntaḥsthāni bhūtāni
yena sarvam idam tatam

Translation

O Partha (Arjuna)! This is the eternal supreme person, the indwelling soul, in whom all beings reside and by whom He is manifested and realized in those with extreme devotion.

Metaphorical Interpretation

God is the abode of all. Earth, water, fire, air and sky, stars, planets, trees, animals, man, and so on are born in God and living in God. God is the cause of everything. He is everywhere—*sarvam, idam*, and *tatam*. All that one perceives is nothing but God's presence. The power of God is hiding and living in the body house. The soul is called Purusha, the indwelling self. The almighty God is called Parama Purusha, the supreme self, the conductor of everything. The existence of the body is possible because of the breath inhaled and exhaled by the indwelling self, but the supreme God is beyond breath. He is Purushottama, the supreme person and the almighty father. He is all-pervading, omnipotent, and omniscient.

In this verse, the Lord speaks of the essential factor for self-realization saying, *bhaktya labhyas tv ananyaya:* "Become realized through extraordinary devotion." What is devotion?

Devotion is the foundation for spiritual progress. *Bhakti paranuraktih ishvare*—devotion can be obtained by maintaining extreme attachment to the Lord. People are attached to the objects of the senses, but one should practice perceiving the presence of God in all objects. This is real attachment to the Lord, or true devotion. Implicit faith in the words of the master is the foremost requirement for devotion. Inquiry into one's own self is the other aspect of true devotion. Emotion is not devotion. Rather, devotion brings proper understanding and the motionless stage. Devotion is superior to *karma* (action) and *jñana* (knowledge). Devotion brings constant association with the supreme self.

If one wants liberation and realization, then one must try to love God from the core of the heart. God is life and God is the breath. During every breath, one must maintain deep devotion for God.

Verse 23

yatra kāle tv anāvṛttim
āvṛttim cai 'va yoginaḥ
prayātā yānti tam kālam
vakṣyāmi bharatarṣabha

Translation

Best of the Bharatas (Arjuna)! Now I shall tell you of the time (path) when the yogis depart and do not return and also of when they depart and do return.

Metaphorical Interpretation

In a previous verse, while describing supreme movement the Lord mentioned *akshara brahma*, which is *parama gati*: the supreme goal, the supreme path, and the supreme abode. The supreme almighty father is formless. In the Bhagavad Gita (9:4) the Lord says: "I am pervading all over the world. I am everywhere. I am in all human beings and all of creation. I remain in the formless stage although I am in body form. The invisible counterpart of God is hiding in all body parts and in the entire universe."

God's power is activated through the nine gates of the body house. These nine gates are extrovert, but the practice of meditation techniques like Kriya Yoga, one can introvert these open doors in order to achieve liberation. In this verse, when the Lord speaks of *kala*, it does not mean time, but rather refers to a state of realization possible through meditation. When one practices regular meditation, God's presence is perceived everywhere. One can perceive *ham* and *sa*, and their unity or yoga in every breath. *Sa* is the imperishable soul, the conductor of the gross body, *ham*. This *ham* body is full of delusion, illusion, and error; it is perishable. Without the imperishable soul, *sa*, this gross body, *ham*, cannot survive.

In this verse, the Lord calls Arjuna "Bharatarshabha", which means the best of the Bharatas, that is to say the best among spiritual seekers. Arjuna is intelligent and sincere. These two qualities combined bring quick success. The Lord is saying: "O Arjuna! There are two paths. Man may choose one of the two to follow. One path is full of temptation, it is the path of delusion. The other is the path of perfection, it is free from all tempting desire. I will describe this path in detail."

Verse 24

agnir jyotir ahaḥ śuklaḥ
ṣaṇmāsā uttarāyaṇam
tatra prayātā gacchanti
brahma brahmavido janāḥ

Translation

Fire, light, day, the bright lunar fortnight, the six months of the northern path (of the sun); by proceeding along it, man realizes the absolute and merges in the absolute.

Metaphorical Interpretation

Agni is a fire that not only removes darkness, but also burns. *Jyoti* means illumination. Daytime is full of all-pervading light. During the waxing phase of the moon, the bright fortnight, there is light in the night. *Uttarayana* means the presence of the sun in the northern hemisphere, which occurs six months out of the year. During this period, the days are longer than the nights, so there is more light than darkness. Here however, the Lord is speaking about the light connected with spiritual progress and realization.

In general, people remain in darkness; they are not aware of spiritual life; they are not after God. They spend most of their time eating, drinking, and merrymaking. Their valuable life is wasted in vain. Where there is no light, life is full of misery. In the grip of darkness, there is a life of delusion. But in each human body, the marvelous power of God is hiding. The body is called *tad dhama paramam mama*, the supreme abode of God (See the Bhagavad Gita 8:21). This divine abode is located within a ten-finger span—from the pituitary, the *ajña* chakra, to the fontanel, the *sahasrara* chakra. Each person should try to come up to this presence, where the power of God is hiding and breathing.

When one's mind becomes introvert trying to perceive the power of God inside the cranium, one can visualize the divine illumination, as well as divine vibration and the *aum* sound. This is the light of the fire, the soul sun, which is always inside the cranium. Those who meditate and perceive the illumination of the soul sun are in daytime. This one fire, the soul fire, becomes the seven fires (*sapta archis*) that are in the seven centers. (See the Mundaka Upanishad 2:1:8).

Meditation is a spiritual journey from the bottom center of the spine up to the top center, from the ordinary plane of human existence of money, sex, food, and so forth, up to the divine plane located in the pituitary and the fontanel. In the human body, the coccygeal center, the *muladhara* chakra, is to the south while the fontanel, the *sahasrara* chakra, is to the north. Through deep meditation, one moves from the south to the north. The six centers from the coccyx to the pituitary are the six months of illumination following the winter solstice.

Those who practice the scientific technique of Kriya Yoga know how to cover the six centers and come up to the presence of the soul sun. This is the path to realizing the absolute. It is not possible to progress spiritually until and unless one moves up from the propensities of the lower centers and remains in God consciousness at the top.

During deep meditation, the breath is extremely fine and one is able to withdraw from the mind and senses. In Kriya breathing, the exhalation moves down the front of the spine, whereas the inhalation moves up the back of the spine. Since there are no sense organs in the back of the body, there is no delusion, illusion, or error. This is a special path that each seeker of Truth must follow to achieve liberation and become *brahmavid,* the knower of Brahman.

The four great vedic proclamations state: 1) *prajñanam brahma* (Rig Veda), "Wisdom is Brahman." Through deep meditation, one goes to the state of wisdom, the *samadhi* stage. 2) *aham brahmasmi* (Yajur Veda), "I am Brahman." In thi s body form, I am the formless, the supreme. 3) *tattvam asi* (Sama Veda), "That thou art." and 4) *ayamatma brahma* (Atharva Veda), "This soul is Brahman."

Verse 25

dhūmo rātris tathā kṛṣṇaḥ
ṣaṇmāsā dakṣiṇāyanam
tatra cāndramasam jyotir
yogī prāpya nivartate

Translation

Proceeding through smoke, night, the dark lunar fortnight, and the six months of the southern path (of the sun), the yogi perceives moonlight and returns back.

Metaphorical Interpretation

Dhuma means smoke. *Ratri* means night. *Krishna* means the dark fortnights and *dakshinayanam* is the time when the sun is in the southern hemisphere. All the sense organs are found in the front side of the spine and on the front part of the body. In the front, there is temptation; people are engrossed in matter and memory, delusion, illusion, and error. Fire covered with smoke does not allow one to perceive the beauty of the fire. In addition, smoke is uncomfortable. People busy with material activity forget the indwelling self and are full of confusion. They do not feel the marvelous power of God is inside them. This is delusion, night, and darkness.

Darkness is the symbol of spiritual ignorance and suffering. People who are extremely engrossed in sense objects—sound, sight, smell, touch, and taste—are very deluded and have a lot of attachments. They are in body consciousness. They forget the truth. They are like animals. This is the common behavior of the front side of the body. Remaining attached to material activities such as money, sex, food, ego, and so on, draws life force downward. Consciousness flows down from the fontanel to the coccyx. Without the power of God, people cannot really enjoy the material world, but they don't realize this.

Going from the pituitary down to the coccyx is the movement of the soul sun from north to south. This is called *dakshinayamam*, the six months of the sun's southern path from July to December. People in this condition perceive the moon plane. The moon and the mind are related; therefore, people give a lot of importance to the desires and passions of the mind when they are enjoying the material world. This is *chandra loka*, a state that cannot give real peace, bliss, or joy. Real joy is in the soul sun in the pituitary and the fontanel. Those who practice Kriya Yoga come up the back of the spine perceiving divine illumination; they constantly feel the unity of *ham* and *sa*. *Ham* and *sa* are, respectively, the six months of waning light and the six months of waxing light—twelve months, conducted by one soul.

Verse 26

śuklakṛṣṇe gatī hy ete
jagataḥ śāśvate mate
ekayā yāty anāvṛttim
anyayā 'vartate punaḥ

Translation

These are the two paths of the world, the light and the darkness. They are considered to be everlasting. Proceeding one way, one does not return and proceeding the other way, one returns.

Metaphorical Interpretation

In this verse, the Lord describes two ways of life. Every day people see day and night. In the daytime, there is light and in the night, darkness. Similarly, in each human body there is light in the back of the body and darkness in front. The front is full of delusion. Here people are engrossed in the world of the twenty-four principles and the five sense organs. This is *maya*. But there is another way, in the back of the human spine. Here, people can perceive the marvelous power of God breathing through the spine. He is the Lord of everything. He loves His creation.

By the practice of Kriya Yoga, *ida* and *pingala* in the spine are separated, and the subtle passage of *sushumna* is opened. Once this occurs, people can perceive that the power of God is breathing from the top. Breath is the cause of life. Through breath, people have endless desires and satisfactions. Those who are truly intelligent come to the realized master and follow and practice the spiritual life. With deep love, loyalty, and faith, they gain a desire to progress from the bottom to the top.

God-realization is the birthright of each human being, but not animals. Those who proceed on the northern path taste divine love and ultimately reach liberation. Those who follow the downward path of darkness must come back again. This is the way as given by the Lord.

Verse 27

nai 'te sṛtī pārtha jānan
yogī muhyati kaśćana
tasmāt sarveṣu kāleṣu
yogayukto bhavā 'rjuna

Translation

O Partha (Arjuna)! The yogi who knows these paths is never deluded. Therefore, O Arjuna! Be steadfast in yoga, all the time.

Metaphorical Interpretation

This verse is a beautiful direction from the Lord to Arjuna, which indirectly gives direction to all human beings. Each human being is an image of God. God has given divine rationality to all people so they can decide what is good and bad. With this ability, everyone should try to follow the right direction, the divine path.

The Lord is saying: "O Partha! I address you by the name of your mother who is truly spiritual. You have inherited that quality. I have told you in detail about the two paths. People are attracted to the path of enjoyment; they do not remember that this will cause a lot of difficulties. This will not enable them to be realized. But you are born as a warrior, to fight with all the evils of your own life. I also told you about the path of illumination which requires directing your focus to the north, which is the path of emancipation and realization. Practice Kriya Yoga. Come down the front of the spine with every exhalation and go up the back of the spine with every inhalation. Perceive the divine power in the fontanel with every breath. Practice this and be free from delusion."

A yogi is always seeking the Truth, always speaking the truth. He does not rest in emotion or attachment. A yogi's life is the life of discernment. His mind is always at the top, in the north. A yogi's life is full of light. Inner light guides him all the time. There is no ignorance. A yogi remains compassionately detached. The yogi is in the back of the spine and in the fontanel and is therefore free from all delusion, illusion, and error.

"O Arjuna! Many people follow some spiritual way, but only for a short period. Spiritual life is for all time. This yoga is yoga for life. With every breath, perceive unity with the Lord. He is breathing; your breath is possible only due to the constant union of *ham* and *sa*. Be a true yogi, all the time, in all situations, and in all activities. If you perceive *kri* and *ya* constantly and continuously, you will not be deluded. *Tasmat sarveshu kaleshu yogayukto bhava:* Be constantly united with the almighty. You will be liberated."

Verse 28

vedeṣu yajñeṣu tapaḥsu cai 'va
dāneṣu yat puṇyaphalam pradiṣṭam
atyeti tat sarvam idam viditvā
yogī param sthānam upaiti cā 'dyam

Translation

The yogi who realizes this profound Truth is undoubtedly beyond the fruits of meritorious deeds as described in the scriptures, which come from the study of the Vedas, sacrifices, austerities, and charities, and he ultimately attains the beginningless supreme state.

Metaphorical Interpretation

In this verse, the Lord explains the impermanence of virtues that arise from religious activities like studying the Vedas, *yajña* (sacrifices), *tapas* (penance), and *dana* (charity). Many people practice different techniques to achieve some desired goals of enjoyment. People study the scriptures like the Vedas to know the Truth, but they may not be able to realize the Truth just by study of the scriptures. The word Veda comes from the verb *vid*, which means to know, but which really means to know one's indwelling self. If someone spends his precious time studying instead of trying to know his divine self, then he cannot reach the goal.

A sincere seeker realizes the impermanence of human life and is not so attached to the study of the scriptures; instead, he studies his own life and uses every moment for soul culture. Ordinarily, *yajña* is a ritualistic fire ceremony where people offer oblation to the holy fire and chant mantras. It gives some results or benefits, but these are only temporary. Real *yajña* is perceiving the soul in every breath and touching the soul fire with each breath. One must sacrifice all negative qualities to be established in the soul. Performing all actions as a worship to God in a spirit of selflessness is also *yajña*.

Tapas means austerities. People undertake many forms of penance, fasting, and so forth, and even follow many painful practices, but the soul is ever present in all living beings. The soul is the sole doer. The soul is breathing. The soul is maintaining the body heat (*tapas*). If one watches the breath and loves the soul in every breath, this is true *tapas* or austerity.

Dana means charity. People donate money, food, medicine, and clothing to the needy, poor, and sick. This is virtuous, but true *dana* is having the discrimination to correctly perceive spiritual knowledge. One who is established in Truth can truly help people.

When a seeker knows the true purpose of the Vedas, *yajña*, *tapas*, and *dana*, he will always remain on the top, in the state of constant God awareness. Such a yogi, who is self-controlled and well-disciplined and whose mind is not after temporary achievement is able to reach the supreme goal of self realization.

Kriya Yoga is a marvelous technique. If a person follows this meditation technique as taught by an able, realized master, he will reach real knowledge, consciousness, super consciousness, and cosmic consciousness. All ignorance will disappear. He will become well established, constantly perceiving divine sound, light, and sensation. Through meditation, such a person will enter the beginningless stage where he can perceive the imperishable power of the supreme Lord in the whole body. Then, he reaches the stage of *samadhi*. This is the attainment of a yogi—the state of supreme bliss.

Summary

This chapter is called the "Yoga of the Imperishable Brahman" (*akshara brahma yoga*). It is also called *taraka brahma yoga*, the "Yoga of Realizing Brahman." Each individual endowed with a body nature is called a *jiva*, the perishable aspect of God. Behind this perishable nature, remains the imperishable soul—Brahman. One should try to realize this during every moment and with every breath. Continuous and constant God awareness is the source of inner peace, bliss, and joy. This is real love. To perceive the presence of God in all activities is the manifestation of divine love. Everyone should try to fight their inner weaknesses and impurities to achieve and experience peace within.

In this chapter, Verse 8, the Lord explained *abhyasa yoga*, the yoga of practice. An ounce of practice is better than tons of theories. Knowledge is good, but knowledge applied in practical life is better. Knowledge transformed into experience is the best; this is the state of wisdom. Spiritual life is not a dream, but a life of sincere practice ultimately leading to success. Success in life is the result of one percent inspiration and ninety-nine percent perspiration.

This chapter also highlights how to control the doors of the body house and how to thoroughly control one's life (Verse 12). To merge into the ocean of cosmic consciousness, one should continuously listen to *aum*, the divine sound.

This chapter, consisting of twenty-eight verses, can be divided as follows:

Verse 1-2 contain Arjuna's questions related to practical spiritual life and philosophy.

Verses 3 and 4 present the Lord's explanations about Brahman, *adhyatma, adhibhuta, adhiyajña,* and so forth.
Verses 5 to 8 discuss continuous God awareness, daily spiritual life, and the path to achieve constant liberation.
Verses 9 to 13 explain how to be free from body consciousness, how to awaken spiritually, and the state of a liberated being at the time of death.
Verses 14 to 16 discuss how, with an unwavering and concentrated mind and constant soul consciousness, one can realize God.
Verses 17 to 19 elucidate the repetition of the cycle of creation, day and night, exhalation and inhalation—through all these changes, one must realize the imperishable, Brahman.
Verses 20 to 22 state that the unmanifest imperishable *purusha* (the indwelling spirit) is beyond the play of changing nature.
Verses 23 to 28 describe the paths of liberation and bondage.

In the two concluding verses, the Lord explains how one can remain in the state of yoga all the time. Ordinary people consider yoga to be a difficult path, but this conception is wrong. Yoga is life and life is yoga. Without yoga—the union of body and soul—life is impossible. Yoga is as easy as incoming and outgoing breath. Everyone must practice perceiving Brahman's presence in *adhibhuta*, *adhiyajña*, and *adhidaiva*. This is the way to liberation.

Chapter 9

Raja vidya raja guhya yoga

The Yoga of the Secret Royal Science

Introduction

In the Mundaka Upanishad (1:1:4), the *rishi*, the man of right vision, instructs the disciple, *dve vidye veditavye iti ha sma yad brahmavido vadanti, parā caivāparā ca*: "One must be well versed and competently trained in two branches of knowledge..." The first is *apara vidya*: material science, knowledge of the phenomenal world; the second is *para vidya*: the ultimate knowledge, self knowledge, the knowledge of the absolute. Most people are after the first, and neglect the second. A few are after the second, looking down on the first. But the *shruti* (Vedas) declares that one must be proficient in both.

Material science is the domain of observation: the experience of the senses and the mind. This mundane knowledge comes very easily. Self knowledge is the inner journey to reach the goal of human perfection. This knowledge comes with sincere effort. Material science discusses life. Philosophy explains life. But spirituality experiences life. This experience is easily available through the path of yoga. Yoga is the art of living in constant soul awareness.

In the last two verses of Chapter 8, the Lord encouraged Arjuna to be a yogi and to reach the supreme abode. Where is the supreme abode? How do you get there? The objects of the material world are external; the experiments in the material world are outside in the world laboratory. But where is the supreme abode, where one is to experiment and experience the spiritual inquiry? These questions are latent in the mind of Arjuna, not expressed in words.

On the spiritual journey, the guru is the preceptor and true guide who helps the student advance toward self realization. The omniscient guru preceptor, looking at the face of the student and knowing his inner thoughts, exposes and explains the secret doctrine of spiritual life. But the spiritual science is supreme, royal, and divine—it cannot be expressed by the mouth, through limited words. The divine abode is not outside, it is within: The kingdom of God is within you. (See Luke 17:21).

So, following the instructions of the guide, the disciple progresses on the inner journey of self realization and tries to become enlightened by the light of the soul. The flame of spiritual life is burning in the secret chamber of the spiritual heart, in the cave of the cranium. While going there, one should be extremely cautious and careful.

After explaining *akshara brahma* in the previous chapter, the Lord now tells of the secret and hidden royal treasure of spirituality that is covered with a veil of ignorance, waiting to be discovered through constant meditation. This chapter is therefore called *Raja vidya raja guhya yoga*, which means "Yoga of the Manifestation of Divine Knowledge."

Verse 1

śrībhagavān uvāca
idam tu te guhyatamam
pravakṣyāmy anasūyave
jñānam vijñānasahitam
yaj jñātvā mokṣyase 'śubhāt

Translation

The Lord said:
To you who are free from jealousy, I shall reveal the most secret, hidden knowledge with its application, which will free you from all evils.

Metaphorical Interpretation

The previous chapter taught how to perceive God in everything, *vasudeva sarvam*, the omnipresence of God. But it is human nature to find fault, which makes one unfit for receiving this higher knowledge. If people don't sincerely prepare themselves to receive divine knowledge, they will not be qualified.

"O Arjuna! You are a true disciple. You are free from jealousy, and your vision is clear." In Sanskrit, the qualified disciple is called *adhikari*, which means to attain inner fitness. *Anasuya* is the word for those who are free from jealousy, who don't find fault in others. This is what it takes to be a true disciple. By focusing on the faults in others, a person not only uses precious time, but also subconsciously takes those negative qualities into himself.

Knowledge can neither be purchased nor borrowed; although one can learn from books, real knowledge is communicated from the master to the disciple. This real knowledge is extremely secret. The master may talk about spiritual truth, but if the disciple is not qualified, fit, or sincere, then he cannot understand. Such a situation is described in the Bible. When Jesus was teaching, many came to him again and again asking questions; he explained everything with the utmost care, but many were not able to understand or even perceive his teachings (See Matthew 13:10 and Mark 4:34). When a disciple is ready, when his mind is pure, when he perceives divine love and follows the master, then, the compassionate guru will reveal the wisdom to him. Sincerity and love for the master, and implicit faith in and loyalty to the guru will enable him to understand. The eagerness and worthiness of the disciple and the compassion of the master enable the manifestation of divine wisdom in one's life.

The Lord is saying, "O Arjuna! I will teach you this secret knowledge in such a way that you will attain *jñana* and *vijñana*." *Jñana* means knowledge. *Vijñana* means the way to reach or realize the truth, which is the application of knowledge, the states of super consciousness and cosmic consciousness.

"O Arjuna! I will impart the knowledge to you and the way to realize it." This knowledge is *guhyatamam*, which literally means hidden or secret. But the real meaning of *guhya* is *guhayam nihitam guhyam*, that which remains in the cave (the cranium). In the scriptures it says, *dharmasyatattwa nihitam guhayam*: "The essence of *dharma* (that which holds the body and soul together) is in the cave of the cranium." The hidden but marvelous power of God is inside the brain and is breathing day and night. Most people do not realize this.

"O Arjuna! I will give you this divine knowledge because you are spotless and sincere. If you follow Me and realize the Truth, you will be free from all that is evil and inauspicious." What is truly evil and inauspicious in the world? To ordinary people, it is death. Those who know *jñana* and *vijñana* perceive the state of immortality and are free from all worries, anxieties, and troubles and free from the fear of death.

Verse 2

rājavidyā rājaguhyam
pavitram idam uttamam
pratyakṣāvagamam dharmyam
susukham kartum avyayam

Translation

This is the supreme royal knowledge, the greatest secret (hidden) science, the most holy and excellent, known through direct perception, attainable through morality (*dharma*), extremely easy to practice and also imperishable.

Metaphorical Interpretation

In this verse, the Lord describes the glory of divine knowledge.

The mind is restless, due to the extroverted sense organs. The sense organs become restless from the restlessness of the vital breath. The restless mind constantly roams from one object to another; it is never at rest or in peace. The mind does not realize that everything is pervaded by the power of God. When one treads the path of spiritual practice with faith and love, as described in the scriptures and taught by the master, and if this practice is accompanied with knowledge (*jñana*) and inner detachment *(vairagya)*, then one will quickly and steadily make progress on the path and will become realized.

In this scientific age, people undertake many different types of work using scientific knowledge. Spiritual practice is called *rajavidya*, the royal science. Spiritual practice is neither based on blind belief, nor is it an ordinary science. The practical aspect of Kriya Yoga is the science of meditation and soul culture. This meditation is also *rajaguhyam*, which means royal secret or extremely hidden, because without purity of mind and extremely sharp intellect, one cannot penetrate into the cave of the cranium (*guha*) and become realized.

Meditation and the mind are correlated. Meditation purifies the mind. With a pure mind, one can meditate better. During meditation, one can enter a state of no-mind. This is the royal secret. Meditation such as Kriya Yoga is extremely pure, clear, and divine. It cleans the inner life and makes one continuously aware of the indwelling self.

Meditation is the highest method of soul culture and self realization. This technique is *uttama,* the supreme. It leads to the perception of the highest, located on the top of the head. *Uttama* consists of two parts, *ut* and *tama*, which mean that it helps to go in an upward direction, to the north, to the cave of the cranium in the body; the fontanel is in the north and the feet are in the south. This supreme (*uttama*) technique also leads to realization of the supreme self, *uttama purusha*.

Pratyakṣa avagamam means to know through direct perception. The soul cannot be perceived by indirect processes such as reading books or hearing discourses. In the Mundaka Upanishad (3:2:3) it says, *nāyam ātmā pravacanena labhyo na medhayā na bahunā śrutena:* "Self knowledge is the subject matter of direct perception of which only the soul is the object." Apart from the soul, whatever man perceives is indirect, because man perceives everything with the help of the senses, mind, and soul. To know the soul, one must close the doors of all the senses and keep the mind still. Soul is beyond the perception of the senses; it is transcendental.

Dharmyam means to perceive the soul through the link of the breath. *Dharma* means to hold. The breath holds the body. The breath is going in and out through the soul. Through breath control, one can reach the state of self-control and God realization. One may think that spiritual practice is extremely difficult, but the Lord tells us it is *susukham kartum*, extremely easy to practice—there is no need for ostentatious show, it is free from any physical hardship.

Avyayam means imperishable. Although easily attainable, divine perception is not temporary. Self knowledge is the supreme One, beyond all modification and change. It is the supreme state of spiritual achievement. Those who follow the master with implicit faith, love, and loyalty, and who practice a scientific technique like Kriya Yoga, can attain supreme truth in this very life.

Verse 3

aśraddadhānāḥ puruṣā
dharmasyā 'sya paramtapa
aprāpya mām nivartante
mṛtyusamsāravartmani

Translation

O Oppressor of Enemies! (Arjuna) Men who have no faith in this way (the path of spirituality) are unable to reach or realize Me, and they return to this mortal world of *samsara*.

Metaphorical Interpretation

When the Lord Himself describes this beautiful and effective technique, why doesn't everyone follow the path? Even after hearing of the glory of meditation and the spiritual life in the previous verse, doubt will still arise in the minds of many. This verse addresses that doubt.

In this verse, Arjuna is addressed as Paramtapa, the oppressor of enemies. One who has achieved victory over passion, anger, ego, and all the inner enemies is *paramtapa*. The inner enemies are more harmful than the outer enemies. The Lord is saying, "O Arjuna! You have gained thorough control over your inner weaknesses and enemies. Those who want spiritual progress must be like you."

A quality of the true spiritual seeker is *shraddha*, which means faith—faith in the words of the scriptures and in the words of the master. The spiritual master is the mouthpiece for divine wisdom. A disciple must be a faithful follower of the master. Those who lack faith in this divine path of God realization are far away from peace, bliss, and joy. They will remain in the mortal world of suffering and misery: Although truth may be very near, it will still be extremely far.

"O Arjuna! You listen to my every word carefully and try to practice sincerely. When you have any doubt or confusion, if you are not able to understand, then you immediately ask me."

A spiritual technique such as Kriya Yoga is extremely easy to practice. Follow it joyfully and you will be merged in the almighty father, constantly united with Him. If you do not perceive Him, follow and practice Lord Krishna's teachings; then you will see that the Lord is the nearest of the near and the dearest of the dear—He is with you always.

Verse 4

mayā tatam idam sarvam
jagad avyaktamūrtinā
matsthāni sarvabhūtāni
na cā 'ham teṣv avasthitaḥ

Translation

The whole universe is pervaded by Me as the unmanifest divine form. All beings are within Me, but speaking the truth, I am not abiding in them.

Metaphorical Interpretation

In the previous two verses, the Lord revealed the beauty of the divine path of self-realization, and the suffering in the demonic path that is devoid of faith in yoga and meditation. The Lord is telling the efficient disciples, followers, and friends, "O Arjuna! Please listen to Me very carefully. Ordinary people engage themselves in arguments, interpretation and analysis, but this is only the play of the ego."

Maya tatam idam sarvam jagat means that this entire universe is pervaded by God who is formless and all-pervading: He is in the left and right and in the north and south; He is in the front and back; He is in and out. But His form is *avyakta*, unmanifest, and beyond the perception of the senses. Although His presence is everywhere, the physical eye and the power to see cannot perceive Him. He is transcendent.

"O Arjuna! If the intellect is not pure, then you cannot really perceive, conceive, and realize Me. When you realize this, you will be free from all inauspiciousness. If you want to realize Me, perceive My presence everywhere.

"Try to understand that although I am in all the senses, I am beyond all the senses. I am pure consciousness. I can see without eyes and hear without ears. I have no legs or hands, but being infinite, I am at all times, in all places. As the life principle, I make everyone full of life, vitality, and activity. I am purer and finer than the sky, I am compassionate and detached, I am the soul in all living beings. I am not limited, I am neither male nor female, I have no name and no form, I am not affected by the triple qualities of nature. I am self-effulgent; no one can illumine Me; I am illumination for everyone. I am the cause of breath. I am, therefore, everyone and everything that is alive."

Consider how air permeates living beings; then you can easily understand this verse. The Lord is saying, "O Arjuna! I am the breath in everything, but you cannot say that I am inside all beings, or that I am outside of them. I am both inside and outside—everywhere at once. In this way, all living beings are born in Me, living in Me, and are merging in Me."

Also remember the analogy of the waves and the ocean. All waves are in the ocean. Waves cannot exist without the ocean. Waves ultimately merge in the ocean, but you cannot say that the ocean is in the waves. God is the ocean of pure consciousness and all created things and beings are the waves.

Verse 5

na ca matsthāni bhūtāni
paśya me yogam aiśvaram
bhūtabhṛn na ca bhūtastho
mamā 'tmā bhūtabhāvanaḥ

Translation

And yet the beings (elements) do not abide in Me. Behold My divine yoga. Though I am the sustainer and creator of all beings (elements), My Self, in reality, dwells not in those beings (elements).

Metaphorical Interpretation

In the previous verse, the Lord said, *matsthani sarvabhutani,* "All living beings (including the gross elements) are within Me." In this verse the Lord says: *na ca matsthani bhutani*, "All beings (or the gross elements) are not within Me." These two statements appear to be contradictory, but in reality they are not. When the mind becomes pure and fine, when the intellect is sharp, then one will be able to conceive and realize this truth.

Maya tatam idam sarvam: The Lord is saying, "I am everywhere. All beings or gross elements are within Me. I am pervading in the entire universe. I am the sustainer of everything." When a person is able to perceive that God is the creator and maintainer of everything, he experiences joy and happiness. He will also realize that he is completely detached, that he is pure consciousness, that he is not gross or elemental.

"O Arjuna!," says Lord Krishna, *Pashya me yogam aishvaram*: "Behold my divine yoga. I am the Light of lights. I am the supreme Lord." And also, *Mamatma bhutabhavanaḥ*: "My soul, the self, maintains all beings and activates all the centers."

When you practice meditation and come up to the fontanel and perceive the divine illumination, then you can easily realize that the Lord supplies the power to all the centers in the spine (all the gross elements); yet at the same time, you can also realize that He is beyond the centers (the gross elements). All the gross elements are created by the Lord: earth, water, fire, air, and sky. In the whole universe, one can see the five gross elements. Inside the human body, one can see the activities of the five gross elements in the lower five centers. All gross elements, as well as all living beings, have form and are limited. A limited object cannot contain the unlimited.

"O Arjuna! Meditate nicely, then you will be able to perceive my divine nature."

Verse 6

yathā 'kāśasthito nityam
vāyuḥ sarvatrago mahān
athā sarvāṇi bhūtāni
matsthānī 'ty upadhāraya

Translation

As the mighty wind, which is everywhere, dwells eternally in space (vacuum center); so know clearly that in the same manner, all beings dwell in Me.

Metaphorical Interpretation

In this verse, the Lord beautifully explains a subtle spiritual truth through the metaphor of sky and air. It is similar to the Taittiriya Upanishad (2:1:1) where it says, *etasmād ātmana ākāśaḥ sambhūtaḥ, ākāśād vāyuḥ...*: "The sky was born from the supreme self, and from the sky was born the air..." Among the five elements of creation, sky is the first, then came air.

As ornaments are created from gold and gold is the substance in ornaments—sky (vacuum, the ether, space) is the substance of air. Without gold, there would be no gold ornaments. Without substance, there would be no creation. The sky is the cause of the creation of air. Air is born in the sky, remains in the sky, and blows in the sky. The sky is more subtle than the air: Sky is static, steady, and changeless, while air is changing and restless. Everything you see, any living being, or even any of the gross elements, even your body is born from God, and exists only because of God.

In this verse, every individual and living being is symbolized by the air. Also in this verse, air is associated with the adjective *mahan*, which means the great. Is every individual great? There is no doubt about it. Every living being is the formless image of God. From air, one is to go to the state of vacuum—from manhood, one can reach the state of Godhood—the formless divine state.

The Lord is saying, "Arjuna! The path of self-knowledge is extremely slippery, but it is also extremely easy and natural. Just as the sky and the air remain together, you and I are always together, always united. You always remain in my divine lap. This is yoga."

Verse 7

sarvabhūtāni kaunteya
prakṛtim yānti māmikām
kalpakṣaye punas tāni
kalpādau visṛjāmy aham

Translation

O son of Kunti (Arjuna)! All beings enter into My divine being (nature) during the final dissolution (the end of one cycle, one *kalpa*). Again, I send them forth at the beginning of creation.

Metaphorical Interpretation

Lord Krishna is saying, "O Son of Kunti (Arjuna!) You are extremely intelligent. I have explained how the air constantly remains in the lap of the sky, just as you, every living being, and all material substance are in My lap, always. Creation is a constant cycle: Existence and dissolution occur everywhere, at all times, in the form of My divine nature." Whatever is created is done through the Lordship of God and His divine nature, which is eightfold. In each human being, the dominance of this eightfold nature can be seen in the spine. (See the Bhagavad Gita 7:4.)

In this verse, the word *kalpa* has many meanings. One meaning is the calculation of time. The other meaning is the cycle of creation. But it's real meaning in this verse is *kalpana*, the modification of mind, thoughts, or desire.

"O Arjuna! When a *kalpana* (a desire) is born in you, your whole system changes: your physical blood circulation, your breathing pattern—everything." Both good and bad desires are born in the waking and dream states. *Kalpakshaya* means the dissolution of all these desires. This state occurs either during deep sleep (the absence of all activity) or during deep meditation (the state of extreme tranquility). This state is called *avyakta*, the unmanifest. There is a subtle difference between deep sleep and meditation. Deep sleep is meditation without consciousness. Meditation is deep sleep with consciousness. Deep sleep is a play of nature; it has nothing to do with spiritual evolution. Meditation, however, accelerates spiritual evolution.

When a person wakes up from deep sleep, this is called *kalpadau*, the beginning of creation. Similarly, when one gets up from meditation, there is a transition from *kalpakshaya,* or dissolution, to *kalpadau*, the beginning of creation. After deep sleep, although a person is full of refreshment, he is still the same old person. On the other hand, after meditation, a person's entire system is new; he is a better person. Meditation accelerates human evolution and enables one to be more spiritual and divine and to realize the absolute.

Verse 8

prakṛtim svām avaṣṭabhya
visṛjāmi punaḥ-punaḥ
bhūtagrāmam imam kṛtsnam
avaśam prakṛter vaśāt

Translation

Resting in My own divine nature, I send them forth again and again. This multitude of beings is truly helpless, by the power of My divine nature.

Metaphorical Interpretation

The Lord is saying, "O Arjuna! You are overpowered by the play of nature, but I am the Lord of nature. My nature is eight-fold, extremely active from the coccyx (*muladhara chakra*) to the pituitary *(ajña chakra)*; therefore you are always tempted and engrossed with activities related to money, sex, food, emotion, religious rituals, mind, intellect, and ego. You do not know that the play of nature is possible through these activities only because of My power, the power of breath.

"Just as all creation is done through me and people are busy in the play of the world; similarly, all thoughts come from above, from the brain, and you are playing with your thoughts. You do not realize that thoughts and God are one and have been one, always."

Everything is possible only through the breath. When the breath is restless, people are restless. People do not know how to achieve calmness through breath control; they feel extremely helpless. This is the state of beings who are under the power of nature. Those who are intelligent, however, will try to bring their awareness up to the pituitary and above it, to the fontanel. In this state of constant God awareness, restlessness disappears; the stage of God communion has been reached.

"Arjuna! Constantly perceive that I am with you, that I am the charioteer in the body chariot in the battlefield of life. If through meditation and breath control you remain always in My presence, then you will not be affected by the turbulent dance of nature."

Verse 9

na ca mām tāni karmāṇi
nibadhnanti dhanamjaya
udāsīnavad āsīnam
asaktam teṣu karmasu

Translation

O Dhanamjaya! (Arjuna, conqueror of wealth!) These actions do not bind Me, for I sit indifferently, unattached to those actions.

Metaphorical Interpretation

Ordinary people are attached to action and its fruits; they do not understand that they cannot work without the breath. As a result of their body consciousness and ego, they feel that they are doing the work. Ego and attachment are the causes of bondage and are qualities of the rajasic nature. But the body is merely an instrument of action; the real action remains on the top. Always remember who is breathing.

"O Arjuna! You are Dhanamjaya. You are extremely powerful to have achieved victory over all the lower propensities. You know the art of breath control. You know how to bring your awareness to the pituitary, and you can even reach the state of formlessness in the fontanel; therefore, you become one with Me and reach My state of divinity."

All karma (action) is born from *avyakta* Brahman, the unmanifest one (See the Bhagavad Gita 3:15). When you practice Kriya and reach this state of soul consciousness, which is true karma, true action, then you will perceive inaction in action. In this state, the spiritual seeker perceives the divine and remains *udasinavat*, indifferent, and *asakta*, detached, which means compassionately detached. The Lord is revealing the beautiful teaching of *udasinavat*. *Udasina* is *ut,* above, and *asina*, seated, and means seated on the top. *Udasina vat* also means not attracted. Differentiation and distinction in the world brings the sense of attachment, but someone who can keep his attention on the top, not below, achieves the divine state of indifference and is not affected by the dualities of pleasure and pain. The Lord also mentions another important quality, *asakta,* which is compassionate detachment. This detachment is not an external show; it is an inner state of mind.

Indifference and detachment are two divine qualities one can gain by regular practice of Kriya. Although someone may live in the material world, inner purity from the practice of Kriya Yoga can free him from the bondage of ignorance. He then works in the material world as an actor—the actor in a drama knows that he is acting, that in reality he is someone else.

Verse 10

mayā 'dhyakṣeṇa prakṛtiḥ
sūyate sacarācaram
hetunā 'nena kaunteya
jagad viparivartate

Translation

O Son of Kunti (Arjuna!) With Me as the supervisor, divine nature produces all things animate and inanimate. This is the cause of the universe.

Metaphorical Interpretation

In the previous verse, the Lord said that although all actions come from Him, He remains detached and indifferent because He knows that He is the actor. In this verse, the Lord is speaking of creation: "O Arjuna! I and My eightfold nature, made from earth, water, fire, air, vacuum, mind, intellect, and ego, are the causes of creation. Under My supervision, nature produces all things, animate and inanimate. I abide in the fontanel. When I am in the fontanel, I am the supreme, when My presence is experienced below, I am manifested in all the chakras and all the universe."

The Shvetashvatara Upanishad (6:11) declares,

eko devas sarva bhūteṣu gūḍhas
sarva vyāpī sarva bhūtāntarātmā
karmādhyakṣas sarva bhūtādhivāsas
sākṣī cetā kevalo nirguṇaśca,

which means: "The one God is hiding in all beings, all-pervading, the indwelling self of all; at the same time He is the all-pervading supervisor, the Lord of all activities, abiding in everything, the witnessing consciousness, the only One, devoid of qualities."

The Lord is formless. Whatever one can see, living and non-living, is pervaded by the Lord alone. Without the Lord, nature has no value; it is inert and non existent. Similarly, without the soul, the body is dead. Human thoughts and everything are from the one and the absolute. Nature is nothing but God's manifestation. Alone, nature cannot create. Alone, God has no form. Divine nature and God are one and are the cause of everything. United, the body and soul are active, alive, and the cause of all activities.

The Lord is saying "O Arjuna! Please look at Me. I am eternal and ever free. So are you. You can perceive this if you are constantly united with Me. Practice the way of soul culture: An ordinary piece of iron constantly attached to a magnet becomes magnetic. Be constantly associated with Me and perceive that you and I are one and always have been one." This is divine transformation.

Verse 11

avajānanti mām mūḍhā
mānuṣīm tanum āśritam
param bhāvam ajānanto
mama bhūtamaheśvaram

Translation

Being deluded, they despise Me, as I am assumed to be in the human form. They do not know My supreme nature as the great Lord of all existence.

Metaphorical Interpretation

"O Arjuna! Those with impure minds who are deluded cannot perceive My divine nature. They have a gross outlook, attached to the body. They ignore Me personified in all forms, especially in the human form. Although I am omnipresent, my divine quality is manifested more strongly in human beings. Animals cannot develop intellect or knowledge.

"O Arjuna! I am the self, beyond the body nature. I am the soul, abiding in every human being. At the same time, I am the Great Lord, Maheshwara, the Lord of everything. I am in everyone, the weak and the strong, males and females, the young and the old, animate and inanimate. If I do not remain in the body and the breath, then you would not exist. Even when you are sleeping, I am awake and breathing.

"Try to perceive My divine presence in every cell of the body. If you remain attached to your body, you will think that you are that body. And as long as you are body-conscious, you cannot achieve divine wisdom. Look within and perceive that you are really the self, the pure, and the divine. The state beyond the body is called *parambhava*, the supreme nature."

Failing to perceive the soul as the supreme is to despise and ignore the Lord. Deluded man is ungrateful; he does not perceive his real nature, the divine soul, the charioteer driving the body chariot. Truly, this dishonors the Lord who is always with you, constantly serving you, who is your eternal companion, friend, philosopher, and guide.

Those who do not perceive their real nature are not human beings; they are animals in human form. So, cast away all your delusion and ignorance! Practice meditation and perceive your indwelling self, in you and in everyone. Then you will achieve liberation.

Verse 12

moghāśā moghakarmāṇo
moghajñānā vicetasaḥ
rākṣasīm āsurīm cai va
prakṛtim mohinīm śritāḥ

Translation

Those with vain aspirations and fruitless knowledge, whose actions are futile, and those who are devoid of discrimination, who abide in a fiendish and demonic nature, are attracted by enchanting delusion.

Metaphorical Interpretation

"O Arjuna! Those who ignore or despise Me must face three difficulties: their aspirations are futile; their activities are fruitless; their knowledge is useless."

People cherish their endless aspirations and expectations, but they become restless waiting for their desires to be fulfilled. They are bewildered with extremely passionate desire. They roam in the lower centers. Their work is not God-oriented. These people don't know the true source of aspiration, that which is the true achievement in human life. Devoid of discrimination, they search outside themselves for material achievement, but desire is the cause of their material activity. Real action leads to upward progress.

Man, attracted by multiplicity, runs after a multitude of things. He cannot perceive unity in everything—the presence of one divine being. He is completely deluded. He is devoid of peace, bliss, and joy. This type of person is called *rakshasa*, a person of fiendish nature, extremely worldly and materialistic, performing different rituals while being full of fear of pain or loss. He is extremely selfish and tries to appropriate everything for himself. He is full of self-love, devoid of real love. The Lord also speaks of another category of deluded people who are called *asura*, those who are of a demonic nature or ungodly. They are monstrosities, extremely body-conscious and sensual. On the other hand, one who is engrossed in spiritual practice and divine illumination is called *sura*.

Restlessness and peace exclude each other, like darkness and light. Material experience and skill may bring some pleasure in the lower centers, but true peace, bliss, and joy can only be perceived in the state of extreme calmness. Deluded people, extremely restless and bewildered, don't search for the divinity in everything. As their desires multiply, so do their activities. For them, peace is far away. People who are extremely engrossed in material activities eventually lose their energy and strength; this action gives birth to knowledge.

Verse 13

mahātmānas tu mām pārtha
daivīm prakṛtim āśritāḥ
bhajanty ananyamanaso
jñātvā bhūtādim avyayam

Translation

O Partha (Arjuna!) Those who are great souls, who have embraced divine nature, worship Me with an undistracted mind, knowing Me as the origin of beings and also as the imperishable.

Metaphorical Interpretation

"O Partha! People in this world are of two types, demonic and divine." The nature of demonic people was described in the last verse. Now please learn about the divine nature of spiritual people. Spiritual people are *mahatma. Mahatma* ordinarily means great soul, but it has a deeper meaning. *Mahan* and *atma* together create *mahatma.* One who perceives the soul, *atma,* constantly is great, prime, and supreme—a great soul. In another meaning, *mahat* means divine nature, and *atma* means the Lord of everything. Those who perceive that the divine nature and the Lord are one are truly the great souls. Their minds are extremely pure. They have thorough control over mind, thought, intellect, and ego. They perceive the presence of soul everywhere. Lord Krishna is describing these great souls: "They never ignore Me. Their mind is so concentrated that they have no other thoughts while meditating. They worship Me with a single and undistracted mind. Their worship is of a special type: By following divine nature, they worship Me."

By following the words of the scripture and the master, and by practicing meditation sincerely, people of divine nature achieve constant spiritual progress and liberation. Even after meditation, when they return to the ever changing world, they are extremely calm and divine. They perceive the changeless presence in everything, in every name and form.

Verse 14

satatam kīrtayanto mām
yatantaś ca dṛḍhavratāḥ
namasyantaś ca mām bhaktyā
nityayuktā upāsate

Translation

They meditate constantly remembering Me, striving with strong determination (vows), and honoring (bowing to) Me with devotion; they are ever united with Me.

Metaphorical Interpretation

A person of many virtuous deeds is embraced by divine nature. His life and activities are full of love and divinity. In this verse, the Lord explains in detail the practices of those with divine qualities:

Satatam kirtayantam: "Constantly remember Me." The ordinary meaning of *kirtan* is to chant the name or to sing the glory of God, but the real meaning is to use the faculty of speech in such a way that every word becomes a prayer to God. The aspirant with divine qualities perceives that the power of God is talking through the mouth, that every word is divine and full of love. He never misuses his tongue. Every word should be both truthful and pleasing.

Yatantah: "Strive sincerely to realize Me." There is a price for everything. Without self-effort, self-realization is impossible. Self-control and a disciplined life is the price of the state of God realization. He whose endeavor is stronger, is always nearer to God.

Dridhavratah: "Seek Me with strong determination." Self-discipline is the foundation of the spiritual life. All the sense organs and the mind are usually extrovert and restless. In the beginning of the spiritual life, every seeker must try to regulate his life with a set of maxims or principles. Daily, disciplined spiritual and material activity in God consciousness, is necessary for spiritual evolution.

Namasyantah mam bhaktya: "Bow to Me with devotion." *Bhakti* is devotion or love. This love for God is the absolute, supreme love. To love objects or others, forgetting God, is passion. This brings emotion. To love God in everything, is devotion. Devotion is not emotion, it is self-surrender. This love is the cause of the realization of God. To bow to God with devotion means to perceive God's presence everywhere. The aspirant with these divine qualities manifests this divine love in all his words, thoughts, and actions.

Nitya yukta: "Be ever united with Me." One who loves God perceives constant unity with the indwelling self. The body and soul are ever united. This is yoga, *ham* and *sa*. To perceive this state of unity continuously, constantly, and in every breath is *nitya yukta*. Another meaning of *nitya yukta* is to be united with *nitya,* the eternal one.

Upasate: "Meditate." *Upasana* means to sit near, *upa* (near) and *asana* (sit). A true spiritual person does not sit in the lower centers, rather, he comes up to the divine presence, in the pituitary and the fontanel. His mind is engrossed in divine love, and he constantly perceives the Lord's presence, in every breath and every thought.

Verse 15

jñānayajñena cā 'py anye
yajanto mām upāsate
ekatvena pṛthaktvena
bahudhā viśvatomukham

Translation

And by the path of knowledge, they meditate upon Me and worship Me as the One, and as the manifold, variously manifested, facing in all directions.

Metaphorical Interpretation

In the previous verse, the Lord explained the necessity for devotion; in this verse, the path of knowledge is explained. In reality, knowledge and devotion are one. In fact, action, knowledge, and love for God are inseparable. In the beginning of this chapter, the Lord told Arjuna that he must understand *jñana* through *vijñana*, knowledge with its application. Here the Lord is saying, while bowing, one must understand three aspects: whom to bow to, who is bowing, and how to bow. So, bow to God (soul in the body), by the living power of God!—in reality, the aspects are inseparable. When a river bows to the ocean, it becomes one with the ocean. This is divine knowledge.

The Lord is saying: "O Arjuna! When one meditates and bows to Me, sitting in the cranium, he is really practicing *jñana yajña*." *Yajña* means oblation in fire. Whatever is offered to fire is burned into ashes. Each one should sacrifice ego in the fire of yoga. When the ego is burned, constant unity with the indwelling self is perceived: one becomes well established in knowledge. This knowledge is not acquired by reading the scriptures or hearing explanations of the holy books. This is not theoretical knowledge; it is direct perception of the truth—the breath becomes extremely fine, not coming out of the nostrils; the divine illumination, the flame of knowledge, is extremely bright; one hears the continuous and spontaneous divine sound. Opening the eyes after meditation, the divine presence is perceived everywhere—a state of unity like the waves with the ocean—unity in diversity and diversity in unity.

One who closes all the doors of the body, who comes up from the lower centers and sits in the fontanel and offers the whole mind, thought, intellect, ego, body sense, and worldly sense to the fire of knowledge, is practicing *jñana yajña*, another name for *paravastha*.

Verse 16

aham kratur aham yajñaḥ
svadhā 'ham aham auṣadham
mantro 'ham aham evā 'jyam
aham agnir aham hutam

Translation

I am ritualistic action. I am sacrifice. I am the offering for the diseased. I am the medicinal herbs. I am the holy words. I am the *ghee* (clarified butter). I am the fire and I am the offering.

Metaphorical Interpretation

Lord Krishna says,

Kratuh: "I am *kratuh*"—a Vedic, ritualistic ceremony where *somarasa*, a special oblation, is offered to the holy fire. In fact, *kratuh* is *somayaga*, essentially an inner spiritual practice. What is real *somarasa*? In the *Agamasara* scripture, it says, *somadhārā kṣaret yā tu brahma randhrāt varānane pitvātān ānanda maya...*: "When one practices a special *mudra* (Kriya Yoga technique), a nectar-like secretion flows from the fontanel." This is "*soma rasa.*" Oblation of this *somarasa*, by keeping the tongue rolled up, is called *kratu*. By this, the mind becomes calm and quiet. One experiences inner tranquility.

Yajña: "I am the *yajña*, sacrifice." The breath is constantly offered as an oblation to the soul fire in the cave of the cranium. In a broader sense, every activity of every living being that is in the form of enjoying sense objects, is sacrifice *(yajña)*.

Svadha: "I am *svadha*, the offering of love to the deceased, the dead." Whatever actions have been done in the past are dead. Yet, their impressions remain in the midbrain, the seed of memory. Every thought accessed from memory is also *svadha*, which means the power of God.

Aushadhi: "I am the medicinal herbs." Medicine is necessary to treat disease. Everyone suffers from *bhava vyadhi*, diseases of the world. Ease means calmness. "Dis-ease" means restlessness. People of the world are suffering from the disease of restlessness; they are devoid of peace and joy. The Lord is the medicine, the process by which people can free themselves from restlessness. They can be calmly active and actively calm. *Aushadhi* is the technique of breath control.

Mantra: "I am *mantra*, the holy syllable." *Mantra* is that which makes the mind free from all restlessness, worries, and anxieties. The true *mantra* is to listen to the divine sound *anahata nada*, the nonstopping, continuous inner sound that gives extreme inner silence.

Ajyam: "I am the *ghee* (clarified butter)." In meditation and even in daily life, a spiritual person perceives the power of God in every breath. *Ghee* in a fire keeps the fire burning; similarly, the soul fire is kept burning with every breath.

Agni: "I am the fire. I am the fire present in all the centers. I am the one fire, who has become the seven flames in the seven centers, creating seven types of propensities."

Hutam: "I am the offering or oblation." The Lord is saying "I am the practice of Kriya Yoga in meditation as taught by the master. I am the oblation means that *kri* and *ya* are united during every activity—every action is offered to the divine fire."

All these principles are easily perceived by regular practice of meditation.

Verse 17

pitā 'ham asya jagato
mātā dhātā pitāmahaḥ
vedyam pavitram aumkāra
ṛk sāma yajur eva ca

Translation

I am the father, mother, sustainer, and grandfather of the universe. I am the object of realization, the holy syllable *aum*. I am Rik, Sama, and Yajur as well.

Metaphorical Interpretation

"O Arjuna! I am everything in this universe (*jagat*)." *Jagat* means that which is ephemeral. In this ever changing world, as well as in the body universe, perceive God as the father and the mother. God is the father as well as the mother. He is the father, remaining in the cranium. He is the mother, remaining in the body nature. The Bhagavad Gita (14:4) says, *aham bija pradah pita:* "I am the father who implants the seed in the womb of the mother, mother nature." Mother nature is the mother in whose womb one lives. All of creation is in the womb of God. There is constant copulation going on inside the cranium in the form of ingoing and outgoing breath.

The Lord says, *dhata*: "I am the sustainer." God sustains the entire universe. He also sustains every human body in the form of breath. Without His presence, there is no life.

> *Pitamaha*: "When there is creation, I am the father as well as the mother. I also existed before creation. I am the absolute. I am also the cause of creation of father (soul) and mother (body nature). As I was present before creation, I am the grandfather, the cause of all causes."
>
> *Vedyam*: "I am the knowable. I am the object of realization. I am present in everything you see, hear, smell, touch, or taste. I am to be known as the essence in all names and forms, in all beings and things."
>
> *Pavitram*: "I am the holy. I am free from all impurities. One who perceives or realizes Me becomes pure and holy."
>
> *Aumkaram*: "I am *aum*. I am present in the gross, astral, and causal. I am present in creation, preservation, and dissolution. I am in the past, present, and future. I am the eternal divine sound *aum*."
>
> *Rik*: "I am the Rig Veda." Rig means that any words coming out of the mouth are hymns to the almighty.
>
> *Sama*: "I am also Sama Veda. I am the divine sound perceived through deep meditation."

Yajur: "I am also Yajur Veda. I am divine illumination." Veda is from the root word *vid*, to know. The Lord is saying, "I am the knower as well as the knowable. I am the Vedas as well as the author of the Vedas. I am divine wisdom manifested in three steps—*jñana, vijñana,* and *prajñana* (knowledge, applied knowledge and wisdom)."

Verse 18

gatir bhartā prabhuḥ sākṣī
nivāsaḥ śaraṇam suhṛt
prabhavaḥ pralayaḥ sthānam
nidhānam bījam avyayam

Translation

I am the supreme goal, the maintainer, the great Lord, the witness, the abode, the refuge, and compassion. I am the place of origin as well as dissolution. I am the treasure-house and the imperishable soul.

Metaphorical Interpretation

In this verse, the Lord explains his divine aspects in every human life:

Gati: "I am the destination, the movement, and the way." *Gati* consists of two parts: *ga*, to go, and *ti,* to stay. Everyone is moving towards God, knowingly or unknowingly. *Gati* also means that God is the supreme destination.

Bharta: "I am the cause of all nourishment. I am the maintainer. I am maintaining everyone with the breath. I am the appetite. I am the food. By taking food and digesting it, I am maintaining all beings."

Prabhu: "I am the Lord. I am the Lord of the body. I am the Lord of the entire universe. I control everything."

Sakshi: "I am the silent witness of everything, good and bad. As a witness, I am compassionately detached."

Nivasa: "I am the abode. The entire universe is in Me. I am the abode of the universe. Every individual is playing in Me. I am the supreme abode of everything."

Sharanam: "I am the refuge. I protect everyone. Whoever comes to Me becomes free from all fear. All ignorance disappears. People think of friends at times of distress and difficulties. But I am the refuge in all situations."

Suhrid: "I am eternal compassion. I am always with you. Silently, without any expectation, I am constantly helping you. My breath is true help for you. Your breath is My presence."

Prabhava: "I am the place of origin. Just as waves are born in the ocean; similarly, everything is born in Me." All thoughts are born from the soul in the brain.

Pralaya: "All the waves are born in the ocean, live in the ocean, and at the end, merge with the ocean. I am this place of dissolution." Thoughts are born in the brain, live in the body. and at the end, dissolve in the brain. This is *pralaya*.

Sthana: "I am the place of everything. Everything lives in My self." I am established in the *kutashtha*, the seat of the soul.

Nidhana: "I am the treasure-house. The treasure is inside the cranium, the brain is the real treasure."

Bija avyayam: "I am the imperishable seed. From the seed, the tree grows; in the tree, the seed is manifested again. The seed is the cause and the effect of the tree. I am the cause and the effect of everything. I am indestructible. I am eternal."

Verse 19

tapāmy aham aham varṣam
nigṛhṇāmy utsṛjāmi ca
amṛtam cai 'va mṛtyuś ca
sad asac cā 'ham arjuna

Translation

I radiate heat; I send or I prevent the rain. I am immortality as well as death. O Arjuna! I am both reality and unreality.

Metaphorical Interpretation

The Lord continues,

Aham tapami: "I radiate heat." In the ordinary sense, the sun radiates heat and collects water in the form of vapor and clouds. *Tapa* means body heat. Body heat is the indication of life. There is combustion of oxygen and the body is kept warm. This body heat is really the living power of God. Another meaning of *tapa* is breath. God keeps life in the body by the breath. Watching the power of God in every breath is true *tapasya*. Those who practice Kriya are doing *tapasya,* which is true meditation.

Aham varshami: "I send the rain from above, down to the earth." Rain cools the earth and causes an abundance of agricultural production. Similarly, in human life, those who practice meditation get *somadhara*, a special saliva secretion from the *brahma randhra*, the fontanel, which gives extreme calmness and divine abundance.

Nigrihnami: "I hold back." In nature, the sun's rays evaporate water. In this way, it has an effect on controlling the rain. The spiritual meaning of this is that the Lord regulates and controls the activities of all men who keep their attention on Him.

Utsrijami: "I send the rain back again." A person's life is a state of creation, possible only through the power of God, the soul sun Who abides in the body. After deep meditation, even after realization, a spiritual person's divine propensities are given only by the Lord.

Amritam caiva mrityumcha: "I am life and death. I am immortality as well as mortality. I am the life (breath) in everything." When the breath stops, there is physical death. Although the body dies, the imperishable soul still lives in every being. In another sense, if body consciousness does not die, then one cannot perceive the immortal soul. This is death and immortality simultaneously.

Sat asat ca aham: "I am reality and unreality, manifest and unmanifest. I am the soul as well as the body. I am the creator along with creation." Through regular practice of Kriya meditation, this divine perception is possible.

Verse 20

traividyā mām somapāḥ pūtapāpā
yajñair iṣṭvā svargatim prārthayante
te puṇyam āsādya surendralokam
aśnanti divyān divi devabhogān

Translation

With sacrifice, those knowers of the Vedas, the drinkers of *soma* juice, and pure beings free from all sins and evils seek the goal of heaven; they, the holy, reaching the holy world, enjoy the divine in heaven (the vacuum), divine joy.

Metaphorical Interpretation

Trai vidya means the three types of knowledge and also the three Vedas. The knowledge of creation, preservation, and dissolution is also *trai vidya*. It also indicates the knowledge of function of three *nadis* in the spine.

In each human body, there is rationality as well as animality. However a conscious person tries to remove the animal and remain rational; yet other people want to go beyond rationality and be established in divinity. These human activities are dependent on the vital air passing through the three different channels: *ida, pingala,* and *sushumna.*

Vital breath in *ida* gives extreme slothfulness, making one lazy with no desire for quick evolution. *Pingala*, on the other hand, is the cause of extreme activity, creating endless desire and restlessness. Vital air in the *pingala* makes one fond of status, pomp, and grandeur, and makes one desire to spend life in enjoyment, which can also cause physical ailments and unhappiness. *Sushumna* is the spiritual channel. By the practice of Kriya Yoga, the *ida* and *pingala* are separated, and the *sushumna* is opened. People whose vital breath enters this channel can achieve thorough control over their activities. Ignorance disappears. This is the first step in spiritual practice.

> *Somapa*: *Soma* means moon, the Lord of the mind. *Somapa* means those who have thorough control over their minds through a self-disciplined yogic lifestyle. Those who practice Kriya know how to drink the divine saliva *(soma)* secreted from the fontanel, which brings extreme calmness and inner soothing.

Puta papah: *Puta papah* means freedom from all evils, or perception of constant purity, which is the next spiritual stage. One who has thorough control over the mind is truly pure. Mind is the cause of desire and bondage as well as liberation. Impure mind is the root of all evil desire and sins, while pure mind is a divine achievement.

Yajñaih: "By sacrifice of all their evils, they practice the technique of breath control."

Svargatim prarthayante: "They seek the goal of heaven." *Svar* means the place of extreme happiness. Although spiritual aspirants meditate a lot, they still desire the state of extreme happiness.

Te punyam asadya: "By virtue of meditation, they can easily reach this state." They can enter into the kingdom of heaven, which is within the cranium (See the Bible, Luke 17:21).

Ashnanti divyan divi devabhogan: "They enjoy the divine bliss in heaven, in the vacuum." Meditation causes all-around development, so many people practice it with some expectation. Here, the Lord is explaining the expectation and the achievement of people who meditate with desire.

Verse 21

te tam bhuktvā svargalokam viśālam
kṣīṇe puṇye martyalokam viśanti
evam trayīdharmam anuprapannā
gatāgatam kāmakāmā labhante

Translation

Having enjoyed the vast world of heaven, they enter the world of mortality when their virtues are exhausted. Thus, sincerely following the dictum of the three Vedas, they reach the state of going and coming, due to their desire for enjoyment.

Metaphorical Interpretation

Desire is the seed of activity, whether it is material or religious. People undertake many rigorous practices even in their spiritual life. Due to ambitious spiritual practice, they enjoy calmness, peace, happiness, and joy. But such a state is not permanent. Eventually they come back into the ordinary plane of consciousness. People seek either *papa*, vice and sin, or *punya*, virtue or noble qualities. Sins are the cause of suffering, while virtues are the factors that create divine joy. But both states are exhaustible and temporary. Those who remain in the domain of *trai dharma*—that is, the three Vedas, the *ida, pingala,* and *sushumna*—obtain the state of going and coming. They practice with desire to achieve physical and mental benefits.

The highest achievement is freedom from the cycle of *gatā gata*, coming and going. But *gatā gata* is also inhalation and exhalation. No matter how spiritual a person may be, if he has ambition for divine joy, then he must come back to the material world, back into the domain of the breath. Only those who want God, and nothing else, can reach the divine state of realization.

Verse 22

ananyāś cintayanto mām
ye janāḥ paryupāsate
teṣām nityābhiyuktānām
yogakṣemam vahāmy aham

Translation

To those who concentrate on Me without any other thoughts, who sincerely meditate (worship) and are constantly united with Me—I bring what they lack and preserve what they possess.

Metaphorical Interpretation

This verse is one of the most beautiful verses; it contains the Lord's divine assurance. By repeated practice of meditation, the mind loses its restlessness, and slowly it becomes free from even the ambition of achieving peace or pleasure. The Lord explains that He will take responsibility for following the duties of His devotees.

This is a beautiful world. Eventually people will get what they strive for. Everything depends upon one's own desire and effort. Ordinary people seek material achievement through ordinary life. Spiritual people pursue higher achievement. Truly fortunate people seek God.

The Lord says,

> *Ananyash cintayanto mam*: "Without any other thought or ambition." As long as there is breath, there is ambition. People are restless with their thoughts. They are even disturbed by thoughts during their spiritual practice. Those who practice Kriya know the secret of thought control and channeling the life force. Their minds become extremely pure and free from even good thoughts. They reach the state of extreme tranquility.
>
> *Ye janah paryupasate*: "Those who meditate on Me." Deep sleep is a state without thought (*ananyash chinta*). But it is not true meditation. Deep sleep is the shadow of meditation—meditation without consciousness. Those who practice true meditation know the beauty of it. In deep meditation, one is absorbed in God consciousness, merged in God, like sugar is dissolved in tea.

Tesham nityabhiyuktanam: "They are constantly united with Me." Spiritual life is not a temporary activity; it is a continuous and spontaneous state of God awareness. Neither a single moment nor a single breath is wasted in vain. Every moment is for the Lord and the Lord alone.

Yoga kshema vahamyaham: "I, the Lord God, take all your responsibilities." Yoga means to achieve what one lacks. Everyone lacks the perception of his own divine nature—the fact that he is the image of God, the living presence of God.

Kshema: "To preserve what one has in his own possession." In the previous two verses, the Lord described the temporary nature of happiness and joy. In this verse, the Lord speaks of the state of eternal peace, bliss, and joy achieved through meditation. Yoga means meditation. *Kshema* means all-auspiciousness or liberation. The Lord gives all-auspiciousness of liberation through meditation.

In this verse, the Lord outlines the steps of meditation:

1. *Ananya*: One is free from all other thoughts through breath control.
2. *Mam chintayantah*: One perceives only the divine, all the time.
3. *Paryupasana*: In every aspect, one sits near Him and remains in His divine presence. God is all around and inside, everywhere.
4. *Nityabhiyukta*: One is in constant unity with the Lord.

With these four steps, one is certain to get liberation. This is the greatest assurance of the Lord.

Verse 23

ye 'py anyadevatābhaktā
yajante śraddhayā 'nvitāḥ
te 'pi mām eva kaunteya
yajanty avidhipūrvakam

Translation

O Son of Kunti (Arjuna!) Even those who worship other gods with faith, also worship Me, though they do so in ignorance.

Metaphorical Interpretation

In the previous verse, the Lord spoke of *ananya*, not any other. The state of *ananya* is the state of formlessness, where there is nothing other than God, the one, the absolute. But many people cannot meditate on the absolute. So, here, the Lord explains *anya*, the others.

People worship different gods—Ganesha, Durga, Kali, Lakshmi, Sarasvati, Surya, Vishnu, Hari, Narayana, Rama, Krishna, Shiva, and so forth. People worship different names in different forms (idols) with different formalities and rituals. They worship through the five sense organs: Through the mouth, they chant or sing; through the eyes, they see different idols, well-decorated; through the ears, they hear hymns and prayers; through the nose, they smell incense; with the hands, they offer flowers and other offerings. In reality, all the gods or deities are in the spine and the sense organs, but behind all names and forms, one God remains. Although He is called by different names, He is still one.

Ordinary people cannot realize this. They are attached to the ornaments; they forget to see the gold from which the ornaments are sculpted; therefore, many names and forms are imposed on gold. In reality, gold and gold ornaments are one. Deities are not separate from the One, the absolute and formless. But people with ignorance and delusion see them as separate.

In the Brihadaranyaka Upanishad (4:4:19) and the Katha Upanishad (2:1:10), it says, *mṛtyoḥ sa mṛtyum āpnoti ya iha nāneva paśyati*: "One who sees the multiplicity, remains in mortality. But in all the differences and divisions, there is one indivisible, and He is God."

The Lord is saying, "O Arjuna! All deities function by My power. In each human being, if I do not breathe, then they cannot see, hear, smell, taste, or touch. All the deities working through these sense organs and chakras are really working through the breath, My divine power. One who worships in any way, with love, really worships me."

Love and faith are the foundation of spiritual life and the key to success. God grants everything to he who possesses these two divine qualities.

Verse 24

aham hi sarvayajñānām
bhoktā ca prabhur eva ca
na tu mām abhijānanti
tattvenā taś cyavanti te

Translation

Indeed, I am the enjoyer and also the Lord of all sacrifices (*yajñas*), but they do not know Me in reality, hence they have deviated from truth.

Metaphorical Interpretation

Sarva means all the senses; *yajña* means oblation or offering. Lord Krishna is saying, "O Arjuna! I am the Lord of all oblation in all the centers and sense organs, and I am the true enjoyer."

This teaching is *jñana* with *vijñana*, knowledge with its application and direct perception. *Vijñana* practice of meditation and a spiritual life. God is the soul abiding in all living beings Who causes the air (breath) to flow. Because of this breath, all the sense organs and the chakras function. There is a fire in each chakra and that fire burns and creates a particular desire. All these fires burn by the breath alone. To every human being and even to animals, the Lord gives different propensities by creating different desires in the chakras.

The life of every human being is a life of *yajña*, sacrifice, oblation to the ceremonial fire. Every action is a sacrifice or oblation to the divine fire. In the seven centers (chakras), there are seven fires, with seven oblations in the form of different activities. For example, when the breath touches the *vaishvanara*, the fire in the navel center, there is appetite, and food can be digested. Thus, taking food is oblation to the *vaishvanara*. The taste of food is the taste of God. Without breath and life, there is no appetite or eating. This is *yajña*. The soul is the enjoyer, or the Lord, of this *yajña*, this fire ceremony.

People undertake different activities through the sense organs: earning money, enjoying sexually, taking food, emotional activities, religious rituals, philosophical and intellectual pursuits, and so forth. All these are *yajñas*. A dead man cannot perform these activities or receive their fruits. Those who do not perceive the presence of the soul in all these endeavors have deviated from the truth. They lead life like animals. They will not experience peace, bliss, or joy.

Those who practice Kriya constantly perceive the truth of human life. They perceive the presence of the soul in all activities. They realize *kri* and *ya*, the soul as sole doer. Without soul, one has nothing.

Verse 25

yānti devavratā devān
pitṛn yānti pitṛvratāḥ
bhūtāni yānti bhūtejyā
yānti madyājino 'pi mām

Translation

Those who are devoted to the gods, go to the gods. Those who are devoted to the ancestors, go to the ancestors. Those who are devoted to the spirits (elements) reach the elements, and those who worship Me, come to Me alone.

Metaphorical Interpretation

Liberation (or self-realization) can only be achieved through soul culture and meditation. Realizing the self makes one free and independent. The foundation of spiritual realization is perceiving the soul in all actions.

The literal meaning of *upasana* is to worship, but *upasana* really means to keep the attention on the top, in the fontanel. This requires practice. When practice becomes regular and repetitive, it becomes a habit, which ultimately leads to direct and constant perception of the soul. In the material world, however, people worship many deities with *mantra*—chanting, prayers, and hymns, and with *tantra*—techniques for acquiring supernatural powers. People thus engaged are motivated by their ambition. In this verse, the Lord speaks of four types of *yajñas*.

1. *bhuta yajña*: Oblation or offerings to animals, spirits, and the elements.
2. *pitri yajña*: Oblation to the deceased.
3. *deva yajña*: Oblation to supernatural powers.
4. *brahma yajña*: Oblation to God, the absolute.

Ordinary people are busy with the ritualistic oblations, full of forms and formalities, motivated by ambition. But the spiritual person offers sincerely, without ambition. In this verse, the four stages of meditation and realization are explained.

The first is *bhuta yajña*. *Bhuta* means lower beings, like animals, insects, and so on. It can also mean departed souls, spirits. Some people feed animals with love, with expectation of some good fruits. Some people worship spirits in cremation grounds to gain supernatural power. But the real meaning of *bhuta yajña* is *bhuta*, the gross elements: earth, water, fire, air, and sky, which are in the five centers, and *yajña,* to perceive the presence of the living God. Those who practice Kriya know how to concentrate and meditate in each chakra and perceive God's presence there.

The second *yajña* is *pitri yajña*, oblation to deceased relatives. It is true, one's ancestors are liberated through deep meditation, but in the scriptures, the real meaning of *pita* is not family. For instance, in the scriptures it says, *pita ha vai pranah*. *Prana*, the vital breath is called, *pita*, the real father, who is the cause of the breath. By the practice of Kriya Yoga one can quiet the mind and can perceive the almighty father.

Deva yajña, ordinarily called oblation to God, is the third sacrifice. *Deva* is derived from the word *div,* which means vacuum. Those who fix their attention on the throat center and above, even up to the pituitary, are doing formless meditation and perceiving the living presence of God. This is *deva yajña*.

The fourth is *brahma yajña*, loving the almighty father. Ordinary people think *brahma yajña* means *vedadhyayana*, to read holy books. But merely reading holy books such as the Bhagavad Gita or the Upanishad*s* cannot produce liberation. Real *brahma yajña* is to know thyself. During every breath whoever knows his own self as the sole doer is doing real *brahma yajña*. In Kriya Yoga, one who constantly fixes his attention on the pituitary and fontanel is continuously touching the formless father. This is *brahma yajña*—the way to liberation and emancipation.

Verse 26

pattram puṣpam phalam toyam
yo me bhaktyā prayacchati
tad aham bhaktyupahṛtam
aśnāmi prayatātmanaḥ

Translation

From he who offers to me with devotion and a pure heart, a leaf, a flower, a piece of fruit, or water, I will accept that offering of devotion.

Metaphorical Interpretation

In this chapter known as *Raja vidya raja guhya yoga*, the Lord is discussing the primary condition of spiritual life—devotion. In this verse, the Lord describes this devotion, *bhakti*. *Bhakti paranuraktih ishvare*, He says, "Devotion is extreme attachment to God." Action or *karma* is the cause of *jñana*. Through knowledge, *jñana*, one gets devotion, which can only come after reaching the stages of knowledge, consciousness, super consciousness, and cosmic consciousness.

Yoga means *jiva atmani eva aikyam*, the perception of constant unity with the almighty father. Devotion is perception of God in everything, and everything in God. By introverting the sense organs and going into the atom point, people can reach this stage. A devotee endowed with such love is truly dear to God. Whatever this devotee does becomes a sacrifice, an offering to God.

The Lord says that a leaf, a flower, a piece of fruit, a little water are enough for Him if it is offered with devotion—He will accept (eat) the love of the devotee. The leaf is the Vedas (See Bhagavad Gita 15:1). Leaves represent the holy scriptures that can give one the sincere desire for soul culture. The leaves are the beauty of the tree; they nourish the tree and provide shade. Similarly, divine knowledge leads to control of the mind, and it brings inner calmness to human life. Each human body is like a tree.

The flower is the teachings of the master. The flower is the principal part of the tree. It not only increases the beauty of the tree, but it also is the cause of further manifestation. The realized master is the direct instructor of divine wisdom. He enables the student to be God-oriented. Flowers also symbolizes divine propensities and thoughts.

Fruit represents achieving success in human life. Those who follow the teaching of the scriptures, *jñana*, with the direct help of the realized master, *vijñana*, reach the stage of *prajñana,* the fruit of human life. Fruits also represent man's memory.

The leaf, the flower, and the fruit are all nourished and ripened with the help of water. Water represents the love for God and guru. One who truly follows the teachings of the scriptures and the master, who practices spiritual life daily, becomes the true lover of God. In this verse, the Lord also tells his devotees to be *prayatatmanah*, one who has thorough control over the senses. This kind of person is free from worldly ambitions and perceives constant unity with the supreme Lord. This is the stage of true love.

The Lord is saying, "When my devotees feel Me and realize Me, they are one with Me. Without such love, I am very far. But I am hungry for their love. I accept and enjoy the love manifested through their wish to learn the teachings of holy books. Following the footprints of the realized master, practicing a scientific method of soul culture, and through a self-controlled spiritual life, they are following the path of supreme devotion."

Verse 27

yat karoṣi yad aśnāsi
yaj juhoṣi dadāsi yat
yat tapasyasi kaunteya
tat kuruṣva madarpaṇam

Translation

Whatever you do, whatever you eat, whatever you offer to the sacred fire, whatever you give (as charity), on whatever you meditate, O son of Kunti, do it as an offering to Me.

Metaphorical Interpretation

God loves the love of the devotee. This love is pure love and is in itself divine. This love purifies life and is the cause of liberation. The Lord is saying "O Son of Kunti (Arjuna!) You want spiritual evolution and liberation, so I will tell you the secret of spiritual life and God realization: Offer everything to Me, your whole life, all of your activities, even your thoughts."

In this verse, the Lord mentions five things: *karosi*, all activities; *ashnasi*, eating and enjoyment; *juhosi*, all sacrifices or oblations; *dadasi*, all charity and donation; and *tapasyasi*, meditation. People eat through the mouth. This mouth is not only the physical mouth, but is every part of the body that is used for enjoyment. People love enjoyment, but they do not realize that this enjoyment is the result of the breath. Whatever a man does or thinks or says should be offered as an oblation to the almighty.

In the eleventh book of the Shrimad Bhagavatam (a rare holy scripture from India) it says,

kāyena vācā manasīndriyair vā
buddhyātmanāva prakṛter svābhāvāt
karomi yad yat sakalam parasmai
nārāyaṇāyetisamarpayāmi

which means: "By the body, the mind, the speech, the senses, the intellect, or ego, even by the habits, whatever I am doing, I am offering it to the Lord."

This offering is not verbal, it must be an inner attitude. People who meditate, who watch the indwelling self, who love God and unite with the almighty in every breath, observe life as *yajña*, a sacrifice. They do everything with the sense of oblation. Dedicating everything to the Lord, they are free from bondage.

The Lord is explaining *madarpanam,* offering to the almighty. In truth, every breath is an oblation to the soul fire in the pituitary, every breath is a fire ceremony. For those who live this principle, all five types of activities—action, eating, sacrifice, charity and meditation—are dedicated to God.

Verse 28

śubhāśubhaphalair evam
mokṣyase karmabandhanaiḥ
samnyāsayogayuktātmā
vimukto mām upaiṣyasi

Translation

You shall no doubt be liberated from the bond of actions that produce good and evil fruits. With your mind disciplined by the yoga of renunciation, you will come to Me.

Metaphorical Interpretation

Ego is the greatest obstacle to spiritual evolution. Ego in Sanskrit is *ahamkara,* or *aham karta iti bhavah*: "I am the doer. I am doing, I have done, Without me nothing will be done, I am the only one," and so on. This attitude is ego.

In reality, when a person does anything, it is done by the breath, the power of God. An ordinary person thinks that he himself is the doer. But without the breath, this person is merely a dead body—good for nothing, without activity. The ego is the cause of bondage to activities and their fruits, good or bad.

The Lord is saying: "O Arjuna! Know that the soul is the doer. You are only an instrument. When you do every action to please the Lord God, your indwelling self—you cannot do negative things." In addition, when all your actions are done as an offering to the Lord, you will not be attached to the fruits of those actions, good or bad. This is the first step to emancipation. But just as a child walks with two legs; similarly, you must know the second step to reaching liberation, which is *sannyasa yoga yuktena*, the practice of the yoga of *sannyasa*.

Sannyasa means accepting the monk's life. *Sannyasa* is not merely a renunciation of the physical world, it is inner detachment. *Sannyasa* is not an outward show of changing the name and dress, it is an inner transformation. One who has thorough control over his own self is a true *sannyasi*. This is the basic requirement of a yogi. So why does the Lord use the term *sannyasa yoga*? Because *sannyasa*, renunciation, and *yoga*, union, are synonymous. Yogi and *sannyasi* are the same (See the Bhagavad Gita 6:1).

Where there is light, there is no darkness. Where there is perception of God, there is no touch of negativity. This is yoga with the almighty Lord. This is also *sannyasa*. If one is well established in the state of *sannyasa yoga*, he will undoubtedly be liberated.

Verse 29

samo 'ham sarvabhūteṣu
na me dveṣyo 'sti na priyaḥ
ye bhajanti tu mām bhaktyā
mayi te teṣu cā 'py aham

Translation

I am the same in all beings, there are none who are disliked or dear to Me. But those who worship Me with devotion are in Me, and I am in them.

Metaphorical Interpretation

In this verse, the Lord is stating the supreme spiritual truth that can be perceived and realized by a person who meditates with a pure mind:

Samo aham sarva bhuteshu: "I am one, unrivaled. I am all-pervading, inside and outside of everything that exists. O Arjuna! Looking at the plurality and multiplicity of the world, you may think, how is it possible to be present in everything? You may also be confused by the world of duality, good and bad, cold and hot, but there is no duality."

Please remember what was taught in verse 5:19 where the Lord said, *nirdosham hi samam brahma*: "I am free from all defects and I am equal, I am Brahman. I am the supreme self. I am the Lord. I am existence (reality), consciousness, and bliss. There is no differentiation or discrimination in Me. Another name of Mine is Sama, equal. To come to Me is to be free from all differences. Although differences are apparent on the outside, still, I am equal in everything."

How can the Lord be equally present in everything that seems so different? The sun shines equally on plain stones and on diamonds, but due to the differences in their natures, the sun reflects on them differently. Also, rain drops may fall equally everywhere, but high mountains cannot preserve water like low valleys. Furthermore, the same air is breathed by all people, but some are good and some are bad.

"O Arjuna! Not only am I omnipresent, but I am the same in everything. I am equally present. No one is dear to me, no one is disliked by Me. There is no discrimination." Those who follow the realized master and practice meditation can realize this truth.

The first precondition is devotion, *bhakti*, and the second necessity is regular practice. From devotion and meditation, a devotee perceives divine omnipresence and perceives God in himself. This is the perception of unity, that God and he are one and always have been one.

Verse 30

api cet sudurācāro
bhajate mām ananyabhāk
sādhur eva sa mantavyaḥ
samyag vyavasito hi saḥ

Translation

Even if a man of the most vile conduct worships Me with undivided devotion, he is to be thought of as righteous, for he has indeed rightly resolved.

Metaphorical Interpretation

Here, the Lord is saying, "O Arjuna! Even people with extreme negative qualities can change their mind from restless to calmness, from duality to unity. Then they are free from all negative qualities, free and pure." This verse is one of the most beautiful verses; it is the expression of consolation from the Lord himself. Due to delusion and ignorance, people commit mistakes and sins. When they become aware of their mistakes, they repent.

A rusty iron wire plugged into an electrical socket can be the conductor of extremely powerful electricity. Here, the Lord says that even vile people, if they meditate upon Him with deepest desire and pinpoint concentration, will become spiritual. Human nature can be changed and transformed depending upon the company kept and the activities performed. Good company and spiritual practice can bring inner transformation.

"Arjuna! Even if a person does extremely immoral work, I am still present in him and his breath still goes in and out. When this person realizes his mistake, by the power of meditation he can look inside and perceive My presence; he can become holy. Sins are washed away by spiritual practice." There is no permanent suffering, but there is eternal happiness and joy.

Throughout human history, this has been evident. Ratnakar, a robber and murderer, became Valmiki, a great spiritual master and author. A prosecutor, Saul, became Saint Paul. Everything depends upon one's desire. Kriya brings inner purity. Those who practice regularly, achieve inner purity. All the bad habits from the past can be removed by deep meditation. *Sudurachara*, the state of restlessness, can be easily changed by the practice of Kriya, the scientific process of breath control.

Verse 31

kṣipram bhavati dharmātmā
śaśvacchāntim nigacchati
kaunteya pratijānīhi
na me bhaktaḥ praṇaśyati

Translation

Quickly, he becomes a virtuous person and goes into the state of eternal peace. O Son of Kunti (Arjuna), be sure, no devotee of Mine is ever lost (out of my sight).

Metaphorical Interpretation

In this verse, the Lord says that a vile person rightly resolved quickly becomes *dharmatma*, a noble soul. What is *dharma*? It is that which upholds the life in the body. Breath holds life in the body. Breath is the binding force and integrating power in each one's life.

Restlessness is the cause of all sins and suffering. Restlessness is due to irregular breathing patterns. Those who calm the breath by the scientific method of meditation, without holding the breath uncomfortably, are free from restlessness and unhappiness. Calmness is liberation. Those who practice Kriya, who can rise above the lower centers to the upper center, are righteous. In one inhalation, they can come up to the top, to His presence, reaching a state of eternal peace, free from all negatives and restlessness. Peace is the bread of life. Without peace, life is miserable. Kriya is the panacea to over come all human suffering.

"Arjuna! You have the strength to come up to the *ajña* chakra. You can find peace. Practice Kriya nicely; withdraw from the lower centers and ascend to the cranium, even to the fontanel. Take it for granted that My devotee is eternally established in Me. Be my devotee, my lover, and perceive my presence in every breath. Such meditation will let you taste immortality and eternal peace."

Verse 32

mām hi pārtha vyapāśritya
ye 'pi syuḥ pāpayonayaḥ
striyo vaiśyās tathā śudrās
te 'pi yānti parām gatim

Translation

Those who take refuge in Me, O Partha (Arjuna!), even if they are of low origin, women, *vaishyas,* or *shudras*, they will also go to the highest goal.

Metaphorical Interpretation

This verse is about spiritual evolution.

Papa means sins; *yonaya* means places of origin. *Papayonayah* means from where the sins are originated. People who are extrovert and always restless are committing sins by the sense organs. They speak evil, hear ill of others, and do many evil things. Their sense organs are abused. So *papayonayah* means born of low origin, but in the sense that the mind is always engrossed in the lower centers.

Striyah means women. Metaphorically, it refers to all those who are body-conscious. In every human being, the soul is male, *purusha,* and the body is female, *stri.* People who are extremely engrossed in the body sense cannot remember the indwelling self are symbolically woman. Instead, they are always seeking enjoyment and comfort.

Vaishyas are the traders, those who are always ambitious and calculating: They always think of material profit. People who are beginning spiritual life often think of the benefits of their spiritual practices.

Shudras are those who are engrossed in body pleasure. In the caste system of India, *shudras* are serving others. But here, those who serve the body instead of the soul are *shudras*.

In this verse, the Lord is telling Arjuna: "O Partha! Whoever comes to the realized master with love, learns spirituality, and leads life accordingly, they are dear to Me."

Spiritual attainment is the result of regular meditation and a soul-conscious life. Impurities are not outside a person, they are inside. Mind is the source of all dirt as well as purity. If someone's mind is made pure by meditation and the practice of Kriya, then this person will automatically attain the supreme stage. If people of sinful activity and polluted minds have a sincere desire for soul culture, then even while they are immersed in the world, they can come up to the pituitary and their delusion can disappear. Slowly and steadily, with the guidance of the master, they will be able to lead a divine life.

Verse 33

kim punar brāmaṇāḥ puṇyā
bhaktā rājarṣayas tathā
anityam asukham lokam
imam prāpya bhajasva mām

Translation

How much easier it is for the pure and spiritual (the Brahmins), and even for the devoted royal seers (the *rishis*). Having come to this impermanent and unhappy world, meditate upon Me, devote yourself to Me.

Metaphorical Interpretation

The human body is the temple of God. Human life is created for God realization. One shouldn't think about past life, what one has done, rather, one should try to perceive the indwelling self and be self realized. The marvelous power of God is hiding in everything. Every single person is potentially divine. Continuous spiritual practice is necessary to achieve this state, and through continuous practice, quick evolution can be achieved. The Lord is telling everyone, "Do not think about what you have done or achieved; instead, remember that your life is precious and spend your every breath in God consciousness."

As explained in the previous verse, from the origin of sin, *papayoni*, one becomes *stri*, woman, then *shudra*, servant, and then *vaishya*, active in business. In this verse, the Lord talks about those who are devoted royal seers and pure spiritual people. *Brahmana* is not a person of the highest caste, rather, it is the highest state of spiritual attainment. *Brahma janati it brahmanah* means a Brahmin is the knower of Brahman, the absolute, the indwelling self. He is always after truth and is enlightened. His life is complete and divine. Spiritual truth is never a monopoly of a particular class or section of the society, it is equally available and attainable to all.

To reach this highest state of realization, one must be *rajarshi* and *bhakta*. *Rajarshi* means *raja ca rishi ca*. *Raja* is the king, born into the royal family, a brave warrior. A warrior is one who is constantly fighting to overcome his negative qualities, his inner enemies: anger, ego, passion, pride, and so forth. By regular practice of Kriya Yoga, one can burn the negative qualities and become a *rishi*. A *rishi* is a man of right vision. This person's vision is purified and divine if he is seeking truth in every step of his life; thus, he has extreme love for God. He is the real devotee. The *rishi* has some perception of duality, but in the state of Brahman, one is completely absorbed and merged in God.

Everything separate from God is temporary and changeable, *anitya*. Only God is eternal, *nitya*. Everything in the world is full of pain, *asukham*. Only God is the source of peace, bliss, and joy. *A su kha* means not in the vacuum. Those who remain in the lower centers experience constant discomfort and difficulties. So, do not go below, come up to the *ajña chakra*, the pituitary. Meditate and be realized. Meditation will make you divine. Meditation will enable you to perceive your indwelling self during every step of your life.

Those who practice the scientific Kriya Yoga daily, regularly, and sincerely cross all the stages of spiritual evolution and ultimately become merged in God.

Verse 34

manmanā bhava madhbhakto
madyājī mām namaskuru
mām evai 'ṣyasi yuktvai 'vam
ātmānam matparāyaṇaḥ

Translation

Fix your mind on Me. Be devoted to Me. Worship Me and bow to Me. Having disciplined yourself with Me as the supreme God, you yourself shall come to Me.

Metaphorical Interpretation

In the previous verse, the Lord spoke of meditation. In this verse, He explains the practical aspects of meditation in detail:

Manmana bhava: "O Arjuna! Please fix your mind on Me." External objects tempt the mind, so the mind is usually distracted and restless. But the mind can be concentrated and directed toward the soul in the fontanel. If at the same time, one seeks truth, almighty God's presence can be perceived everywhere. If one's mind and thoughts are directed toward God, one becomes divine. As one thinks, so one becomes.

Madh bhakto: "Be devoted to Me. Love Me in everything and in every being. Love Me in every breath. I am your life and soul. You have no existence without Me. In every circumstance, please be divine."

Mad yaji: "Worship Me." Meditation is true worship. People worship with flowers, fruit, and many things, but true worship is work in God consciousness. All work is worship and *yajña*, oblation or offering to the almighty. Perceive this. Avoid bad things. Be in reality. Let all your work that is done through the sense organs be directed to God. Perceive *kri* and *ya,* work as worship.

Man namaskuru: "Bow to Me. A person with ego cannot bend himself. A person with love perceives his unity with Me. Bow to Me physically and mentally with love and unity. This will transform you." Be free from ego.

Mat para yana: "Come to Me." One should try to come up from the lower centers to the highest center, from body consciousness to God consciousness, from manhood to Godhood.

Yuktaiva atmanam: This is unity, association with, and merging into the self.

Ayam atma brahma: "This self alone is God." To be united with the soul in every thought, word, and action and to perceive God's presence in every breath is truly divine life.

"O Arjuna! If you follow these few steps, there is no doubt that you will be one with Me."

Summary

By giving one's own life, one will taste eternal life. Ordinarily, people lead a life of possessiveness and selfishness, but a life of divine love is a life of sacrifice—sacrificing and offering all activity to the Lord God. In the Shrimad Bhagavatam (11:2:36) it is written, "Whatever one does with the body, tongue (talk), mind (thought), intellect, and one's own nature must be surrendered and offered to God."

The Lord explains the essence of the secret spiritual doctrine to the sincere seeker. To one who is free from all negative qualities, truth is revealed. Spiritual truth is extremely pure. It sanctifies everything. This truth is not a concept or a precept; it is an experience gained through practice and self-control. Discipline, spiritual life and self-knowledge will provide extreme joy that is imperishable and limitless.

This chapter is one of the few that contains no queries from Arjuna. The supreme truth of spiritual life is revealed beautifully in this section of the Bhagavad Gita.

This chapter consists in thirty-four verses:

Verses 1 to 3 highlight the easy and simple path of the spiritual life, free from so-called hardships and difficulties.

Verses 4 to 6 discuss how to realize the divine state through yoga, the all-pervading power of the unmanifested God through manifestation.

Verses 7 to 10 describe how the supreme self remains compassionately detached in the creation and dissolution of the universe. Attachment is the cause of suffering and detachment is liberation.

Verses 11 and 12 explain that deluded persons devoid of self-knowledge are demonic.

Verses 13 to 15 describe the qualities of the great souls who dedicate their life to soul culture.

Verses 16 to 19 explain that Ishwara is everything in this creation and in its destruction.

Verses 20 and 21 describe the perishable, impermanent nature of ritualistic activities without self-knowledge.

Verse 22 explains God's supreme love for the true devotee. This is one of the most beautiful verses in the Bhagavad Gita.

Verses 23 to 26 contain a description of the benefits obtained as a result of ritualistic activity.

Verses 27 and 28 advise one to offer everything, all activity, to the Lord God, to be liberated from bondage (*kri* and *ya*).

Verses 29 to 34 explain that God is ever compassionate. Those devoted to God get the real taste of divine love and liberation.

He who keeps his attention on the breath and through every breath loves God is very spiritual (*sadhu*) and becomes realized. Offering all thoughts, words, and activities at the feet of the Lord, and living a life in love, peace, and harmony, is the essence of spiritual life. When a yogi meditates and makes his life balanced, he becomes conscious of the indwelling self. The simple spiritual life is the way to eternal bliss.

The end of the ninth chapter is the midpoint of the Bhagavad Gita. With the discipline of spiritual practice, one gets ready for spiritual awakening. The first half of the Gita has highlighted the practice; the second half will describe the experience.

This chapter ends with the injunction to bow to God with love and to surrender to God, so that one's life becomes more enlightened.

Chapter 10

Vibhūti yoga

The Yoga of Divine Glories

Introduction

Man is potentially divine; in the temple of his body, the soul is the presiding deity. Although the body temple is perishable, it is beautiful and radiant with the divine glamour of the soul. But as people play with their body toy, they are usually not aware of the inner spirit.

Those who are really fortunate, however, follow the footsteps of saints and sages, the instructions of the scriptures, and the guidance of the guru preceptor; they make steady progress on the spiritual path. Through the regular practice of spiritual discipline, they are able to have many divine experiences. Thanks to the Lord, who is Krishna, Arjuna's divine charioteer and guide, for His guidance on the inner journey.

The Bhagavad Gita contains eighteen chapters; the first nine are the *purvardhas* (the beginning half), and the last nine are called the *uttarardhas* (the latter half). The first half is theory, the second half is practice and divine experiences. Theory and practice are like a person's two legs, they go together. Without practice, theory is useless. Without theory, practice is not so easy. They complement each other. Through theory and practice, as taught by the master, a disciple gets perfection.

The tenth chapter of the Bhagavad Gita begins to describe spiritual experiences that one gets through practice. They are called *vibhuti*. In Sanskrit, *vibhuti* has many connotations, a few of which can be used to help with spiritual life: divine glory, *siddhis* (yogic powers), material prosperity, superhuman power, strength, and holy ash.

From meditation and from discipline of the senses, great spiritual power comes to seekers. Tempted by these spiritual powers, or *siddhis*, many seekers are overpowered by their egos, and as a result, they deviate from the experience of Truth. In many cases, the *vibhuti*, which are lower spiritual attainments of superhuman qualities, become a spiritual hindrance—all sincere seekers should beware of their allurements.

When *vibhuti* is surrendered to God with devotion, then this hurdle in the spiritual path is overcome. In this case, *vibhuti* becomes part of the spiritual life. This is *vibhuti yoga* to perceive the blessings of God in every spiritual attainment and to thank Him for it.

In *vibhuti yoga*, the Lord explains how to perceive God in all: Do not develop ego for your beauty or strength, your intelligence or wealth, your achievement and success. Love God in every step of your life.

Vibhuti yoga is the yoga of divine glories—to see the glory and presence of God in everything in the microcosm.

Verse 1

śrībhagavān uvāca
bhūya eva mahābāho
śṛṇu me paramam vacaḥ
yat te 'ham prīyamāṇāya
vakṣyāmi hitakāmyayā

Translation

The Lord said,
Again, O Mighty-armed Arjuna! Hear My supreme word, which I shall say to you who are beloved, with a desire for your welfare.

Metaphorical Interpretation

The Lord addresses Arjuna as mighty-armed, with mighty hands. Hands are the symbol of activity. Arjuna was not just strong in his physical hands, but he was very strong in all his endeavors. A person who is capable of perceiving subtle aspects as well as gross aspects is Mahabahu, mighty-armed. The one who is fit to perceive the divine glory—the qualified disciple—is really Mahabahu.

The Lord is saying, "O Arjuna! You are my able student. I have explained in detail about spirituality because you are dear to Me. You have sincerely tried to come up from the lower centers and sit near Me in your body chariot, in the *kutastha* (sixth center). You are also able to understand *jñana* and *vijñana,* how to attain knowledge and its practical application. You have tried to come to the super-conscious stage. I am the indwelling Self, your eternal companion. I am constantly remaining within you, all around and everywhere. I am breathing for you. I am your true well-wisher. Now I am telling you about the supreme truth. Although I am using words, it cannot truly be expressed with words."

In this verse the Lord says, *hitakamyaya,* which means for your welfare, I need your welfare, you are my child, you are really dear to Me, please listen and follow Me. Such is the relationship between body and soul, disciple and spiritual master, creation and God. The master wants the welfare and complete development of the disciple. He wants the student to excel in such a way that he may become greater than the master himself. This is the unconditional love of the master for his students. The relationship of the master and the disciple is based only on love and spirituality. A truly worthy student slowly and sincerely follows the instruction of the master and steadily proceeds to His presence. The master's every word contains supreme spiritual truth, *paramavaca.*

A sincere disciple who practices Kriya can easily hear the continuous and spontaneous divine sound, day and night. This is the supreme word, the *paramavaca,* the divine talk of the almighty.

Verse 2

na me viduḥ suragaṇāḥ
prabhavam na maharṣayaḥ
aham ādir hir devānām
maharṣīṇām ca sarvaśaḥ

Translation

Neither the host of gods, nor the great seers know My origin. In truth, I am the source of the gods and also the great seers.

Metaphorical Interpretation

The Lord is saying, "O Arjuna! I am the cause of the origin of everything. You can see other things, but you cannot see your own eyes. You need the help of other things to see your eyes. I enable the eye to see. So, how can eyes see Me?

"O Arjuna! The gods are not able to know Me. In your body, there are gods presiding in your sense organs: Ganesha in the nose; Durga, Shakti, and so on in the tongue; Surya in the eyes, Vishnu in the skin; Shiva in the ears. These gods are active through My power. Their action is possible only due to My presence. They cannot see Me. They do not know My origin. I cannot be known through the five sense organs. I am transcendent.

"I am *anadi*, beginningless. How can one know My origin? I am formless. How can one see Me? I have only My divine manifestation. *Rishis* are saints of right vision, great seers. Thoroughly controlling their extrovert state, they attain the higher level of consciousness. Still, they are unable to know Me in essence. O Arjuna! If I do not reveal Myself, they cannot realize Me."

In this verse, the Lord uses the word *prabhava*, the real meaning of which is *pra*, essential, and *bhava*, manifestation: thus, the divine manifestation. Those who practice Kriya regularly and who daily and sincerely follow the path of soul culture are *sura*. *Su* means beautiful, *ram* is the seed syllable for fire. Gods are also called *sura*. Those who come up to the *ajña* chakra, the pituitary, perceive beautiful, divine illumination. This is the state of *sura*.

Maharshi is the state that the student perceives during the practice of *jyoti mudra*. But God is beyond that. He is beyond the seven centers. Self-discipline, sincere effort, and the search for Him (the deep desire for self-realization) enables one to receive the true grace of God Himself. He will reveal Himself to him, the dear one, out of His compassionate love.

Verse 3

yo mām ajam anādim ca
vetti lokamaheśvaram
asammūḍhaḥ sa martyeṣu
sarvapāpaiḥ pramucyate

Translation

He who knows me as the birthless and beginningless, as the mighty Lord of the worlds, among mortals, he is devoid of delusion. He is freed from all sins.

Metaphorical Interpretation

In the previous verse, the Lord said that He Himself is the source of the gods and great seers. In this verse, the Lord explains that He is birthless and beginningless, the cause of everything that exists. But He is also beyond cause and effect; He is the supreme almighty father.

The Lord is saying, "O Arjuna! I have no beginning and no end. I have no birth and no death. Those who are born will surely die (See the Bhagavad Gita 2:27). One who realizes that I am Maheshvara, the supreme Lord of all the *lokas* (planes of existence), is truly realized."

Maheshvara consists of two words: *maha,* great or supreme, and *Ishvara*, the Lord. In each human body, there are seven planes of existence *(lokas)* in the seven centers. These seven centers function through the breath, which is inhaled and exhaled by the power of God—*Ishvara*. The supreme Lord is all-pervading, present in all human beings as the indwelling self. In this world, a person is supposed mortal, but is really immortal if he can perceive the indwelling self with every breath. The indwelling self is neither born, nor does it die.

What is sin? Forgetting the indwelling self and being engrossed in the lower centers, in animal propensities, is sin. No one is born a sinner, nor is sin eternal. Everyone is a child of God. God is breathing from the day of birth, but people live in darkness, which is the cause of all evil. Those who remain in God consciousness, bringing their life energy to the top, are truly spiritual. They perceive the marvelous power of God as the cause of the body, the maintenance of life. They are free from delusion, illusion, error, and all negative qualities. They are in truth, far from falsehood, free from all sins. This state is the state of unity and freedom.

Man can become his own friend or his own foe. By the sincere practice of Kriya, he can become pure, perfect, and realized. To know God is to be one with God, to perceive God in human form and a human being as God. Such a person is divine, enjoying eternal peace.

Verses 4-5

buddhir jñānam asammohaḥ
kṣamā satyam damaḥ śamaḥ
sukham duḥkham bhavo 'bhāvo
bhayam cā 'bhayam eva ca

ahimsā samatā tuṣṭis
tapo dānam yaśo 'yaśaḥ
bhavanti bhāvā bhūtānām
matta eva pṛthagvidhāḥ

Translation

Intellect, knowledge, freedom from delusion, forgiveness, truth, control of the senses, control of the mind, pleasure, pain, birth, death, fear, and fearlessness,

Non violence, equanimity (balance of mind), contentment, meditation, charity, fame, disrepute—these diverse traits arise from Me alone.

Metaphorical Interpretation

The quest for knowledge is endless. People are always wanting to know many things, but this search ends with the knowledge of the divine self. When human beings try to turn the mind inward, away from the external world and toward the indwelling self, they become extremely calm and are able to experience extreme divine qualities. All these divine qualities come from God alone. When a person approaches a fire, he is able to perceive more heat and light. Similarly, when one constantly tries to perceive the soul, divine qualities and the glory of the divine self are more manifest. In these two verses, the Lord describes several divine qualities:

Intellect *(buddhi)*: Every human being is endowed with a mind full of desire and ambition. This mind cannot remain in one state for a very long period of time, so it is the source of confusion and restlessness. This fickle state prevents success. Intellect, however, is above the mind. It is the decisive faculty of man, a God-given quality. It is the source of rationality and understanding. Real intellect leads man to the source of everything, the soul. So, with the help of the intellect, one reaches inner peace.

Knowledge *(jñana)*: Intellect gives birth to knowledge. With the help of knowledge, one proceeds to higher states of consciousness, super consciousness, cosmic consciousness, and ultimately to wisdom *(prajñana)*. Wisdom, the state of being and becoming, cannot be perceived through the sense organs. Meditation, through pure intellect, can bring one to such a state.

Freedom from Delusion *(asammoha)*: In the world of temptation and extroverted sense organs, people are deluded. A man afflicted with cataract cannot see the world nicely. Likewise a man with delusion cannot perceive reality. As a good surgeon can operate on the cataract, a true spiritual master can make one free from delusion. Due to delusion, people have misunderstandings, misdeeds, ambitions, attachment, and suffering. A true seeker, in every state of his life, tries to be free from the delusive play of nature.

Forgiveness *(kshama)*: As a person slowly frees himself from delusion, his life begins to be filled with love. Love gives and forgives. Forgiveness is a great divine quality. When others make little wrongs or mistakes, most people grumble and try to retaliate. To quarrel is animal; to love and forgive is divine.

Truth *(satya)*: People are deluded and remain extremely engrossed in the body nature. Truth is covered by a casket of gold, which is full of delusion. Truth is the soul, the breath. In the Upanishads, it states, *sad eva soumya eva atma:* "O Dear, the soul alone is truth." One who perceives the soul in himself and in everything is in truth.

Sense Control *(dama)*: God has given us five senses of perception, five organs of action, and the mind—not for destruction or difficulties, but to unfold the divine life. To achieve this state, one should have thorough control of the senses in the initial period of spiritual life.

Control of Mind *(shama)*: This is another glory of God. Although mind by nature is restless, it can be controlled through regular practice of meditation. Breath and mind are correlated and causally connected. One achieves control over the mind through breath control and regulation.

Pleasure and Pain *(sukha duhkha)*: In Sanskrit, pleasure and pain are *sukha* and *duhkha*. The common ending in these two words is *kha* meaning vacuum, sky, and space (remaining in the neck and above). To remain in the vacuum center is the source of happiness, and to turn away from it, to be engrossed in the lower centers, is the cause of unhappiness and pain. Pleasure and pain are perceived due to breath and life. One who leads a sincere spiritual life can perceive God's presence in all these dualities and can remain detached from their impact.

Birth and Death *(bhava abhava)*: Physical birth and death, inhalation and exhalation, creation and destruction—everything originates from God.

Fear and Fearlessness *(bhaya abhaya)*: Duality is the cause of fear. People think of separation and loss because of duality. This thinking generates fear. To be merged in God perceiving the divine presence in every breath is the real cause of fearlessness.

Non violence *(ahimsa)*: True non-violence or non-injury is not thinking ill of others, not harming anyone in thought, word, or action.

Equanimity, or Balance of Mind *(samata)*: This is the state of tranquility of mind. When one gets an equal pressure of breath flowing through both nostrils, or reaches the state where warm breath does not come out of the nostrils at all, one will attain balance of mind. Equanimity comes from erasing the ego. In *paravastha,* one enjoys a state of perfect equanimity.

Contentment *(tushti)*: Through equanimity, one reaches inner contentment. Contentment is the real quality of the yogis. When the stomach is full, the yogi will not appreciate or accept even the most palatable dishes. Similarly, as he is ever content and merged in God consciousness, he is free from all other extroverted desires and ambitions.

Meditation *(tapas)*: The seven chakras are called the seven *lokas*, the seven planes of existence. The *ajña chakra,* the sixth center, is called the *tapa loka*. One who keeps his awareness constantly above the *ajña* is really doing *tapas*. In every breath, he is offering oblation to the supreme fire. This is continuous meditation.

Charity *(dana)*: To give food to the hungry, medicine to the diseased, education to the poor children, help to the needy, assurance and love to the destitute is charity. This charity must be done without any expectation of praise or appreciation. Real charity is to lead a spiritual life and to encourage others to live such a life.

Fame and Disrepute *(yasha ayasha)*: If one really leads a divine life, it is the cause of fame. If one does not follow the divine path and lives with the objective of sense gratification, this brings disrepute.

The Lord is saying, "O Arjuna! Whatever you see in this world or universe, whatever quality you see in each living being, even in yourself, it is nothing but My manifestation. I am omnipresent. I am the supreme almighty father. Perceive this. Lead a spiritual life. This will bring complete fulfillment to you."

Verse 6

maharṣayaḥ sapta pūrve
catvāro manavas tathā
madbhāvā mānasā jātā
yeṣām loka imāḥ prajāḥ

Translation

The seven great seers of the past, the four mental sons of Brahma, and the fourteen Manus are of My nature and born of My mind, and from them all the creatures of the world originated.

Metaphorical Interpretation

In the ancient scriptures, the Upanishads, and even in mythology, elaborate descriptions are found of the seven great seers, the four sages (the mental sons of Brahma), and the fourteen Manus. The seven great seers, the *maharshis*, are Marichi, Atri, Angiras, Pulastya, Pulaha, Kratu, and Vasistha. The four Sages, *sanakadis*, are Sanaka, Sanandana, Sanatkumara, and Sanatana. The fourteen Manus are called: Svayambhuva, Svarochisha, Uttama, Tamasa, Raivata, Cakshusha, Vaivasvata, Savarni, Dakshasavarni, Brahmasavarni, Dharmasavarni, Rudrasavarni, Rauchyadevasavarni, and Indrasavarni.

In this verse, the Lord is saying, "O Arjuna! Whatever creation you see in this world is from Me and merges in Me. I am the cause and the source. I created the vacuum; from the vacuum, I created air, fire, water, and earth successively. It took millions of years. Then from the ground, slowly, fungus, insects, plants, and animals were born. At last I created man in My own image. I made human beings not as animals, but as rational beings, so they gradually became cultured and advanced. Although all men are created in My image, in relative existence, all are not equal. Many are living in delusion, illusion, and error; they have many troubles, worries, and anxieties. But those who are truly intelligent overcome all the hazards and become superhuman beings. Through their sincere effort, they perceive Me and My presence. As a result, they find peace, bliss, and joy."

Ordinarily speaking, all the great seers (the *maharshis*), the four divine sons, and the fourteen Manus are divine personalities. But the metaphorical meaning is completely different. *Rishi* means man of right vision and *manu* means the indwelling self manifested in the mind's activities. By practicing meditation one has spiritual experiences and realizations. All these experiences and perceptions are explained in the words of the great Lord.

In the beginning, when people sit for meditation, they face many disturbances and restlessness. These disturbances occur from the bottom center up to the heart center. When they are truly able to lift their consciousness up to the neck center and above, they can perceive calmness. Only by breath control, can one achieve self-control. There are fifty types of breath. Beyond these, there is the breathless breath, the true spiritual breath, which is tranquil. This is the breath of meditation and calmness.

Those who practice a meditation technique such as Kriya Yoga, will be able to have divine experiences such as perceiving brilliant light, namely, *koti surya smah prabhah*: the rays of millions of suns, or many stars twinkling in the darkness of the vacuum. All these perceptions are symbolically explained by the states of *rishi, muni,* and the children of Brahma, the creator.

Verse 7

etām vibhūtim yogam ca
mama yo vetti tattvataḥ
so 'vikampena yogena
yujyate nā 'tra samśayaḥ

Translation

He who really knows the yoga of My manifested glory and power is certain to be united with Me by unshakable yoga. There is no doubt about it.

Metaphorical Interpretation

Many people think that they are practicing yoga. In reality they neither know what yoga is, nor do they really practice and perceive the beauty of yoga. Yoga is the way one can perceive divinity manifested in the whole universe as well as in the entire body. A constant union of body and soul keeps life in the body of each living being. The breath is the gross, divine manifestation in each one of us. People engaged in the divine pursuit can realize it. He who is really practicing yoga, perceiving constant union with the divine self, perceives everything as God's divine glory. His manifestation is known as *vibhuti yoga*.

When one practices a meditation technique such as Kriya Yoga, he constantly remains in the *ajña chakra* and the fontanel. He perceives divine glory while meditating with the eyes closed and perceives divine manifestation with the eyes open. His every breath is utilized for God perception. His life is for God alone. The perception of divine glory and power, in reality and essence, cannot be achieved by reading books or intellectual analysis. He who sincerely follows the instructions of the realized master and practices the techniques to quiet the restless mind is really fortunate; he perceives God's glory and power.

By the regular practice of the yoga of meditation, one reaches the state of *avikampa yoga*, unshakable yoga. *A-vikampa* also means no breath, no vibratory state. In this state, there is firm footing in the yogic lifestyle. The yogi is free from ego. He may have tremendous spiritual power, but he is devoid of vanity and arrogance because he realizes that all glory and power belong to God alone. Power and glory are the manifestation of God's omnipotence. With such spiritual knowledge and practice, one makes constant progress in leading a divine life. Being free from all ambition and expectation, this fortunate devotee becomes well established in divine consciousness. This is the path to *samadhi* and realization.

Verse 8

aham sarvasya prabhavo
mattaḥ sarvam pravartate
iti matvā bhajante mām
budhā bhāvasamanvitāḥ

Translation

I am the source of all creation, everything proceeds from Me. Thus, thinking of Me, these intelligent people worship Me with devotion.

Metaphorical Interpretation

In the previous verse, the Lord explained the state of unshakable yoga, the ultimate goal. In this verse, the Lord speaks of the way, the path to that divine attainment. Lord Krishna says, "O Arjuna! I am the cause and effect. I am the source of all creation. I create everything from Myself alone. Whatever you see in any name or any form is nothing but My manifestation. There is nothing existent without Me."

Gold ornaments are nothing but gold with different names and forms; gold is the ultimate source of all gold ornaments. Gold as gold itself remains changeless in the ornament. A new ornament is born or created from the gold, lives or exists in gold, and at the end, disappears in gold. God is like gold, and all of creation is like the different ornaments.

"O Arjuna! Whatever you perceive through the senses or feel through the heart is nothing but Me. I am the supreme self, the creator, maintainer, and destroyer. Those who are truly intelligent perceive My divine presence."

Material intelligence is not true intelligence. A person endowed with the faculty of discrimination is really intelligent. He is rational. He can really understand what is good and bad, real and unreal, true and false, temporary and eternal. God alone is real. God alone is existent, everywhere. Intelligent people worship omnipresent God with devotion. Ordinarily, people think of worshipping with flowers, fruit, and so forth, but that is not real worship. A truly intelligent yogi, due to his self-regulated spiritual life, can perceive God's presence constantly. He is always in truth. His life is full of love and devotion. He has neither ego nor emotion. He is a true lover of God. His entire life is only for God, nothing else. This is worship with devotion. All of his work activity becomes worship. Work is worship. This is Kriya. This is God consciousness.

Verse 9

maccittā madgataprāṇā
bodhayantaḥ parasparam
kathayantaś ca mām nityam
tuṣyanti ca ramanti ca

Translation

Those whose thoughts are directed to Me, whose *prana*, the breath, is channeled toward Me, are awakening or enlightening each other, constantly speaking of Me, remaining content and delighted.

Metaphorical Interpretation

Here the Lord explains the practical aspect of the spiritual life. People with divine motives go to the realized master, and with his help and guidance, practice meditation. The Lord says, *mat chitta*, "In every thought, perceive Me." This is perception of constant unity. All thought is directed to God. The mind is engrossed in soul. A real yogi perceives that thoughts and the indwelling self are one.

The Lord says, *madgata pranah:* "In every inhalation and exhalation, they perceive My living presence." In every exhalation, life energy flows downward, and in every inhalation, upward to God in the fontanel. The yogis constantly practice *prana-karma*, awareness of breath as the flow of God's life in the spine.

"I am all-pervading, yet, in the multiplicity of My manifestation, I am inhaling and exhaling in all living beings from the time of their birth. Those absorbed in breath awareness (in Me) feel My blissful presence moving in the whole body." These people can hear divine, melodious sound. They achieve the higher stage and perceive divine illumination. As they advance from consciousness to super consciousness and to cosmic consciousness, their body sense and worldly sense gradually diminish. Then, they may attain wisdom, the *samadhi* state, where there is no pulse, no breath, oneness with God, where there is no darkness. This is true, divine illumination. A true spiritual seeker constantly gets self-satisfaction and perception of peace, bliss, and joy. All agonies and negative qualities slowly disappear. In this way, they achieve constant advancement.

The spiritually advanced teach about the almighty Lord, who is hiding as the imperishable soul, formless in each living being, remaining compassionately detached. Such advanced people always speak of truth and love. They are realized and help others to become realized. They teach about love and God in daily life. Proper explanation of spirituality will give real evolution to all human beings. As a rich and generous person can distribute his wealth to make others comfortable, a spiritually rich person always distributes his spiritual treasures among true seekers. Material wealth is diminished through distribution, but spiritual wealth is multiplied because the spiritual person is constantly united with the infinite and formless.

If one practices the scientific technique of soul perception, supernatural power develops. A life of God consciousness and love brings sound health and a divine state. One can be free from doubts, delusions, worries, anxieties, ups and downs, pitfalls, and shortcomings. Strong desire and willpower will make one free from all negative qualities. Body, mind, intelligence, and soul are developed simultaneously. There is constant contentment. Soul culture is the path to attaining peace, bliss, and joy. A life of love is the way to reach complete satisfaction and joy.

Verse 10

teṣam satatayuktānām
bhajatām prītipūrvakam
dadāmi buddhiyogam tam
yena mām upayānti te

Translation

To those who are constantly united with Me, who worship Me with love, I give the yoga of discrimination, by which they come to Me.

Metaphorical Interpretation

Spiritual practice is not a temporary, leisurely, or part-time effort. It is continuous and constant self-effort and self-inquiry. In this verse, the Lord speaks of *satata yuktanam,* which means to be constantly and consciously united with the indwelling self in every breath and in every activity. Life is manifested because of yoga, the union of body and soul. Without the soul, the indwelling spirit, the body is inert and dead. Because of the soul, the breath is going in and out. Without soul, people cannot work. Perceiving *ya*, the soul, and *kri*, in every action, is Kriya, the state of constant union.

Here the Lord also describes worship with love. Worship does not refer to prayers or to worship in a temple or church. It is the manifestation of divine love in every action. Work is worship. Animals work. But only humans can participate consciously in all work. Everyone should avoid bad things and should always be in the state of God consciousness. When a true seeker is endowed with these twofold divine qualities, he is truly blessed by God with *buddhi* yoga, the yoga of discrimination.

What is the yoga of discrimination? Man is a rational being who has the divine quality of discrimination. Man knows what is good and bad, right and wrong. A spiritual person keeps his intellect constantly alert with love for God so that he can be free from negative qualities. This divine quality enables this person to live in the world with a sense of discrimination and detachment. Then it is possible to remain compassionately indifferent and unattached. Life becomes divine.

A devotee's life is so God-oriented that God's presence is perceived constantly in every breath. They are inseparable. The essence of this teaching can be directly understood with regular practice of meditation and contemplation. Thus, a man becomes truly spiritual.

Verse 11

teṣām evā 'nukampārtham
aham ajñānajam tamaḥ
nāśayāmy ātmabhāvastho
jñānadīpena bhāsvatā

Translation

Out of compassion for them, I who dwell in them destroy all darkness born of ignorance with the brilliant lamp of knowledge.

Metaphorical Interpretation

A deluded person, devoid of self-knowledge, thinks of himself as a limited human being, weak in the face of troubles, difficulties, and obstacles. He is body-conscious, always afraid of disease, death, and suffering, and unable to perceive his own divine nature. But in reality this person is the imperishable, deathless, eternal soul, the image of the almighty.

He who leads life as described in the previous verses gets inner spiritual strength. By seeking good company—the company of the realized master—and by the study of holy scriptures, the practice of meditation, and spiritual life, he gets a clear conscience and pure vision. His intellect becomes sharp. Through his discriminative faculty, he can be established in God-consciousness.

The Lord is saying, "O Arjuna! I am the indwelling self in everything, good and bad, rational and irrational, divine and demonic." If a person approaches a fire, he not only feels the fire's warmth and energy, but he can also perceive everything more clearly. Those, who by the instruction of the realized master, come to the pituitary and fontanel, perceive God's presence, the divine illumination. True divine illumination is not only perception of different colors of inner light, but it is also the divine knowledge, which arises out of deep meditation. Knowledge is light. Ignorance is darkness. Darkness does not create true vision. Divine illumination brings God perception to everything. In the forehead, inside the brain, there is the place of the third eye, the eye of divine illumination. In the Bible, there is a description of this third eye—the eye of divine light. (See Matthew 6:22 and Luke 11:34).

"O Arjuna! I am ever compassionate. I have compassion for all My creation. But due to ignorance born out of their deluded deeds, people remain far from Me. They are engrossed in the lower centers and evil actions. But those who come up, who are free from negative deeds, are truly fortunate. I, being self-effulgent and present in them, and through the illumination of self knowledge, destroy all their doubts and delusions. Where there is light, there is no darkness."

Spiritual people are children of light, lovers of light, living in light. Evil doers love darkness, because they want to hide their misdeeds in it; they do not realize that nothing can be hidden from the eyes of the omnipresent God. God is the light of eternal wisdom. He sees everything. His divine wisdom shines brilliantly in the life and deeds of all spiritual people whose lives are an example to all.

Verse 12

arjuna uvāca
param brahma param dhāma
pavitram paramam bhavān
puruṣam śāśvatam divyam
ādidevam ajam vibhum

Translation

Arjuna prayed:

You are the supreme Brahman, the supreme abode, the supreme purifier, the eternal, divine indwelling spirit, the primal God, unborn and all-pervading.

Metaphorical Interpretation

In the previous verses, two things were mentioned by the Lord: sincere effort in spiritual practice, and the grace or compassion of the Lord. *Sadhana* as prescribed in the scriptures and described by the realized master is the first step; realization by the grace of the Lord is the last. Sincere spiritual endeavor is highly essential for reaching divine grace. Arjuna is the true seeker who through his sincere effort is trying to realize the divine gospel.

Arjuna is praying, "O Lord! You are the supreme Brahman. You are formless, absolute and infinite, beginningless and eternal. You are all-pervading. A seeker can perceive your divine presence in the whole body as well as in the whole universe. In deep meditation one goes to the atom point in the fontanel and realizes your absolute divine manifestation.

"O Lord! You are the supreme abode. You have created everything out of Your desire and You are abiding everywhere. The scriptures say that heaven is the supreme abode, but the yogis realize that You are remaining in Your own self. You are Your abode. In the *sahasrara chakra*, yogis realize Your essential nature.

"O Lord! Ignorance is the cause of impurity. One who realizes You in every breath is pure. You are not only pure, You dispel all impurities and ignorance. You are the supreme purifier. The mother cleans her child's body. You are the divine mother who purifies the entire lives of those who come up from the lower centers to the cranium.

"O Lord! You are eternal. You are beyond all changes and modifications. You are immutable. You are unconditional and infinite. O Lord! You are divine. O Lord! You are the indwelling spirit. You are in everything. You are hiding in everything. You are the formless counterpart of all forms. O Lord! You are self-effulgent. You are subtler than the vacuum *(div)*. You are the supreme illuminator who illumines everything. No one can illumine You. You are one without a second. O Lord! You are the primal God, before creation You alone existed. You are the cause of everything. O Lord! You are unborn. Those who are born will die. You are birthless, therefore You are deathless. O Lord! You are omnipresent, omniscient, and omnipotent."

Such is the experience and inner realization of seekers such as Arjuna.

Verse 13

āhus tvām ṛṣayaḥ sarve
devarṣir nāradas tathā
asito devalo vyāsaḥ
svayam cai 'va bravīṣi me

Translation

Thus they address You, all the seers *(rishis)*, the divine seer Narada, also Asita, Devala, and Vyasa, and even You Yourself have told me.

Metaphorical Interpretation

In this worldly life, the mother knows the father of the child and she gives the father's knowledge to the child. In the same way the realized master, like the mother, gives the knowledge of God and the self to the sincere disciple. Ultimately, God reveals Himself.

In this verse, the divine disciple Arjuna is uttering the names of great seers like Narada, Asita, Devala, and Vyasa. They are *rishis*. *Rishis* are men of right vision, great seers, who through their self-effort and a disciplined life have realized the indwelling spirit, the eternal soul, inside and outside.

Narada means *naram dadati iti*, one who gives knowledge and bliss. Narada is a divine seer, the guru, the preceptor. In mythology, Narada is said to move in the sky, which means when one goes from the neck center (vacuum) up to the pituitary, one reaches the ecstatic stage of Narada.

Asita is another *rishi* considered to be the disciple of Vyasa. Asita has a dark complexion. The metaphorical meaning of Asita is *a,* not, and *sita,* in bondage or entangled. Asita is the state of liberation, the freedom from all bondage.

Devala is the son of Asita. He is also called Ashtavakra, a very powerful master, even in his childhood. There is a beautiful book written under his name called the Ashtavakra Gita—the Gospel of the Great Seer Ashtavakra. The metaphorical meaning of Devala is *deva,* vacuum or heaven, and *lam*, the root of the earth principle. Through meditation one reaches the state of *devala*—the perception of God's presence from the earth principle in the *muladhara* to the sky principle in the neck center.

Vyasa is the great spiritual master, compiler of the Vedas, author of the Brahmasutras, Bhagavad Gita, Mahabharata,

Bhagavatam, and Puranas. As a realized master, he has spoken, taught in detail, and written about spiritual life, the path of God-realization, and who God is. The metaphorical meaning of Vyasa is the divine wisdom that enables man to discriminate the real from the unreal and reach the state of realization.

In this verse, after mentioning the names of the great seers, Arjuna says, "O Lord! Only You can describe Yourself. None but you can reveal Yourself, Your state, and Your being. You showed me Your essential nature." To learn through reading or to be told something is indirect information, but to practice and realize is direct perception. Spirituality is being and becoming one with the divine.

Verse 14

sarvam etad ṛtam manye
yan mām vadasi keśava
na hi te bhagavan vyaktim
vidur devā na dānavāḥ

Translation

Everything You told me, I believe to be true. Indeed, neither the gods, nor the demons know your divine manifestation, O divine one (Lord).

Metaphorical Interpretation

God is absolute and formless. His divine manifestation is in every form in creation. To perceive God in all these aspects and to realize Him is not so easy. The first step for spiritual practice and realization is belief. This is not blind belief. Belief is the foundation of learning. A child initially believes what he is taught in primary school, but when he grows up he gradually realizes the truth of it.

In this verse, Arjuna, the enthusiastic student, expresses his strong belief in the words of the master. Arjuna addresses the Lord as Keshava. There are many meanings for this name, but let's consider *ka* plus *isha* plus *va*: *ka* means Brahma, the creator; *isha* means Shiva, the destroyer; and *va* means Vishnu, the preserver and sustainer. So, Keshava is the total of these aspects of God as creator, maintainer, and destroyer. At every moment, in every human being, a thought is created, it lives for awhile, and then it dissolves. Then, another cycle of thought will begin—and so on. This is possible only because of the breath, and ultimately, the soul. Keshava is the indwelling self.

So Arjuna is saying, "O Keshava! My indwelling self. You are my real master, my guru. You have spoken in detail about Your own divine nature. You Yourself are a mystery. None but You know Yourself. Only You Yourself can reveal Your own divine nature. Neither the gods nor the demons know You in reality." *Atmaiva gurur ekam*—the soul is the real master.

In Sanskrit, a "god" is *deva*, which means the state of vacuum, divine light, and divine qualities. When people come up to the *ajña chakra*, the pituitary, they reach the state of the *devas,* the gods. But self-realization is beyond this. *Danavas* means the demons, those who are always engrossed in the lower centers, sense gratification, and restlessness. They are unable to know the glory of God. In mythology it is said that these *danavas* meditate at times to gain more strength of body and more power to enjoy.

Arjuna is asking, "O Bhagavan, O divine one, O Lord, I believe your teachings and descriptions. Please teach me more about spiritual life and realization."

Verse 15

svayam evā 'tmanā 'tmānam
vettha tvam puruṣottama

bhūtabhāvana bhūteśa
devadeva jagatpate

Translation

You know Yourself through Yourself alone, O supreme person, Lord of the universe, source of all beings, Lord of creation, God of gods and Lord of the world.

Metaphorical Interpretation

In this verse, over and over again Arjuna through the divine quality invokes the ultimate reality:

"O Lord! You are Purushottama, the supreme self, hiding in everything. The real nature of every person is the spirit, the self. Without this self, one is essentially dead."

"O Lord! You are Bhutabhavana." *Bhuta* means the gross elements. There are five gross elements—earth, water, fire, air, and vacuum. *Bhavana* means the creator. *Bhutabhavana* means the creator of the five gross elements. In the Upanishads it says, "From God alone, creation began." From Him came the vacuum, then air, from air came fire, from fire came water, and from water came earth. These five gross elements are the fundamental principles of all living beings as well as inanimate objects. God created all these elements from Himself and He permeates everything.

"O Lord! You are Bhutesha, the Lord of these elements and of the universe." The five elements make the five lower centers active, and each center in turn is dominant. But all five centers gain their strength through the breath; they are the presence of the soul.

"O Lord! You are God of the gods. You control all the good

qualities of people. You also give light to the sense organs and the inner instruments such as the mind, thought, intellect, and ego.

"O Lord! You are the Lord of the world, *jagat*." *Jagat* means that which undergoes constant change and modification. The world is changing every moment. Each human body is also changing constantly. The changing world as well as each human body is *jagat*. At the same time, God is all-pervading in the world and in each human being. "O Lord! You are *jagat pati*," meaning that, You are the controller of the world and every human life.

"O Lord! No one can know Your self. You know Yourself alone. O Self-effulgent Lord! You, by Your divine illumination, help others to obtain Your knowledge. Nothing is possible without Your grace."

Verse 16

vaktum arhasy aśeṣeṇa
divyā hy ātmavibhūtayaḥ
yābhir vibhūtibhir lokān
imāms tvam vyāpya tiṣṭhasi

Translation

You are able to express completely the manifestations of Your divine self, by which You pervade these worlds and abide in them.

Metaphorical Interpretation

God is infinite. His creation and divine manifestation are also infinite. Only the infinite can know the infinite. So Arjuna is praying to the Lord, "Whatever is seen, perceived, or even unseen or unperceived is nothing but Your manifestation. You have created everything. You are present in everything. You are in and out of everything. There is nothing without You. No one can express, explain, or enumerate Your divine manifestation. Only You are aware of Yourself and Your glory. None but You can reveal Your divinity."

To perceive, realize, and understand the divine manifestation, one must sincerely tread the path of spirituality. Sincere seekers can reach the divine, but as long as the ego is there, they cannot progress on the path of realization. Self-surrender is the essential step for self-realization.

In this verse, Arjuna, because of his inner understanding, is able to surrender his individuality to the great master, the Lord Himself. God alone knows His own glory. God alone can reveal Himself. This revelation is the state of realization. In this condition, the seeker perceives the divine glory in the sky of inner consciousness, *chidakasha*.

Every spiritual seeker must try to realize God's manifestation in every thought, word, and action. In every center *(chakra)*, in every disposition, he must seek God's love, which is *kri* and *ya*, perceiving divinity in every activity. This person will make progress on the path of soul culture. God is in three periods of time. He is in three worlds. He is everywhere. With the eye of inner awareness, one can try to perceive the manifestation of God.

Verse 17

katham vidyām aham yogims
tvām sadā paricintayan
keṣu-keṣu ca bhāveṣu
cintyo 'si bhagavan mayā

Translation

O Master of Yoga! How can I know you through constant

meditation? O Lord! In what particular aspect of Your being am I to meditate upon You?

Metaphorical Interpretation

Arjuna addresses the Lord as *yogin*, the master of yoga. In the scripture it says, *hiraṇyagarbha yogasya vaktā nānyat kadācana*: "Only the Lord is the master, author, and teacher of yoga, no one else." Here, Arjuna is accepting the Lord not only as the master of yoga, but also as the true guide. He is also asking a practical question about constant God awareness, nonstop meditation.

Arjuna is saying, "O Lord! I know the mind is restless, always roaming from one object to another. To regulate the mind, I have tried to perceive your eternal presence in every thought, word, and action." People tend to think that spiritual practice is a pastime done for a few minutes or hours. They do not know that it is *tvam sada parichintayam*—to remember You continuously. "O Lord! I am trying to perceive your presence in every breath, as You are breathing through me. Through this practice, I have achieved calmness, but please tell me how I can meditate more deeply to realize You. Please teach me: You are the real master of yoga."

This verse is an expression of love, regard, and self-inquiry by the sincere seeker, the *sadhaka*, to his master, the Lord. He is not only asking his master what he should do, but he is also asking what essence should he perceive in order to reach self-realization. The human life span is extremely short and transitory. Every exhalation is a slow death. Most do not realize this. Each person should make the best use of his precious time to perceive God's presence in every moment.

Verse 18

vistareṇā 'tmano yogam
vibhūtim ca janārdana

bhūyaḥ kathaya tṛptir hi
śṛṇvato nā sti me 'mṛtam

Translation

Explain to me again in detail, O Janardana (Krishna), Your yoga and manifestation, because I am never satisfied with hearing Your nectar-like words.

Metaphorical Interpretation

Janardana is a name of the Lord Who creates and sustains creation and Who destroys ignorance and negative attitudes. It is also the state of tranquility, where there is no inhalation (birth) or exhalation (death). "O Janardana," Arjuna asks, "Please explain to me again in detail about spiritual life. I want to know about yoga as well as the divine manifestation."

Yoga means to perceive constant unity with the Lord, in every breath and thought. Yoga is also the state of extreme tranquility, the waveless mind and inner realization. Yoga is the cause; the knowledge of *vibhuti,* the divine manifestation, is the effect. Arjuna wants to know yoga as well as *vibhuti*, the divine glory of the Lord.

Arjuna expresses, "O Lord! I am never satisfied with hearing your nectar-like words." When one practices Kriya Yoga and comes from the lower centers up to the pituitary (vacuum), one hears a beautiful and melodious sound, which is enchanting. This divine sound, which occasionally changes, is the song of the Lord. The devotee reaches a state of inner calmness by listening to this sound; the mind dissolves into it. The more one hears it, the more one is eager to hear it. In the yogic scriptures it says, *salayah nadam ashrita*: "When the devotee attains some realization, he is not satisfied, he wants more realization and progress." To achieve more, the devotee expresses the wish to hear, see, and perceive more. This is a demand, request, and expectation from the devotee (disciple) to the Lord, the divine master.

Verse 19

śribhagavān uvāca
hanta te kathayiṣyāmi
divyā hy ātmavibhūtayaḥ
prādhānyataḥ kuruśreṣṭha
nā 'sty anto vistarasya me

Translation

The Lord said:
Listen, O best of the Kurus (Arjuna)! I shall show you the manifestations of My divine self, but only the prominent ones, for there is no limit to My magnitude.

Metaphorical Interpretation

Kurushreshtha is a name the Lord uses to address Arjuna. *Kuru* means action; *shreshtha* means the best; thus, Kurushreshtha is one who does the best action. What is the best action? In verse 3:5, the Lord said, "Everyone is active without pause. No one can exist without performing action." But here, the Lord explains the best action to Arjuna. The power of God, hiding in each human body is doing the work. A dead man is free from any action. Ordinarily, people work with many expectations; as a result their minds are preoccupied with desires and dispositions, and they cannot act in the best possible way. One who fixes his attention on the top and perceives the power of God, the cause of all action, is Kurushreshtha. Kurushreshtha meditates and loves God in every breath and spends his time in God consciousness. One who constantly sits near the soul, Krishna, in the body chariot, on the battlefield of life (*kurukshetra*) is Kurushreshtha, the best of the Kurus.

God is infinite. His names, divine play, activities, and nature are also infinite. Infinite, unlimited, divine manifestation cannot be expressed with finite, limited words. But the Lord says to

Arjuna, "O Arjuna! You are truly sincere. You have extreme desire for soul culture and self-realization. You love My company. You are trying to practice as I direct. The ordinary mind is attracted to sense objects, *visaya*, but your mind is after the perception of My divine manifestation, *vibhuti*. As there are countless waves, bubbles, and ripples in the ocean, so also is My manifestation and glory infinite. Nonetheless, I will describe some prominent aspects of My divine glory."

Verse 20

aham ātmā guḍākeśa
sarvabhūtāśayasthitaḥ
aham ādiś ca madhyam ca
bhūtānām anta eva ca

Translation

I am the self, O Gudakesha (Arjuna)! Abiding in the core of all beings, I am the beginning, middle, and end of all beings.

Metaphorical Interpretation

Arjuna is truly spiritual. He has many good qualities. The Lord knows this, but Arjuna does not. His spiritual guide, the master, addresses Arjuna by different names, each indicating some aspects of a spiritual person. In the previous verse, Arjuna was called Kurushreshtha; here, Arjuna is addressed as Gudakesha. *Gudaka* means sleep or slumber, *isha* means the master, the Lord, the conqueror. So, Gudakesha is the conqueror of sleep. In the Ramayana, the most ancient mythological book, a narration of the life and mission of Rama, Lakshmana conquered sleep, as did Arjuna in the Mahabharata. To be a yogi, one must give up idleness, slumber, laziness, and even sleep. Sleep is the state of forgetting. One who forgets God in daily life is spiritually sleeping. Arjuna is always in God consciousness. Gudakesha also means constant alertness, trying to perceive the indwelling self in every breath, in every moment.

The Lord is saying,

"I am the indwelling self, abiding in all living beings. I am not only living beings, I am also in all *bhutas*, the five gross elements. In each human being, the five gross elements are present in the five lower centers—earth in the coccygeal, water in the sacral, fire in the lumbar, air in the dorsal, and vacuum in the cervical.

"I remain inside the cranium; from there, I cause the breath to move in and out; from there, I give My power to each center, to create different propensities.

"I am in the beginning—I am in the father and mother, in the conception of the baby. If I do not inhale, the father and mother are not able to make a baby. I am in the beginning—I existed before creation, I am in the creation of the universe—and even beyond. I exist without creation, but creation cannot exist without me. The soul can remain without the body, but the body cannot remain without the soul.

"I am in the middle; I am life. I am between birth and death in the span of life, breathing through the nostrils of each being. I am sustaining and maintaining everything.

"I am in the end—everything dissolves in Me. I am the cause of creation, sustenance, and dissolution. In each human being a propensity is created through breath, and then it dissolves in breath.

"O Arjuna! Remember Me as everything in every breath. I am life as well as death. I am the supreme almighty father. Those who remain engrossed in the lower centers, in body consciousness, cannot truly perceive my presence. By leading a moderate and yogic lifestyle, those who come up to the soul center can reach the state of constant alertness. O Arjuna! You are Gudakesha, the conqueror of sleep. Sleep means not only to rest of the body, but it also means forgetting the soul. Most people are deluded in slumber. You are trying to rise up to higher level awareness, to the state of immortality.

"O Arjuna! I am everything in creation. Now I will show you my principal manifestation."

Verse 21

ādityānām aham viṣṇur
jyotiṣām ravir amśumān
marīcir marutām asmi
nakṣatrāṇām aham śaśī

Translation

Among the twelve sons of Aditi, I am Vishnu; among the lights, I am the radiant sun; I am Marichi among the *marutas*; of the stars, I am the moon.

Metaphorical Interpretation

Diti means duality. *Aditi* means non-dual, the perception of unity. Aditi's sons are called *adityas*, which also implies the divine illumination arising from unity with the indwelling self. The *adityas* are twelve in number. They are known as Bhaga, Amsha, Aryama, Mitra, Varuna, Savita, Dhata, Vivasvan, Tvashta, Pusha, Shakra (Indra), and Vishnu. "Among these twelve, O Arjuna! I am Vishnu."

Vishnu means *vishnati pravishyati iti*, He who is penetrating and manifesting everywhere, all-pervading consciousness, or divine illumination. Thus, "In every part of the body, in every aspect of creation, I am Vishnu." In the yogic scripture, it says, *pranah vishnuh*, "The vital breath present in every cell is Vishnu."

"Of all lights, I am the radiant Ravi, the sun." The metaphorical meaning of *ravi* is *ram*, fire or illumination, and *vam* is water, love, and *ing* is *shakti*, which is energy or power. The perception of divine illumination and love through the power of meditation, is Ravi.

"I am Marichi among all *marutas*." *Maruta* means *vayu*, the air, and *marichi* means light and the power by which ego is destroyed. When people have different dispositions, they have different types of breath, air, that is, *maruta*. Among these, is the Lord Marichi—the very slow, feeble, and fine breath. When there is no ego, this state is Marichi.

"I am the moon (*sashi* or *chandra*), among the stars *(nakshatras)*." *Nakshatra* means that which is beyond destruction. This is immortality. Man attains immortality by keeping his attention on the top and perceiving the light, the white light of the moon.

Verse 22

vedānām sāmavedo 'smi
devānām asmi vāsavaḥ
indriyāṇām manaś cā 'smi
bhūtānām asmi cetanā

Translation

Of the Vedas, I am Sama Veda. Of the gods, I am Vasava.

Of the senses, I am the mind and I am the consciousness in all beings.

Metaphorical Interpretation

The Lord continues,

Vedanam samavedo smi: "Among the Vedas, I am Sama." *Veda* means knowledge; another name for it is *shruti*, to hear without any utterance. When a person meditates and enters into the state of inner tranquility, he is able to perceive the inner voice, the *aum* sound. This is the essence of the Vedas. When one fixes his attention on the top, he perceives black and white light. *Sa* means white illumination and *ama* means black. In the sound, he is perceiving divine illumination. This is Sama Veda. *Sama* also means the song. If knowledge cannot be expressed nicely, then it is of less use. Samaveda means the expression of divine knowledge beautifully.

Devanam asmi vasavah: "Of the gods, I am Vasava (another name for Indra)." Vasava is *vasa* and *ava*, which mean one who lives in the vacuum. In different parts of the body, divine power is manifest. But when one goes to the vacuum, from the neck center up to the top of the head, he reaches the state of divine illumination and tranquil breath. Vasava is the king of the gods because he is in the top, in soul awareness, living in the paradise of the cranium.

Indriyanam manashca 'smi: "Among all the senses *(indriyas),* I am the mind *(manas).*" The scriptures mention the senses in different ways. There are five senses of perception: sight, hearing, smell, taste, and touch. But the Bhagavad Gita speaks of the mind as the sixth sense (See Verse 15:7). The mind is the ruler of the senses. If the mind is not associated with the sense organs, they lose their power of perception. When the mind is pure, one's own spiritual nature can be realized.

Bhutanam asmi chetana: "I am the consciousness of *bhuta,* which is the elements, the living being, and even the past." *Bhuta* is changeable and mutable. Among all the changing worlds, God is pure consciousness. The soul is present in all living beings; *bhuta* and the soul are present in the form of consciousness.

Verse 23

rudrāṇām śamkaraś cā 'smi
vitteśo yakṣarakṣasām
vasūnām pāvakaś cā 'smi
meruḥ śikhariṇām aham

Translation

And of the Rudras, I am Shankara; among the Yakshas and Rakshasas, I am Kubera; among the Vasus, I am Pavaka; among the mountains, I am Meru.

Metaphorical Interpretation

Rudranam shamkarash cha 'smi: "I am Shankara among all the Rudras." There are eleven Rudras: Aja, Ekapada, Ahibradhna, Pinaki, Rita, Pitrurupa, Tryambaka, Brishakapi, Shambhu, Hara, and Ishvara. Rudra means prana, the vital life force: *ye rudrah te khalu pranah.* Shankara means *sham*, all auspiciousness, and *kara*, bestower. He who gives all auspiciousness, peace, bliss, and joy is Shankara.

Vittesho yaksha rakshasam: "I am Vittesha (Kubera) among the Yakshas and Rakshasas." *Vitta* means wealth or prosperity and *isha* means the Lord; hence, Vittesha is the lord of wealth and prosperity. True wealth is inside the cranium. The head is compared to a mountain. According to mythology, Kubera, the king of wealth, lives on mount Kailas. One who goes to the mountaintop, in other words, the fontanel, and attains the real wealth of spirituality is Vittesha or Kubera. Yakshas and Rakshasas refer to the protectors of all properties.

Vasunam pavakash cha asmi: "I am Pavaka among all Vasus." *Vasu* means illumination. There are eight Vasus according to the scriptures: Bhava, Dhruva, Soma, Vishnu, Anala, Anila, Pratyusha, and Derabhava. Another name for Anala is Pavaka. Pavaka is the purifying fire. When one remains constantly above the pituitary, one perceives the light of fire and becomes truly pure. Meditation brings purity of body, mind, and thought; thus, I am Pavaka of all the Vasus.

Meruh shikharinam aham: "I am Meru among all the mountains." In the Shiva Samhita 2:1, it says, *dehe 'smin vartate meruḥ satpadvīpa samanvitaḥ:* "Mount Meru exists in this body, surrounded by seven islands." The spine is called the axis of Meru *(meru-danda)*. The Meru is in the cranium and its summit is the *sahasrara*, the thousand-petaled lotus in the fontanel. Etymologically, Meru comes from *me,* to project, and *ru*, brilliance. When one keeps his attention on the top, he perceives brilliant divine light projected from all around.

Verse 24

purodhasām ca mukhyam mām
viddhi pārtha bṛhaspatim
senānīnām aham skandaḥ
sarasām asmi sāgaraḥ

Translation

Of the household priests, I am the chief, I am Brihaspati, O son of Pritha! Of the commander of the armies, I am Skanda. Of the lakes or rivers, I am the ocean.

Metaphorical Interpretation

Purodhas or *purohita* means he who always wants the good for creation. He is called a priest. God is the real guru who wants the good of everything. Brihaspati is called the guru of the gods or the *deva-guru*. Another meaning of Brihaspati is *brihati* and *pati*. *Brihati* means speech and *pati* means the Lord; thus, the Lord of speech—the air, in the vaccum. Man and animals talk through the breath. "I am the breath;" this is Brihaspati.

Each human being has góod and bad qualities. Each person should fight the negative qualities because they are weakness. One who fights is a soldier. With positive qualities, willpower, and inner strength, one must fight all the evil propensities present in him or herself. "I am the commander of the army, Skanda," refers to the state of purity and freedom from passion.

Sarasam asmi sagarah: "Among all the lakes and rivers, I am the ocean." Sarasa is a restless and changing river that always flows downwards. The inner meaning of *sarasa* is mind. The mind is always fickle and restless. When the river meets the ocean, it loses its restlessness and flows into the ocean. The ocean symbolizes vastness, tranquility, infinity, and God. Through meditation and the practice of Kriya, when one attains *paravastha* with the tranquil breath, the restlessness of the mind disappears. One perceives eternity, infinity, and extreme tranquility. This is the state of the ocean, of cosmic consciousness.

Verse 25

maharṣīṇām bhṛgur aham
girām asmy ekam akṣaram
yajñānām japayajño 'smi
sthāvarāṇām himālayaḥ

Translation

Of the great seers, I am Bhrighu; among syllables, I am the one *(aum)*; of sacrifices, I am silent meditation *(japa)*; of immovable things, I am the Himalayas.

Metaphorical Interpretation

Rishis are those of right vision, seers, self-realized masters. They remove the darkness of ignorance from the sky of consciousness. *Maharshi* means the great seer. Among all the great *rishis*, there are seven prominent *maharshis*. They are called *saptarshi*. The Lord says,

Maharshinam bhrigur aham: "Of the great seers, I am Bhrigu." Bhrigu is derived from the root *bhraj*, which means to roast. When the seed is roasted, it cannot be used to germinate. Similarly, when one practices meditation, every desire, ambition, and seed of *samskara* is roasted, making one free from all the effects of past actions stored in the midbrain. This is Bhrigu, who is free from all desire, the seed of good and bad actions, the liberated soul.

Giram asmy ekam aksharam: "Among all syllables, I am the one *(aum)*. In the Bhagavad Gita (8:13), the Lord said: *om ity ekaksharam brahma:* "*Aum* (or *om*) is the one-lettered Brahman." The Lord means that He is *aum* among all the letters. *Aum* is not to be chanted, but to be heard in deep meditation. *Aum* consists of three letters *A, U,* and *M*, indicating past, present, and future; creation, sustenance, and destruction; gross, astral, and causal; and so forth. *Aum* is God Himself. In Patanjali's Yoga Sutras, it says, *tasya vachaka pranava*: "*Aum* is the symbol of God."

Yajñānām japayajño 'smi: "Of all sacrifices, I am silent meditation, *japa*." *Yajña* means sacrifice. Ordinarily, people perform many types of *yajñas* to fulfill their material expectations. They offer oblation to the fire with different mantras. Here, the Lord says, "Of all *yajñas*, I am *japa yajña*." The ordinary meaning of *japa* is chanting. People chant the name of God, even with a rosary in hand. Sant Kabir, a realized master of the fifteenth century said:

mala tȯ hath me phire
jibha phire mukhmahi
manua to chandishi phire
eto sumiran nahi

which means, "The rosary is rotating in the hand, and the tongue is moving in the mouth in *japa,* but one is not aware that the mind is roaming in four directions."
Every spiritual practice aims at calming the restless mind. The easiest way of mind control is to do *ajapa japa*, to perceive the power of God in every breath. One must learn this from a realized master. This can be achieved without any difficulty.

Sthavaranam himalaya: "Of the immovable things, I am the Himalayas (a range of mountains in Northern India)." *Stha* means establishment, *vara* means the best, so *sthavara* means the best establishment. Himalaya does not really mean the mountains, it means *hima*, cold and *alaya*, house. When one penetrates into the cranium through the practice of Kriya and is well established in the fontanel, then his mind is calm and quiet. There is no restlessness. The breath will be extremely cool. Warm breath will not be coming out of the nostrils. The cranium is the real *himalaya.* (See the Bhagavad Gita 5:27 about cool breath, breath inside the nostrils, and so forth.)

Verse 26

aśvatthaḥ sarvavṛkṣāṇām
devarṣīṇām ca nāradaḥ
gandharvāṇām citrarathaḥ
siḍdhānām kapilo muniḥ

Translation

Of all the trees, I am the ashvattha; of all the divine sages, I am Narada; among all the gandharvas, I am Chitraratha; of the perfected, I am Kapila, the sage.

Metaphorical Interpretation

Ashvattha sarva vrikshanam: "I am the ashvattha of all the trees." Every human being is a tree. This human tree is inverted. The root of the ordinary tree is underneath the soil, but the root of the body tree is above, inside the cranium. The branches of the body tree extend downward. Ashvattha (the peepul tree) is a special tree in India. But the metaphorical meaning of *ashvattha* is *a*, not, and *shva*, for tomorrow, and *tha*, to remain—that which will not remain tomorrow, which is the imperment human body. One who realizes that this body will not always exist, that the body is perishable, *ashvattha*, will try to fulfill the purpose of human life, which is God-realization.

Devarshinam cha narada: "I am Narada among the *devarshis* (divine sages)." Devarshi is not a title, it is a state of spiritual attainment from *deva* and *rishi. Deva* means he who roams in the vacuum, in God awareness; *rishi* means the man of right vision, one who meditates and comes up from the lower centers to the neck (vacuum), but more notably one who comes up to higher planes than the vacuum. He is the *devarshi* of the divine sages. Among all the divine sages, Narada is the best. *Nara* means the blissful state, God, and *da* means one who can give and enable; therefore Narada is one who enables people to achieve the state of eternal bliss, one who helps people become self-realized.

Gandharvanam chitrarathah: "Among the *gandharvas*, I am Chitraratha." *Gandharvas* are mythological celestial beings who sing and dance in heaven. One who comes up to the pituitary hears divine sound and perceives many colors. Chitraratha comes from *chitra,* colorful, and *ratha,* chariot. In the body chariot, one perceives many divine colors and sounds. This is Chitraratha among all the celestial beings.

Siddhanam kapila muni: "Among perfected beings, I am Kapila Muni." In the Shrimad Bhagavatam, a holy book of India, it is mentioned that Kapila was perfect, realized from the moment of his birth. He was the best among all the people in the way of self-knowledge. Kapila means copper color. When one meditates, the copper color is perceived.

Verse 27

uccaiḥśravasam aśvānām
viddhi mām amṛtodbhavam
airāvatam gajendrāṇām
narāṇām ca narādhipam

Translation

Of horses, know Me to be Ucchaihshravas, born of nec-

tar. Among royal elephants, I am Airavata and of all men, I am the king.

Metaphorical Interpretation

Ucchaihshravasam ashvanam: "Of horses, know Me to be Ucchaihshravas." The horse carries a load or human beings to their destination, therefore the horse is the symbol of movement and transportation. The horse is the vital breath. There are fifty different types of breath. Among them is the spiritual breath that is able to take the consciousness toward the soul. This breath, *udana,* is called *uchchaihshravas*. Through this breath, one will reach the state of immortality, the nectar. The Lord said that this horse is born of the breath of *udana* or *uchchaihshravas*.

Airavatam gajendranam: "Among royal elephants, I am Airavata." An elephant is an example of extreme attachment to the sense of touch (See the Viveka Chudamani of Shankara, Verse 76). An elephant becomes blind out of sex joy. A royal elephant means one who is not after sense joys, but rather the joy of God-realization. In the Ashtavakra Gita, it says that the mind is an elephant. Airavata is a white elephant. When the mind is clean, pure, and God conscious through meditation, it helps the seeker in their spiritual upliftment. This is Airavata.

Naranam cha naradhipam: "Among men, I am the king." He who knows how to control, rule, and administrate is the king. He maintains discipline. A person who knows the secret of controlling the senses, ruling the mind, and disciplining life is really a king. Jesus was called the King of kings. Monks in India are called *maharajas*, which means great kings.

Verse 28

āyudhānām aham vajram
dhenūnām asmi kāmadhuk
prajanaś cā 'smi kandarpaḥ
sarpāṇām asmi vāsukiḥ

Translation

Of weapons, I am the thunderbolt; of cows, I am the wish-fulfilling cow. I am sexual desire that leads to procreation; of the serpents, I am Vasuki.

Metaphorical Interpretation

Life is a battlefield. The real battle is the battle of the spiritual life, the battle to achieve perfection and God-realization. In each human being, there is a mixture of good and bad qualities. Everyone must sincerely try to avoid negative habits through meditation. In the battle of the spiritual life, one needs the weapons of self-discipline, truthfulness, honesty, and love.

The Lord says,

> *Ayudhanam aham vajra:* "I am *vajra*, the thunderbolt of all weapons." The real weapon of the spiritual battle is the breath. With breath control, one can regulate and channel all activity. Another meaning of *vajra* is strong determination and willpower. Those who really want spiritual evolution must lead their life with determination and not deviate from the truth. They must meditate and learn to regulate the breath.

> *Dhenunam asmi kamadhuk:* "Among the cows, I am Kamadhenu." Kamadhenu is a mythological cow who fulfills all wishes, ambitions, and expectations. The soul in the body is the wish-fulfilling cow. Those who want sense pleasure, get it and enjoy it by the soul and the power of the

breath; those who want God-realization, can achieve this through the grace of the Self. Man is his own friend or his own foe. Man can change his life and activities, but it depends upon desire. If the desire is strong for spiritual progress and self-realization, by the grace of the Self and by leading the divine life, this wish of self-realization will be fulfilled.

Prajanash chasmi kandarpah: "I am the desire of sexual procreation." *Prajana* means creative power. In each human being, there is creative power. It is not only sexual desire, procreative energy, but every aspect of creative power. The farmer, artist, scientist—everyone has his own creative power which comes from the breath. "I am the soul abiding in everything, breathing and giving the desire for creation and procreation." Creation is made above the navel center and procreation is below the navel center.

Sarpanam asmi vasukih: "I am Vasuki among all the serpents." Many snakes have jewels on their head. Vasuki is *vasu,* jewel, and *ka,* the head. One who sees the self-effulgent light on the head, is Vasuki. Many people also call the power of serpents, *vasuki.*

Verse 29

anantaś cā 'smi nāgānām
varuṇo yādasām aham
pitṛṇām aryamā cā 'smi
yamaḥ samyamatām aham

Translation

Of the snakes *(nagas)*, I am Ananta, I am Varuna among the aquatic creatures. Of the ancestors, I am Aryama. I am Yama of those who maintain discipline.

Metaphorical Interpretation

Anantash cha 'smi naganam: "Of the snakes, I am Ananta." The snakes in the body, the serpent movement of *prana*, the life energy, are experienced through breathing and respiration. In the human body, there are fifty types of *vayu*, vital airs. Among them is the *udana vayu,* also called *ananta. Ananta* also means infinite. One is able to go to the state of the infinite through the help of *udana* or *ananta*. Through meditation, when one is able to reach the *udana* state of breath, it gives extreme calmness. In Indian mythology, *ananta* is a special serpent coiled in the ocean of milk on which Vishnu takes rest. It symbolizes the divine illumination in the pituitary, white, golden, and blue in color.

Varuno yadasam aham: "Of all aquatic creatures, I am Varuna." Varuna is *rasa tattva*, the water principle. It is the life of all creatures, not only those living in water, but also those who live on the earth and even birds. In each human body, there is *rasa tattva*, water. The blood circulation in the whole body is the water principle. The digestion and circulation are possible due to *vyana vayu,* a special vital breath. This is Varuna.

Pitrinam aryama cha 'smi: "I am Aryana of all the ancestors, *pitrinam. Pitrinam* in Sanskrit is from the word *pita,* which is from the root *pa* meaning one who maintains. Like the parent maintains the child, the breath maintains the body. In the Jñana Shankalini Tantra 8:2 it is said, *vayu rupa sthito harih:* "The *vayu* or breath sustains, maintains, and activates the body. Without the breath, man cannot survive. The Upanishads state: *pita ha vai pranah,* "The vital breath is *pita,* the ancestors."

Yamah samyamatam aham: "I am Yama of those who maintain discipline." In Indian mythology, Yama is the god of death. *Yama* also means the art of self-discipline. In the Yoga Sutras of Patañjali it says, *trayah ekatrah samyamam:* "When there is *dharana* (concentration), *dhyana* (meditation), and *samadhi* (realization) together, this is *samyama* (discipline). This state is achieved by leading a disciplined life. The Lord is saying, "I am the self-discipline *(yama)* of all those who try to be disciplined."

Verse 30

prahlādaś cā 'smi daityānām
kālaḥ kalayatām aham
mṛgāṇām ca mṛgendro 'ham
vainateyaś ca pakṣiṇām

Translation

I am Prahlada of the Titans; of calculators, I am time; of the beasts, the king of beasts (the lion); of the birds, I am the son of Vinita (Garuda).

Metaphorical Interpretation

In Sanskrit, *daitya* ordinarily means demons or titans. *Daitya* also means inner propensities or thoughts, full of aggression and cruelty. These thoughts are mostly very strong and demonic. These thoughts are mostly dualistic. Among these thoughts, the Lord says, *prahladash cha 'smi:* "I am Prahlada." *Pra* means perfect and *hlada* means joy, so *prahlada* means perfect joy. After practicing Kriya, a person enters into the state of *paravastha.* In this state, there is no restlessness of mind. The mind is absorbed in God consciousness. This state can also be called *prahlada*—the state of perfect joy.

Kalah kalayatam aham: "Of the calculators, I am time." People calculate everything with numbers—their wealth, prosperity, activity, material achievements—they even try to calculate their age and life with numbers. But the Lord is saying, "I am the time of all the calculators." The Lord enumerates all human beings through their spiritual life. Human life cannot be measured with days, months, and years; rather, it is measured with the breath. Every breath is precious. This is *ajapa-japa,* the breath that is constantly going in and out in each human being. If one is truly conscious of the indwelling self in every breath, one can be free from *kala* and realize *mahakala,* the supreme time, God Himself.

Mriganam cha mrigendro 'ham: "Of all the beasts, I am the lion, the king of beasts." Each human being has animal qualities such as anger, pride, ego, infatuation, and many more. These animal qualities make one extremely disturbed, restless, and extroverted. The Lord says that of all these animal qualities, He is the lion. The lion is the king of animals who controls, regulates, and can even kill animals. With determination and detachment, one can get thorough control over all his animal qualities, thoughts, emotions, and extroversion. To meditate, one needs determination.

Vainateyash cha pakshinam: "Of all the birds, I am the son of Vinita (Garuda, a fabulous bird)." Birds can fly high in the sky and they can also fly down. The human mind is like a bird, roaming in the vast sky, sometimes at a good altitude, sometimes with negative thoughts. *Garuda* means one who can eat and digest even poison. *Vinita* means humility. With humility and freedom from ego, one can be free from the downward movement of poisonous qualities and can fly to reach the state of God consciousness. This is the quality of Garuda.

Verse 31

pavanaḥ pavatām asmi
rāmaḥ śastrabhṛtām aham
jhaṣāṇām makaraś cā 'smi
srotasām asmi jāhnavī

Translation

Of the purifiers, I am the wind. Of the warriors, I am Rama. Among the fishes, I am the alligator. Of the rivers, I am the Ganga.

Metaphorical Interpretation

People want to cleanse their body and life, but they usually give more importance to outward cleanliness and purity. They wash their body and put on freshly cleaned clothes. Very few know that inner purity is more important than outer purity. Inner purity implies purity in thought, propensities, and state of mind. This purity can be achieved through breath control.

Pavanah pavatam asmi: "Out of all the purifiers, I, the Lord, am the wind." Wind implies *pranayama*—breath control through prana regulation. By the easy process of breath control, the practice of Kriya, one can really be free from emotion, worries, anxieties, and restlessness. One can reach the state of perfection, constant inner purity.

Ramah shastabhritam aham: "Of the warriors (holders of weapons), I am Rama." In the Ramayana, Rama is always holding a bow and arrow. The spine is the bow and the breath is the arrow. One who can hold the bow of the spine in the hand, who has thorough control of all five inner spinal centers, and who has regulated his breath, the arrow, is *atmarama,* merged in soul consciousness. Rama is the son of Dasharatha.

Each human body is *dasha* (ten doors) and *ratha* (chariot), the chariot of the ten doors of the sense organs, out of which nine doors are open and the tenth door, the fontanel, is closed.

Jhashanam makarash cha 'smi: "Of the fishes, I am the alligator *(makara).*" Fish live in water. In the body, the flow of blood is equal to the flow of rivers; the restlessness of the blood circulation is symbolically represented by fish *(matsya).* In Tantra, there is the spiritual practice of the five *M*'s *(panchamakara sadhana)*; one of these *M*'s stands for *matsya* (fish). The inner meaning of this is to perceive everything as coming from God and to avoid bad things through breath control. *Makara* means *ma* (time) and *kara* (action)—action in proper time. To do right action at the right time is *makara.*

Srotasam asmi jahnavi: "Of the rivers, I am the Ganga." *Srota* means the flow of the river. The Ganga is the holy river, which also symbolizes the river of knowledge, *jñana ganga,* flowing from the Himalayas down to the earth. Divine knowledge flows from the top of the head, which is the mountain peak, and purifies the entire body land.

Verse 32

sargāṇām ādir antaś ca
madhyam cai vā 'ham arjuna
adhyātmavidyā vidyānām
vādaḥ pravadatām aham

Translation

Of creation, I am the beginning, the end, and the middle. O Arjuna! Of all knowledge, I am the knowledge of the Supreme Self. I am the right type of reasoning in debaters.

Metaphorical Interpretation

In this verse, the Lord is describing the process of creation *(shrusti tattva)*, "In the beginning I am. From Me, creation started. I am also in creation and creation abides in Me. At the end, creation dissolves in Me." Creation in the mother's womb starts with the breath of the parents, but if the soul does not breathe, then the parents cannot be instruments of creation. This is what I am in the beginning. When the child is born; I remain in the body and the breath; this is the middle. Finally, the soul leaves the body through exhalation; this is the end. This is the breath (soul) in the beginning, in the middle, and at the end." Similarly, the Taittariya Upanishad (3:6:1) says, *ānandādd hy eva khalv imāni bhūtāni jāyante, ānandena jātāni jīvanti, ānandam prayanty abhisamviśanti:* "Beings are born from bliss, survive and live by bliss, and return back to bliss again." Bliss or divine joy is the beginning, the middle, and the end of creation.

Adhyatma vidya vidyanam: "I am *adhyatmya vidya,* knowledge of the Supreme Self among all knowledge *(vidhyas)*." In the Mundaka Upanishad (1:1:4), there is a description of two types of *vidya*: *para*, the supreme absolute, and *apara*, which is relative, material science. *Vidya* comes from the root *vid,* to know. People want to know and study many things, but real knowledge is the knowledge of the self. By knowing gold, all ornaments are known. By knowing earth, all earthen pots are known. By knowing the self, one knows the entire divine manifestation. This is self-knowledge. Through the practice of Kriya, when the mind becomes pure, one perceives the presence of the soul in everything and everywhere.

People argue, discuss, and dispute about many things, thereby wasting their precious time. The Lord says, *vadaḥ pravadatam aham*: "I am the right type of reasoning in those who debate." For this, one requires meditation, developing the intellectual faculty, and attaining right vision and understanding. The Lord is also saying, "I am the right type of understanding." This means using one's own intellect and discriminative faculty to see the difference between the real and the unreal. Only the self is real. Everything else is unreal and temporary.

Verse 33

akṣarāṇām akāro 'smi
dvandvaḥ sāmāsikasya ca
aham evā 'kṣayaḥ kālo
dhātā 'ham viśvatomukhaḥ

Translation

Of the letters, I am A. Of the compound words, I am the dual. I alone am infinite time. I am the sustainer of everything, having My face on all sides.

Metaphorical Interpretation

Alphabets and letters are useful for speaking, writing, and understanding. In English, there are twenty-sixletters, starting with A. In Sanskrit, there are fifty letters, also starting with A. In Sanskrit these fifty letters are associated with fifty types of air or breaths *(panchasa vayu)*. Real knowledge of the *akshara* (the imperishable one) as well as knowledge of the letters and alphabets are possible only through the realized master. "A" means *avyakta brahma,* the unmanifest Brahman.

A compound word is two or more words joined together. In Sanskrit grammar, there are six ways of forming compound words; one way is *dvandva,* which means dual. This duality is the union of two aspects of one thing. This is also the basic principle of yoga. *Dvandva* is the two, which leads from duality to unity—body and soul, individual self and supreme Self uniting to become one. That is why the Lord says, *dvandvah samasikasya*—"I am *dvandva*," the dual of the compound forms. This is to achieve the state of unity from all duality.

People divide time into past, present, and future. The future is coming to be present. The present is becoming transformed into the past. This division of time is relative only to man's use. Time, in reality, is beyond all division. It is the spontaneity of the one time. It is endless. That is why God is called Mahakala, absolute time.

Dhata aham: "I am the sustainer." In the Yogic scriptures, it says, *ayur vāyuḥ, balam vāyuḥ, vāyu dhātā śarīrinaḥ*: "Breath is life, breath is strength, breath maintains this body." Vayu means the breath of life—one's lifespan. Breath is also the strength of the person, sustaining life in the body. Without breath, man cannot live. The air drawn into the body is the breath; the air remaining outside is formless, remaining all around.

Vishvato mukham: "God's face is everywhere." God is omnipresent. No one can hide anything from God. God is inside and outside. To perceive this constantly and continuously is real meditation. This is the perception of the omnipresent consciousness.

Verse 34

mṛtyuḥ sarvaharaś cā 'ham
udbhavaś ca bhaviṣyatām

kīrtiḥ śrīr vāk ca nārīṇām
smṛtir medhā dhṛtiḥ kṣamā

Translation

I am the all-destroying death and the origin of everything that shall yet be born. Among the feminine qualities, I am fame, prosperity, speech, memory, intelligence, firmness, and forgiveness.

Metaphorical Interpretation

Mrityuh sarva harash cha'ham: "I am the all-destroying death." Everything is created from God, everything lives in God, and at the end merges in God. This is death. Death is the end. The Lord says, "I am death." Ordinary people are afraid of death. They think death is terrible. But one who loves God will also love death. With the death of a seed, a new tree germinates; with the death of exhalation, inhalation is born. With the death of the wave, it becomes formless like the ocean.

Sarva means the sense organs; *hara* means to destroy. The state in which all the sense organs are thoroughly controlled by breath control is *mrityu*, that is, *samadhi*. In the state of *nirvikalpa samadhi* all the senses are withdrawn and there is no breath, no pulse, a state similar to death. This state is Godhood.

When one comes back from the state of *samadhi*, one leads a divine life with love and God consciousness. God is the origin of everything, therefore without God, there is nothing. In this verse, the Lord is speaking of seven divine qualities. These are manifested through divine love. The seven divine qualities are also called feminine qualities. With the help of these seven divine qualities, one will progress in meditation and spiritual life, crossing the seven centers and becoming established in truth. The seven following spiritual qualities are also the manifestation of God's power:

1. *Kirti:* fame. This is the fame arising out of a noble and spiritual life, not from material passions in the *muladhara* (coccygeal) center.
2. *Shri:* beauty or prosperity. By leading a spiritual, self-disciplined, yogic life, one is able to reflect inner beauty, not the physical beauty of the male and female.
3. *Vak:* speech. Speech is the fire. Through sweet and divine speech one can achieve higher levels of spiritual awareness.
4. *Smriti:* memory. People try to remember many things, but they forget the reality of life which is God, their indwelling Self. To remember God in every breath, in every step of life, is true or perfect memory.
5. *Medha:* intelligence. People think of themselves as intelligent or cunning in the material life, but real intelligence means discrimination and the ability to distinguish between the real and the unreal, truth and falsehood.
6. *Dhriti:* firmness. Determination, devotion, and dedication are highly essential for soul culture and spiritual evolution. Firmness in one's own divine life and being well established in truth in the fontanel is *dhriti.*
7. *Kshama:* forgiveness. Forgiveness comes from tolerance. To forgive is divine.

Verse 35

bṛhatsāma tathā sāmnām
gāyatrī chandasām aham
māsānām mārgaśīrṣo 'ham
ṛtūnām kusumākaraḥ

Translation

Likewise, of the hymns, I am Brihatsaman. Of the meter *(chhanda)* I am *gayatri;* of the months, the *margashirsha;* of the seasons, the flowering spring.

Metaphorical Interpretation

Brihatsama tatha samnam: The Vedas, the ancient scriptures of spiritual life and God-realization are divided into four parts: Rik, Yajur, Sama, and Atharva. The Sama Veda is the poetic description of spiritual life. The highest spiritual truth contained in the Sama Veda is in the Brihat Sama which is helpful for meditation and God-realization. Sama means tranquility, harmony, and balance. The highest state of tranquility is also called *brihatsama.*

Gayatri chhandasam aham gayatri: The ordinary meaning of *gayatri* is to reach liberation through singing. The real meaning is to hear the song of the divine. When one meditates, one can perceive the inner voice in extreme silence.

Gayatri is a mantra that is considered very sacred. But the real aspect of this mantra is to perceive the divine power in the seven centers:

om bhuh (*muladhara chakra,* the money center)
om bhuvah (*svadhisthana chakra,* the sex center)
om svah (*manipura chakra,* the food center)
om mahah (*anahata chakra,* the emotion center)
om janah (*vishuddha chakra,* the religion center)
om tapah (*ajña chakra,* the soul center)
om satyam (*sahasrara chakra,* the God center)
tat savitur vareṇyam (on that Ishwara fit to be worshiped)

bhargo devasya dhīmahi (resplendent sun we meditate)
dhiyo yo naḥ pracodayat (may He illuminate our mind.)

In the *Gayatri sadhana,* one must try to perceive the triple divine qualities in the seven chakras. This is the essence of Kriya Yoga practice, which must be learned from the master.

Masanam margashirsho 'ham: "Of the months, I am

margashirsha." A month represents the motion of time and is associated with the position of the sun in different zodiacs. *Margashirsha* is a month in the Indian calendar which corresponds to November–December in the Western system. *Margashirsha* is a beautiful word. *Marga* means path or passage' *Shirsha* means the top or climax of spiritual evolution. *Sahasrara* is the top of the passage of this path. This is *margashirsha*. Everyone must try to fix his attention on the top, in God awareness.

Ritunam kusumakarah: Of all the seasons, spring is considered the best because it is colorful, and the trees are full of leaves, flowers, and fruit. The birds sing. It is the season of moderation, neither extreme cold nor extreme heat. *Ida* is cold and *pingala* is hot. The harmony of the two is *sushumna*. When the breath is going in the *sushumna*, it is the state of extreme serenity. The mind is free and pure. This is spring. Spring is the best season for meditation and spiritual life.

Verse 36

dyūtam chalayatām asmi
tejas tejasvinām aham
jayo 'smi vyavasāyo 'smi
sattvam sattvavatām aham

Translation

Of all deceitful practice, I am gambling. I am the glory of the glories. I am victory. I am effort. I am the goodness of the good.

Metaphorical Interpretation

Dyutam chhalayatam asmi: "Of all deceitful practice, I am

gambling." The mind and senses, through temptation, pull man downward in deceitful ways. One should be extremely careful to be free from temptation and pretense. Temptation is the greatest enemy. *Dyuta* is a dice game, but its real meaning is *dyotana*—illumination. To be in the vacuum center through meditation and divine illumination is the real meaning of *dyuta.*

Tejas tejasvinam aham: "I am the glory of the glories." When one comes up to the *sahasrara* and meditates, he comes across the light of the stars, planets, sun, and man. One will even perceive extremely brilliant light. This is the glory.

Jayo 'smi: "I am victory." Life is a battle: the battle between good and evil, purity and impurity, truth and falsehood. But truth always triumphs. Light is victorious over darkness, because where there is light, there can be no darkness. Victory implies freedom from the mind, senses, temptation, thought, ego, and evils. This is possible only through meditation and sincere effort. The Lord also says, *vyavasayo 'smi*—"I am effort." The goal of life—self-realization and eternal peace—can only be achieved through constant effort and endeavor.

Sattvam sattva vatam aham: "I am the goodness of the good." *Ida* is *tamas*: idleness. *Pingala* is *rajas*: restlessness. *Sushumna* is *sattva*: calmness, goodness, and serenity. When one practices the scientific technique of Kriya Yoga, he or she slowly becomes free from restlessness and idleness. The breath flows through the *sushumna;* there is equal pressure of breath in both the nostrils. At that time, the mind is pure. The devotee comes up to the *ajña chakra* through the *sushumna,* then reaches the *sahasrara,* the state of extreme goodness or realization. In this state, the breath is extremely tranquil. All these states are experienced by Kriya Yoga, when it is practiced regularly and with love for God and the masters.

Verse 37

vṛṣṇīnām vāsudevo 'smi
pāṇḍavānām dhanamjayaḥ
munīnām apy aham vyāsaḥ
kavīnām uśanā kaviḥ

Translation

Of the Vrishnis, I am Vasudeva. Among all the Pandavas, I am Dhanamjaya (Arjuna). Among all the sages, I am Vyasa. Among all the poets, I am Ushana (Sukracharya).

Metaphorical Interpretation

Vrishninam vasudevo 'smi: The clan of the Vrishnis was a dynasty into which Shri Krishna was born as the son of Vasudeva; that is why Shri Krishna is also called Vasudeva. The metaphorical meaning of this is more beautiful and spiritual. *Vrishni* means one who has control. It also means to radiate illumination. *Vrishni* is from the root *vrish* (desire). *Vasudeva* means all-pervading consciousness. To remain in the state of soul awareness in the pituitary and the fontanel is the best of all desire. In this state, there is more divine light and love. This is the state of Krishna consciousness or Vasudeva.

Pandavanam dhanamjayah: "Among the Pandavas, I am Dhanamjaya." In this verse, the Lord is speaking about the unity of the soul and God. The Pandavas are five in number, each corresponding to a chakra in ascending order from bottom to top: Sahadeva *(muladhara),* Nakula *(svadhisthana),* Arjuna *(manipura),* Bhima *(anahata),* and Yudhishthira *(vishuddha).* The Pandavas are the children of Pandu. Pandu means divine knowledge. Arjuna has many names, one of which one is Dhanamjaya. Therefore, *Dhanam* means wealth. Wealth is the cause of delusion, negative dispositions, distraction and ego. *Jaya* means victory. Therefore Dhanamjaya is one who tries to achieve victory over delusion and dejection. Arjuna is Dhanamjaya; he is following his guru and guide Shri Krishna, trying to sit near him and follow his instruction. He is the best of all the Pandavas, trying sincerely to come up to the pituitary and fontanel.

Muninam apy aham vyasah: "I am Vyasa among all the sages (*muni,* man of meditation)." By the power of meditation, the *muni* achieves thorough control over mind, thought, intellect, and ego. He is pure, divine, and God-realized. Among all the *munis,* Vyasa is the lord. Vyasa is the sage who edited and divided the Vedas, who authored the eighteen Puranas, the Mahabharata, the Bhagavatam, the Brahma Sutras, and many other texts. The metaphorical meaning of Vyasa is divine wisdom or divine illumination.

Kavinam ushana kavih: "I am Ushana (Sukracharya) among all the poets." Sukracharya is a mythological master with tremendous spiritual power and the capacity to bring life back to a dead body. He was a poet *(kavi),* a man of vision. One can reach this state through meditation and God's grace. *Sukra* means semen, vitality, and strength. God is the strength and vitality in every person. Without Him, man is dead.

Verse 38

daṇḍo damayatām asmi
nītir asmi jigīṣatām
maunam cai 'vā 'smi guhyānām
jñānam jñānavatām aham

Translation

I am the power in the rulers. I am the wise policy for those who want victory. Of all the secrets, I am silence. I am the wisdom of all knowers of wisdom.

Metaphorical Interpretation

Danda (the restraint or power) *damayatam* (the rulers) *asmi:* "I am the restraint or power in the rulers." *Danda* and *damayatam* both come from the word *dama,* which means to control, regulate, and restrain. The senses, mind, and thoughts are extremely restless and should be controlled. The easiest way to regulate or control is by means of *pranayama*—Kriya. In the practice of Kriya Yoga, the disciple is taught the easiest way of breath control. Through breath control, he achieves self-control, self-mastery, and becomes the ruler of his mind, thoughts, and senses. This is the state of God awareness.

Nitir asmi jigishatam: "I am the wise policy for those who want victory." *Niti* means morality and a self-regulated life. Remaining in truth and righteousness is the wisest policy. Those who lead a moral life with truth and righteousness reach victory over restlessness and all the lower propensities. They achieve freedom from all the negative qualities and complete victory over temptation. The person who practices Kriya Yoga regularly gets victory in life. Victory means success.

Maunam chaiva 'smi guhyanam: "Of all the secrets, I am silence." Ordinary silence means not talking, but real silence is to be free from all thoughts—the state of inner tranquility. This state is perceived in *paravastha* during meditation. *Mouna* means gaining control over the tongue. The tongue always wants to speak. The more one talks, the more there is trouble. In Psalm 39:1, it says, "I will watch my ways and keep my tongue from sin, I will put a muzzle on my mouth, as long as the wicked are in my presence." To maintain inner silence is the secret of all spiritual practice.

Jñanam jñanavatam aham: "I am the wisdom of all knowers of wisdom." *Jñanam* means self knowledge, divine wisdom. Wisdom cannot be perceived by reading books, listening to discourses, or through the five sense organs. Wisdom can only be perceived by going to the atom point. One achieves wisdom by closing the doors to extrovert life and going up to the fontanel to His presence. Wisdom is the hidden knowledge in everything, yet to be discovered.

Verse 39

yac cā 'pi sarvabhūtānām
bījam tad aham arjuna
na tad asti vinā yat syān
mayā bhūtam carācaram

Translation

And further, O Arjuna, I am the seed of all creatures. There is nothing that could exist without Me, whether moving or not moving.

Metaphorical Interpretation

One meaning of the name Arjuna is *shubhra,* the color white. White is the combination of all colors and the symbol of inner cleanliness and purity. Cleanliness and purity are next to godliness. Every seeker must try to be clean and pure inside and out. With a self-disciplined life and regular meditation, one can achieve this state. To maintain whiteness in clothes is very difficult. Similarly, to maintain a clean life, one must be extremely careful and cautious.

Here, the Lord addresses Arjuna as pure, clean, and divine.

The Lord says, *sarvabhutanam bijam tad aham*: "I am the seed of all creatures." A seed is hidden under the soil, but a big tree eventually appears above the ground. It comes out of the seed, which is out of sight, down below. Likewise, God is the seed of all creation. *Aham bija pradah pita*: "I am the giver of the seed (See the Bhagavad Gita 14: 4)." He has created everything from Himself. As ornaments and gold are one, God and creation are one and the same, which is why everyone is beautiful. He is air, He is breath, and He is breathing. He is not only in all living beings, He is all-pervading and everywhere. He is in the movable and the immovable. He is in the five gross elements, in the stars, the planets, the earth, the trees, the plants, the insects, the animals, and humans. Everything is in Him. He is the inseparable presence. Through deep meditation, one really can perceive this unity in the almighty.

Verse 40

nā 'nto 'sti mama divyānām
vibhūtīnām paramtapa
eṣa tū 'ddeśataḥ prokto
vibhūter vistaro mayā

Translation

There is no end to My divine manifestation. What has been declared by Me is only an example of the extent of My manifestation and glory.

Metaphorical Interpretation

Now the Lord addresses Arjuna as Paramtapa, *paran tapayati iti paramtapah*—one who destroys all enemies. The enemies are not outside, but rather inside. Every sincere seeker is aware of inner enemies such as anger, pride, ego, vanity, jealousy, and others. These enemies should be ruthlessly destroyed. These enemies are born of ignorance (See the Bhagavad Gita 4:42). But Arjuna is Paramtapa. He is not only aware of the enemies, he destroys them. Arjuna is the real *sadhaka* who is trying his utmost to follow the directions of his master and guide Shri Krishna in the battle of life.

The Lord is saying, "O Paramtapa! O Arjuna! I have explained to you in a nutshell the divine manifestation and My glory. The one thing you must always keep in mind is that the entire universe is My presence. I am infinite, omnipotent, and without a second. Being infinite, My glory is endless. Limited words cannot express or explain the unlimited and infinite glory. You are dear to Me. I love you. So I explained in brief some of My principal manifestations. Arjuna! Please remember that whatever you see or perceive is nothing but My presence, My divine extension. In every thought, word, and deed try to perceive God's play. Looking at the waves, people get some idea of the vastness of the ocean. Listening to this talk of Mine, you must comprehend divine manifestation with inner awareness."

Every *sadhaka,* every meditator, who treads the paths of spirituality has visions, experiences, and perceptions in their daily spiritual life. These experiences are endless. As the picture of a mountain peak is reminiscent of the vast mountain range, similarly, daily spiritual life enables us to recall the infinite divine manifestation of the Lord our God.

Verse 41

yad-yad vibhūtimat sattvam
śrīmad ūrjitam eva vā
tat-tad evā 'vagaccha tvam
mama tejo'mśasambhavam

Translation

Whatever is being manifested with glory, grace, and power, know that in every case it is only a fraction of My glory.

Metaphorical Interpretation

The entire universe is the divine manifestation of the Lord. Each human life is His glory. The Lord in His brief explanation of *vibhuti* (divine manifestation) spoke of the movable, the immovable, hills, mountains, rivers, animals, human beings, and everything. In the Shiva Samhita 2:1–2, an ancient treatise on yoga, the master says:

dehe 'smin vartate meruḥ sapta dvipa samanvitaḥ
saritaḥ sāgarāḥ caivāḥ kṣetrāṇi kṣetra-pālakāḥ
ṛṣayo munayaḥ sarve nakṣatrāṇi grahāstathā...

which means that existing in this body are the poles, the seven islands, rivers, oceans, mountains, holy places, presiding deities, *rishis, munis,* stars, planets, and so on. Through the practice of Kriya Yoga, one is able to understand the mysterious human body and God's play in each human body. Each human being is potentially divine and able to perceive divine manifestation. By God's grace, a person can achieve some excellence in life. Everyone must meditate and perceive the power of God playing and manifesting in his life. This is essential. Instead of having ego, vanity, or pride, he or she must be thankful and grateful to Him. Anyone's physical beauty is God's glory. Anyone's intelligence or success in any field of life is by His grace. When a person meditates and goes inside, he attains some spiritual experience and power. That is also God's divine play.

In this verse, the Lord says, *mama tejo'mshasambhavam*: "Whatever one sees, perceives, or experiences, whatever one has or possesses, (including the body and life) is a ray of light from the infinite Lord sun." In this changing world, the body and life are but a fraction of God's glory. God is infinite and beyond human comprehension, but through meditation when one becomes absorbed in God consciousness, one perceives the vastness and the infinite state.

Verse 42

athavā bahunai 'tena
kim jñātena tavā 'rjuna

viṣṭabhyā 'ham idam kṛtsnam
ekāmśena sthito jagat

Translation

But by knowing all this in detail, O Arjuna, what will you gain? I support this entire universe with a single fraction of Myself.

Metaphorical Interpretation

The Lord is saying, "O Arjuna! I have explained the divine manifestation with an external example. It is really difficult to comprehend the infinite with limited and finite words or examples. Take it for granted that this little world, this little universe, and everything in it, is created and born of Myself, the supreme Lord." Looking into the sky, one cannot really imagine what it is—one cannot comprehend its size. But when the vast sky is reflected in a little lake, and shadows are created by immense clouds, one gets an impression or idea of the vastness of the sky. In a similar way, one can start to grasp the incomprehensibility of the Lord, God.

"O Arjuna, hearing, reading, or looking outside or understanding in detail is of no gain. All these experiences are external, temporary, and limited. To have divine experience, one must go to the inner world, the inner sky. Then slowly through deep meditation, one will be able to come to the state of realization.

"O Arjuna! I hold and sustain this entire universe. Similarly, I also hold this human body, the micro-universe. Breath supports life. No one can live without breath. O Arjuna! There is no need to tell you all these things. Meditate, have your own experience, and be realized.

"Arjuna! The entire manifested universe is but a fraction of Myself. Knowing this, you will be able to realize My great, divine manifestation. By listening to Me talking, you may have some distinctive thoughts that God is here or there, but to remove this state of mind, please meditate and be realized."

Summary

In this chapter, God reveals His divine glory to the worthy seeker and sincere disciple; this revelation ends at the door of realization. People search for God, but seek Him with their senses, mind, and intellect. But the soul, God, is beyond the reach of all the senses. The limited capacity of the internal instruments—the senses, mind, and intellect—is not able to comprehend and recognize the supreme Self.

Through leading a God conscious life, one gets the divine ability to see God in everything. In the Taittiriya Upanishad (2:6:1), this is described as *yad idam kim ca tat sṛṣṭvā tad eva anuprāviśat*: "Having created everything, God permeates every aspect of creation." People are living in the play of names and form, but they do not go beyond that to see the glorious presence of God. However insignificant a thing may be, the living presence of God is contained in it.

In the *Purusha Sukta*, (a Vedic hymn dedicated to the indwelling supreme Self) it says, *pādo'sya viśva bhutāni tripādasyāmṛtam divi:* "One small part of Him is the created, manifest universe, but the major part remains unmanifest and formless." This is the unmanifested presence of the Lord in the manifested world.

Among the forty-two verses of this chapter called *vibhuti yoga,* "The Yoga of Divine Glories," seven verses are attributed to Arjuna, and the remaining thirty-five verses are attributed to the Lord. The entire chapter can be divided as follows:

Verses 1 to 3 explain that liberation comes through the knowledge of the infinite glory of the Lord.

Verses 4 to 7 discuss yoga with the Lord and the manifestation of the divine glories.

Verses 8 to 11 explain that to get the supreme love of God, one must love God in consciousness, super consciousness, and cosmic consciousness.

Verses 12 to 18 contain Arjuna's request to be blessed with the knowledge of the divine glories of the Lord through listening.

Verses 19 to 40 are a brief description of the divine glories of the Lord.

Verses 41 to 42 explain that the entire universe is a small aspect of the unmanifested divine. The Lord is the entire universe and is beyond that.

In sum, the entire creation is the temple of the divine glories. But ordinary people lack the vision to realize this in their daily life. God's grace is always like the rains from the sky, constantly showering, but it is only retained and realized by those who make themselves worthy through self-discipline and by leading a divine life.

People practice spiritual discipline, but after getting some divine power *(vibhuti),* they show slackness in their spiritual life. Little *siddhas* and magical powers are obstacles in spirituality. One must overcome the temptation of such trivial attainments. In this chapter, the Lord has described the greatness of different beings, humans, animals, plants, and elements, where divine glories are manifested to a great extent.

In this chapter, Arjuna listens to all the glories of God. In a state of deep awe, his desire to realize Him grows stronger. He is the true seeker who abandons the glamour of spiritual attachments; he strives to enter the arena of realization.

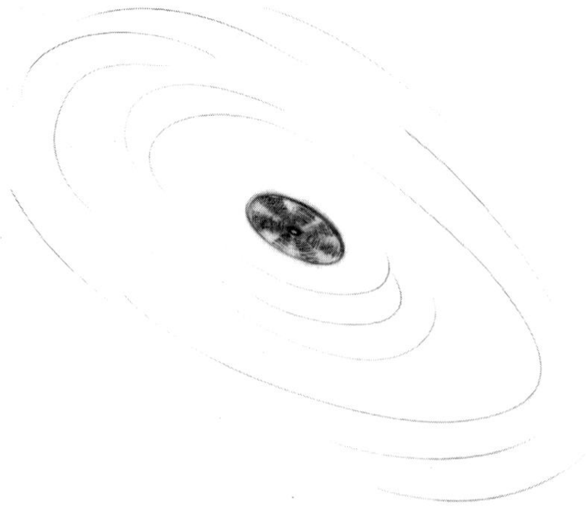

Chapter 11

Vishvarupa darshana yoga

The Yoga of the Cosmic Form Revealed

Introduction

God-realization is everyone's birthright. Every seeker tries to realize God. Whether they perceive Him within themselves or without, the perception of God in all, and the perception of all in God seem to be the same, but there is a very subtle difference. The key is to introvert the senses, control the restless mind, and go within. Perceive the presence of God in yourself, in your body house. Open your eyes, look everywhere, and do not become absorbed in the names and forms of this world; rather, strive to see the divine presence, the glory of the Lord everywhere—beginningless and endless.

It is easy to see the presence of God in good things, but in the beginning, it is difficult to see God in all things. However, as a person develops inner awareness and transformation, his inner perception and outlook gradually change until he grows and glows with super consciousness and cosmic consciousness. There is no end to the glory of God and His divine manifestation.

In the previous chapter, it was as though we looked at the universe through a microscope—the Lord discussed how to feel His presence in the microcosm. This chapter offers a broader vision, an unfocused look rather than a focused one, searching the infinite inner and outer sky to perceive the vastness of God. This is the macrocosmic vision of God.

As a sweet and its sweetness are inseparable, similarly God and His creation are one. In order to have a universal vision of God, to be free from all narrowness of mind and thought, one should seek the grace of God.

Those who have read the Isha Upanishad and have understood its inner meaning will find the beauty of this chapter easier to understand. The first mantra of this Upanishad, *"Isha vasyam idam sarvam,"* or "the entire universe is pervaded by God," is the seed concept of this eleventh chapter.

From the stage of perceiving God in all creation, the seeker must now proceed to the divine experience of perceiving that all of creation is in God.

God is everywhere—inside and outside of everything. Therefore, one cannot separate God from the world. This perception of unity in diversity is the cornerstone of this chapter. Arjuna is questing deeper and deeper into spiritual awareness, in search of the vision of the cosmic form of the formless. The divine guidance of *prana krishna*, the soul, Krishna, is beautifully explained and elaborated upon in this chapter.

O seeker! Open your eyes! Look at the beauty of God everywhere, the love of God everywhere. With this loving outlook, transform your life. Like Arjuna, be a sincere seeker and get the taste of truth.

God is kind and compassionate. Expand yourself. Expansion is life, and contraction is death. People with cataracts in their eyes cannot see clearly, but when the cataracts are removed, their vision is clear. They can have a divine vision in every moment of their lives.

In this chapter the Lord manifests His cosmic form for Arjuna to see.

Verse 1

arjuna uvāca
madanugrahāya paramam
guhyam adhyātmasamjñitam
yat tvayo ktam vacas tena
moho yam vigato mama

Translation

Arjuna said:
As a grace to me, You have spoken about the highest secret, known as the supreme Self; with this, my delusion has entirely disappeared.

Metaphorical Interpretation

Arjuna was deluded. He had so many doubts and questions that he was willing to run away from the battle of spiritual life. But Arjuna is the sincere disciple and the Lord Himself is the divine master. In the beginning of this divine gospel of the holy Bhagavad Gita, Arjuna acknowledges the divine grace of his master, wanting to perceive the hidden spiritual truth. So the master, with boundless grace, tries to remove the clouds of doubt and delusion from the life of the disciple. The master removes this darkness of ignorance with a flash of knowledge.

The able master, through His incomparable compassion and tireless patience, imparts the secret of spiritual life. Man seeks God, but he thinks that God is in high heaven. Man loves himself, but does so thinking that he is his body. Because of these two mistakes, his life becomes troubled. He is not able to perceive either the omnipresent God, or the nature of his soul.

In the previous chapter, the Lord concluded with His statement, *ekamshena sthito jagat*: "The entire universe is a small fraction of My presence." In spiritual life, each seeker must try to seek, to see, and to perceive the presence of the almighty

Lord in everything: flowers, fruit, sky, stars, trees, plants, rivers, hills, birds, animals, and man. This universe is *jagat*: it is constantly changing, modifying, and transforming. However, beyond these changes, there is the changeless soul, the unchanging, eternal Lord. This is the divine vision. This is the secret or hidden spiritual knowledge.

Arjuna is expressing his gratitude: "O Lord! My words cannot express my indebtedness to You. Your divine instructions removed the cloud of confusion from my life. I am able to perceive the spiritual truth, knowledge of the divine Self. I am really grateful to You. You are so kind to help me and to guide me. Now I feel that I am becoming free from the tentacles of doubt and delusion."

Slowly, Arjuna's mind has become clean and clear; in this state of mind, he slowly proceeds toward realization of the highest spiritual truth. Endless is the spiritual journey. A seeker proceeds slowly on the slippery path of spirituality with love, faith, and dedication. The guru guides constantly.

Verse 2

bhavāpyayau hi bhūtānām
śrutau vistaraśo mayā
tvattaḥ kamalapattrākṣa
māhātmyam api cā vyayam

Translation

The creation and dissolution of beings have been heard by me in detail from You and Your imperishable glory, O Lotus-Petal Eyed Krishna!

Metaphorical Interpretation

Arjuna's sincerity has made his inner vision clear. He has

perceived the spiritual potency of his master. The master, the guru preceptor, is not outside, he is inside. *Atmaiva gurur ekam* —the soul alone is the guru. One who takes refuge in the master is able to experience his compassion and grace.

In this verse, Arjuna addresses his divine master, the Lord, as Kamalapattraksha, which means lotus-petal eyed and describes the beauty of the Lord. The name of the Lord has many deep spiritual connotations. The lotus is a beautiful flower. Lotus-petal eyed signifies the beauty of the Lord. True beauty is perceived with inner vision. When Arjuna, following his master, came up from the navel center, the *manipura* chakra (Arjuna's abode), he had the colorful and beautiful vision of the third eye. (See the *Bhagavad Gita in the Light of Kriya Yoga*, Book One.)

Kamala means *kam,* desires and *ala* to decorate. People have endless desires. Instead of endless desires, their desire should be for the endless, the infinite, which is God. This desire for self-realization will give divine vision. Only by loving God and sincerely meditating upon Him are all desires fulfilled. (Please refer to the Bhagavad Gita, 6:22.) So, the Lord is addressed as Kamalapattraksha, the desire-fulfilling eyed.

Arjuna is saying, "O Lord! Your beauty is inexpressible. Your eye is like the lotus petal. When I perceive Your presence in me during meditation (especially while practicing *jyoti mudra*), I see the beauty of the third eye—Your eye. You have explained the creation of the entire cosmos in detail. You have also explained its dissolution in You. Your glory is endless, imperishable, and incomprehensible. I am overjoyed with such knowledge."

Here Arjuna says *shrutau*, which means he has heard. A disciple listens to his master, practices accordingly, advances slowly but steadily, and gains experience. Listening to the master with love is highly essential in spiritual life. The divine master helps the seeker to get the divine vision. God is the cause of creation as well as its dissolution. He is in the beginning, the middle, and the end. Therefore every spiritual seeker must try to perceive His presence in everything.

Verse 3

evam etad yathā ttha tvam
ātmānam parameśvara
draṣṭum icchāmi te rūpam
aiśvaram puruṣottama

Translation

As You have precisely declared Yourself to be, O supreme Lord (Parameshwara)! I desire to see Your divine form, O Supreme Spirit (Purushottama).

Metaphorical Interpretation

In this verse, Arjuna addresses the Lord with two beautiful names: Parameshwara and Purushottama. *Param Ishwara* (Parameshwara) is the supreme Lord. The Lord controls some things, the supreme Lord controls everything. Arjuna is saying: "O my Guru! I am at Your feet. You are not the Lord, You are the supreme Lord. You control the entire universe. You regulate my life as well. The guru tries to make the life of the disciple well disciplined and regulated. O Guru! O Lord! You are Purushottama." *Purusha,* the indwelling self or spirit and *uttama*, the supreme, the best, together become Purushottama, which means the supreme spirit. In each human body, the soul and the spirit are hiding. The Lord pervades the entire universe. He is Purushottama, the supreme almighty father, who is everywhere. (See the Bhagavad Gita, Chapter 15).

The more one hears about something, the more one desires to see it. This creates the thirst for something. This is natures law. When Arjuna hears the glory of the Lord and tries to comprehend Him in his inner self, he has the desire to perceive and realize the glory of God and His divine experience. Arjuna prays to the Lord from the core of his heart, expressing his desire for higher spiritual experience. In the yogic scriptures, it explains,

"When someone comes up from the lower centers to the *ajña* and *sahasrara* chakras, he goes from the state of *jiva* to Shiva, (from manhood to Godhood); he perceives inner awareness and lights of many colors; his ten sense organs are well regulated; he hears the beautiful *aum* sound and perceives the atom point. This atom point, *atmavindu,* is the source of creation and dissolution of everything. He enters into extreme calmness. His breath becomes very slow, feeble, and calm." Thus, he is ready for realization and experience of the absolute.

Verse 4

manyase yadi tac chakyam
mayā draṣṭum iti prabho
yogeśvara tato me tvam
darśayā tmānam avyayam

Translation

If You think it is possible for me to see this, O Lord, O master of yoga, then show me Your imperishable soul.

Metaphorical Interpretation

Yoga is the path of meditation and self-realization. Through yoga, all the sense organs are made pure and one can go beyond the domain of mind and intellect. Yoga transforms life and reveals inner beauty. Yoga is the easy and quick method of soul culture. God is the real master of yoga. God revealed the supreme mystery of yoga, which is Kriya Yoga, to Vivashvan and others. (See the Bhagavad Gita 4:1.)

In this verse, the Lord is addressed as the master of yoga and Prabhu, the Lord. This verse is an expression of self-surrender to the guru preceptor by the disciple. Every disciple, in order to have spiritual realization, must approach the guru with humility.

Arjuna is saying that he does not know whether he is really fit, qualified, and eligible for such realization. He approaches the Lord with the desire for self-unfolding. He is saying, *He prabho*—"O Lord! You are the Lord of this life and of the universe. You know everything. You know me, but I do not know You in essence. I want to realize You. I have heard in detail about Your divine manifestation. Please be kind to me. Am I ready to have divine vision? I do not know whether I am a qualified disciple or not. O master of yoga! By Your grace, everything is possible. I am trying to perceive constant unity with You, in every breath. If I am worthy of divine vision, O Lord! Please show me Your imperishable form."

Each human being has a perishable body and an imperishable soul. Arjuna was able to see the perishable body form of the Lord as the divine master, but he eagerly wanted to perceive the imperishable soul. This is the desire for self-realization. It is the foremost quality of a true disciple. Strong yearning for soul culture with devotion and dedication to the master is essential.

Verse 5

śribhagavān uvāca
paśya me pārtha rūpāṇi
śataśo tha sahasraśaḥ
nānāvidhāni divyāni
nānāvarṇākṛtīni ca

Translation

The Lord said:

Behold, O son of Pritha (Arjuna), My divine form, a hundredfold, rather than a thousandfold, varied, divine, and of various colors and shapes.

Metaphorical Interpretation

Spiritual life starts by breaking the boundary of ego, *aham*, and going to the state of *sa*, the all-pervading soul. The combination of the two creates *hamsa* and *so'ham*. Arjuna, in meditation, approaches the divine master asking for the vision of the absolute. Just as the lamp in a room illuminates all objects, similarly, by the regular practice of Kriya with love, the inner instruments of mind, thought, and ego become pure and enlightened.

In this verse, the Lord is saying, "You are the son of Pritha." In the Mahabharata, we find that Pritha is another name for Kunti's brother. But the real meaning of *prith* is to distinguish.

"You have the power of distinction and discrimination. You have implicit faith, love, and loyalty in your master. You are practicing the path of meditation sincerely, as directed and taught by Me. You are able to come up to the pituitary and fontanel, instead of remaining below in the navel center or elsewhere. In the pituitary and fontanel, there is *akasha*, the sky. Just as the sky is full of beauty, with many colors and manifestations, so is My manifestation, as you will see. I am One, but I am many. I am in many, not only hundreds or thousands, but I am manifest in infinite ways."

When one meditates and practices Kriya Yoga, while staying in the fontanel, one sees many colors and has many spiritual experiences.

Verse 6

paśyā dityān vasūn rudrān
aśvinau marutas tathā
bahūny adṛṣṭapūrvāṇi
paśyā ścaryāṇi bhārata

Translation

Behold, the sons of Aditi, the Vasus, the Rudras, the twin Ashvins and the Marutas, many wonderful forms, unseen before. Behold, O Bharata (Arjuna).

Metaphorical Interpretation

When one closes the nine doors of the senses, and introverts the sense organs, and penetrates into the fontanel, many divine visions, illuminations, and perceptions are possible. At this stage, the mind, thoughts, intellect, and ego are dissolved. One can perceive the twelve sons of Aditi, the *dvadasa adityas*. The twelve sons are the different colors of light seen during meditation. *Ditim* means duality. *Aditi* is the state of non-duality. When the sense of duality disappears, the state of spiritual experience begins.

The Vasus, meaning wealth, are eight in number and refer to the eightfold qualities of nature, *ashta prakriti*, which include the five gross elements, the *pancha mahabhutas*: *bhumi* (earth), *apa* (water), *anala* (fire), *vayu* (air), *kham* (ether) and the internal instruments: *manas* (mind), *buddhi* (intellect), and *ahamkara* (ego). (See the Bhagavad Gita 7:4.)

Rudra is associated with Shiva, but according to the yogic scriptures, *ye rudrah te khalu pranah*: "The Rudras are none but the *pranas.*" There are eleven types of vital breath present in the eleven sense organs, which are the five organs of action, the five organs of perception, and the mind. All these vital (*prana*) breaths are activated from the top.

Ashvins, the twins, refer to the qualities in the money and sex centers. In the Mahabharata, Nakula and Sahadeva are considered to be born of the *ashvinikumara dvaya* (the celestial twins considered to be the divine physicians). All the propensities in the centers come from the top.

Marutas means breath or air. There are fifty types of air present in the universe and in the human body. One experiences all this in meditation. The Lord is saying, "O Bharata! You are *bha*, divine illumination, and *rata*, engrossed. Your mind is always engrossed in God consciousness and supernatural power. You are worthy of divine experiences. Please see the divine manifestation in the body as well as in the universe. It has not been seen before. You are fortunate to have such a vision."

Verse 7

ihai kastham jagat kṛtsnam
paśyā dya sacarācaram
mama dehe guḍākeśa
yac cā nyad draṣṭum icchasi

Translation

Behold now here, the entire universe, standing together, movable and immovable, in Me within the body, O conqueror of sleep (Arjuna)! And whatever else you want to see.

Metaphorical Interpretation

The Lord continues, "O Arjuna, You are Gudakesha", which comes from *gudaka*, sleep, and *isha*, the Lord. "You are the conqueror of sleep. You are free from all slothfulness, drowsiness, and sleep. You are always after the truth. Your love is unique. You do not rest until you reach the divine goal. You have made no compromise with your own divine nature." Sleep means to forget. The real meaning of sleep is to forget the indwelling self. *Gudakesha* is a state in spiritual life where the time of sleep is extremely reduced. It is also the state of constant God awareness, in every breath.

The Lord is saying, "Arjuna! Because of your sincere self-effort for soul culture and self-realization, you are now really ready to have the vision of the entire universe." The universe is called *jagat*, that which changes continuously. The external universe is *jagat*. Each human body is also *jagat*. The difference can be explained by the theory of microcosm and macrocosm. Each human body is also undergoing constant change. Behind this change, there is the changeless presence of the soul. "O Arjuna! Please see everything, movable and immovable. Please see the past as well as the present. You will even be able to see the future too. Past, present, and future are but one. You can perceive all of these in My body. This body is not small, it is all-pervading."

Through meditation, one reaches the state of perceiving the entire universe as the form of God. In every object and living being, one can feel the presence of the almighty Lord. To progress in meditation, one must cast aside all idleness, lethargy, procrastination, and even restrict sleep to a minimum. *Drashtum icchasi* means all the desires of the seeker are truly fulfilled in this state.

Verse 8

na tu mām śakyase draṣṭum
anenai va svacakṣuṣā
divyam dadāmi te cakṣuḥ
paśya me yogam aiśvaram

Translation

Surely, you cannot behold Me, with these, your own eyes. I give you divine vision. Behold My majestic power.

Metaphorical Interpretation

With the two external eyes one is able to see the outer world, the world of duality—good and bad, beautiful and ugly, friend and foe, hot and cold, creation and destruction. In terms of spiritual objectives, these two eyes are blind. These two eyes are the doors of delusion. The temptations of the world enter through these eyes and make people restless. In spiritual life, one must control and regulate the doors of life and the doors of the body. (See the Bhagavad Gita 8:12 and the Bible, Matthew 6:5–6). One must live an introverted life. In meditation, one is to close these doors of restlessness. When the gross eyes are controlled, the real eye, the third eye, is opened. The third eye is the spiritual eye. It is the eye of divine illumination and intuition. At the end of Kriya practice, everyone perceives this third eye of spiritual wisdom.

In this verse, the Lord is saying, "Arjuna! You have heard in detail about spiritual life, which you are following strictly. You have also heard about My divine manifestation, which you desire to see. But your ordinary eyes are unable to see this divine glory. Just as the ordinary ears cannot detect the sound waves in the ether that a transistor can pick up, similarly, you must see this divine manifestation with the third eye.

"Arjuna! You are My loving disciple. Now I am enabling you to have your third eye opened. Through this third eye, you can perceive, conceive, and realize divinity. You will be able to see the glory of My supreme Self. You will achieve perfection in your practice."

In the Guru Gita, The Song to the Divine Master, it is described thus:

ajñāna timirāndhasyā jñānāñjana śalākayā
cakṣur unmīlitam yena tasmai śrī gurave namaḥ:

"I bow to the master who removes the darkness of ignorance with the flame of light and who opens the eye of divine perception."

The realized master, during the initiation and body purification, helps the disciple perceive the opening of the third eye. The disciple perceives multicolored stars and different illuminations. At this moment, the eyes are inwardly transfixed, all the doors of the body are closed. The more the disciple practices such techniques, the more his perception and experience will become clear, and he will proceed on the path of realization.

Verse 9

samjaya uvāca
evam uktvā tato rājan
mahāyogeśvaro hariḥ
darśayām āsa pārthāya
paramam rūpam aiśvaram

Translation

Samjaya said:
O king (Dhritarashtra)! Thus having spoken, Hari, the great master of yoga, revealed to the son of Pritha (Arjuna), His majestic, supreme form.

Metaphorical Interpretation

Samjaya means one who has thorough control of all the senses, the mind, and restlessness. In reality, *samjaya* is a state of spiritual attainment. In this state, one has the power of distant vision and hearing. One can see, hear, and understand things happening in far away places without being physically present. Samjaya in the Mahabharata is a brahmin minister, as well as the messenger of the blind king Dhritarashtra. The blind king is the mind, which has dominance over the body and life of each person. But although the mind takes little interest in spiritual awakening, the inner intelligence, *samjaya*, speaks to Dhritarashtra.

Samjaya describes *vishvarupa*, the universal form, the extraordinary glory and beauty of the Lord, to Dhritarashtra. With the power of discrimination, a blind person (a person with a materialistic attitude and spiritual blindness) can have spiritual vision. Samjaya is saying, "O King! The Lord is not an ordinary person, He is not Shri Krishna, but Mahayogeshwara Hari—Hari, the great master of yoga." In Sanskrit, *hari* has many meanings. One is *harati avidyam iti harih:* "He who dispels the darkness of ignorance is Hari." Hari is the formless God and God alone is the remover of darkness. God, in the form of guru, guides the disciple from darkness to light, from ignorance to knowledge, from falsehood to truth, from death to immortality. God is the supreme master of yoga. He has created everything and has entered into creation. He has permeated everywhere. He and creation are united. This is *mahayoga*, the supreme unification and oneness of the Lord and the world. In each human life, there is union of body and soul. Every sincere seeker must try to reach this divine perception.

"The Lord revealed His majestic power to Partha." This is a spiritual revelation perceived during meditation. This state can only be achieved by sincere practice of meditation with love and loyalty to God and guru. (See the Katha Upanishad 1:2:23)

Verse 10

anekavaktranayanam
anekādbhutadarśanam
anekadivyābharaṇam
divyānekodyatāyudham

Translation

Of many mouths and eyes, of many wondrous aspects, of many divine ornaments, of many uplifted divine weapons.

Metaphorical Interpretation

In meditation, different etheric levels of awareness can be experienced. When one moves above the neck center, the *akasha* vacuum is perceived in the gross form; thus between the *ajña* chakra (soul center) and the *sahasrara* (fontanel) chakra, five levels of subtle vacuum are revealed: *chidakasha, parakasha, daharakasha, atmakasha,* and *mahakasha*. (See the illustration in the *Bhagavad Gita in the Light of Kriya Yoga*, Book One, page 25.) When one is well established in *shunya* (vacuum), he has many divine experiences. The space is directionless and dimensionless. In this space, when the inner gaze is transfixed, one has perception of all directions. The mouths are many and so are the eyes. Many colors are visible in the formless and vast inner sky.

Divya in Sanskrit is related to both divinity and the sky. All experiences and realization dawn in the sky of spiritual awareness. There is extreme beauty beyond the expression of finite words. To reach such a state, one must be well equipped with the weapon of breath control.

Verse 11

divyamālyāmbaradharam
divyagandhānulepanam
sarvāścaryamayam devam
anantam viśvatomukham

Translation

Wearing divine garlands and garments, with divine perfumes and ointments, made up of all wonders, divine, infinite, facing in all directions.

Metaphorical Interpretation

Divya malyam means divine garland; it also implies garlands of the sky. While practicing *jyoti mudra*, which can be learned and practiced under direct supervision of the master of Kriya Yoga, one perceives golden-colored rings with dazzling colors. This is like a divine garland in the sky. *Divya ambara* means divine and luminous dress or garment in the vacuum center. In meditation, with deep consciousness, one perceives a milk-white, snow-white light, pervading everywhere. The vast sky is full of such divine illumination. This is the divine garment. Divine perfumes and ointments bring calmness, coolness, and perception of the formless. Perfume spreads everywhere. When one meditates, one gets a much more sensitive sense of smell. At the same time, smell is associated with the *muladhara* chakra. In meditation, one perceives the formless power of God pervading from the top to the bottom of the spine. This state is beyond the domain of sensory perception.

All these glories of God, seen during meditation, are infinite and wonderful. God is infinite. His glories are infinite. He is formless. His realization is in formlessness. *Vishvatomukham* means the face of God in all directions. He is omnipresent, facing in all directions. This is the state of the absolute perceived in the inner sky of spiritual awareness.

Verse 12

divi sūryasahasrasya
bhaved yugapad utthitā
yadi bhāḥ sadṛśi sā syād
bhāsas tasya mahātmanaḥ

Translation

In the sky, if a thousand suns should rise at once, such brilliance or splendor would hardly approach that of the great self.

Metaphorical Interpretation

In meditation, with awareness introvertedinto the pituitary and fontanel, by the grace of God and gurus, one experiences divine illumination with closed eyes—or even with the eyes open. The illumination is seen in the sky of inner awareness, *divi*. The brilliance of light is compared with the simultaneous rising of one thousand suns. The yogic scriptures describe this experience as *koti surya suprakasha chandra koti sushitala*: "The brilliance of divine illumination is like millions of suns, yet it is not scorching, but soothing like millions of moons." Such experiences are very common for those who meditate regularly and practice the scientific technique of Kriya Yoga.

In this verse, the word *divi* means in the sky. Every meditator must try to remain in the inner sky of soul awareness. It is also said:

anāhatasya śabdasya
tasya śabdasya yo dhvaniḥ
dhvanerantargatam jyotiḥ
jyote rantargatam manaḥ
tan mano vilaygam yāti
tad viṣṇo parama padam:

"When one meditates with love, one perceives spontaneous, nonstop, primordial, divine sound. When one penetrates deep into the sound and seeks the origin of that sound, the state of pure consciousness in that sound is achieved. There is dissolution of mind in God awareness." One realizes the omnipresent God (Vishnu).

To have consistency in meditation and spiritual life, one must remain in the company of the guru, listen to the essence of spiritual practice, practice constant self-analysis and introspection, and read inspiring holy scriptures.

Verse 13

tatrai kastham jagat kṛtsnam
pravibhaktam anekadhā
apaśyad devadevasya
śarīre pāṇḍavas tadā

Translation

There the son of Pandu (Arjuna) beheld the entire uni-

verse concentrated in one place with its manifold divisions, in the body of the God of gods.

Metaphorical Interpretation

In this verse, Samjaya is describing the spiritual awakening of Arjuna. Arjuna's name is Pandava, the son of Pandu. *Pandu* means knowledge. The son of Pandu is someone with spiritual knowledge and aspiration. Knowledge is the stepping stone for entry into higher realms of spiritual experience. Arjuna sees the entire universe concentrated in one place. Human eyes looking at the vast sky, stars, planets, and the Milky Way are amazed and cannot comprehend the greatness of God. But by the grace of God and gurus, and by meditating and entering the sky of inner awareness, one can leave body consciousness and perceive extreme brilliance and the supreme self, the macrocosm in the microcosm. As the different limbs assembled together are pervaded with the flow of life energy in the entire body, similarly one's body is alive because it is permeated by God's power. Arjuna enters into the state of realization with knowledge (*jñana*), meditation (*karma, kriya*), and devotion (*bhakti*). He gets a glimpse of the entire universe. This is akin to how studying the map of the world gives an idea of the world, but seeing this beautiful world firsthand is much more vivid, direct, and divine. Such a state cannot be explained with limited words.

Verse 14

tataḥ sa vismayāviṣṭo
hṛṣṭaromā dhanamjayaḥ
praṇamya śirasā devam
kṛtāñjalir abhāṣata

Translation

Then Dhanamjaya (Arjuna), being greatly amazed, with his

hair standing on end, bowing his head to the Lord with folded hands, said:

Metaphorical Interpretation

This is truly a state of spiritual experience. When one's mind and thoughts are absorbed in God consciousness and perceiving divine illumination and love, the hair on the body stands on end. This is the divine romance. One is greatly amazed. In this state, one is free from the fear or anxiety of birth, death, happiness, sorrow, hunger, and thirst. These six qualities are called *dhana* in Sanskrit. Freedom from these six qualities is the state of Dhanamjaya, the conqueror of *dharma*.

In such a condition, *prana* (exhalation) and *apana* (inhalation) are extremely feeble, faint, and fine. They barely flow through the nostrils as one remains in the *sahasrara* (fontanel) and perceives divine illumination and love.

Pranamya shirasa deva: "Bowing the head down to the Lord." This means not coming down from the head, remaining in the *div* (vacuum), and getting inwardly lost in extreme love and God consciousness.

Kritanjali "With folded hands." Hands are the indicator of activity. Action is the translation of thought. Therefore, folded hands means freedom from thought and action. It is the expression of extreme tranquility and love. Perceiving the incomprehensible, unmanifest, and formless, and stilling the vibration of the material, elemental world brings inner gratitude to God. God is the cause of creation and the continuation of life within creation. God alone manifests.

Abhasata: "Spoke." It is the expression of self-surrender that occurs when one perceives the glory of God. Without God, one cannot have life. Man's strength is due to every little breath. In every breath, we should express our inner love to God.

Verse 15

arjuna uvāca
paśyami devāms tava deva dehe
sarvāms tathā bhūtaviśeṣasamghān
brahmāṇam īśam kamalāsanastham
ṛṣīmś ca sarvān uragāmś ca divyān

Translation

Arjuna prayed:
I see gods, O God! in your body, all kinds of beings assembled there, Brahma, the Lord, seated on the lotus throne, and all the seers and heavenly *nagas*.

Metaphorical Interpretation

After having the divine experience born of deep meditation and the grace of God and guru, Arjuna started praying to God with love and gratitude. The preceding verse contains his prayer and his divine experiences as expressed through limited words. Arjuna had the vision of all the gods (*devas*) in the divine body (formless form of God), all the *bhutas* (beings, also the gross elements like earth, water, fire, air, and vacuum), Brahma (the creator, seated on a lotus seat), the *rishis* (sages), and the *nagas* (serpents).

Each human body is a little universe. This body universe is pervaded by the marvelous power of God, as is the external universe. In terms of this body universe, "all the gods" refers to the divine qualities born of the vacuum, the *div*. In the universe, whatever moving or unmoving beings one perceives, they are nothing but the manifestation of God alone. *Bhuta sangha* means all kinds of beings, birds, animals, humans, and so on. It also indicates the aggregation of five gross elements: earth, water, fire, air, and sky. Each human body is the combination of these five gross elements. The entire universe is the manifestation of these elements, also known as the *bhuta sangha*.

Brahma is the creative aspect of God. He sits on the lotus throne. The perception of creative energy in the four-petaled lotus of the *muladhara* chakra is the state described here. The *muladhara* chakra is called the money, wealth, and material prosperity center. As the fontanel is the place of supreme power, the *muladhara* is the place of creative power. Money and wealth are the cause of hyperactivity of the other four centers (sex, food, heart, and vacuum). The creative power remains in the four-petaled lotus. This is Brahma, seated on the throne of the lotus.

Rishis are men of right vision and right action. Through meditation one gets a clear conscience and decisive qualities. Meditation makes one a *rishi*, a sage.

Uragans means heavenly *nagas* or serpents. These are different vital airs and vital breaths. Breath is the basis of deep meditation and realization.

All these experiences are seen with the divine eye, the third eye of God consciousness.

Verse 16

anekhabāhūdaravaktranetram
paśyāmi tvām sarvato nantarūpam
nā ntam na madhyam na punas tavā dim
paśyāmi viśveśvara viśvarūpa

Translation

I see You everywhere: Your infinite form, with numerous arms, bellies, faces, and eyes. I see not Your end, Your middle, Your beginning, O Lord of the universe, only Your universal form.

Metaphorical Interpretation

If one becomes a seer, one is able to have divine sight. Arjuna, through his meditation and the grace of the Lord, became a seer, perceiving God inside and outside, in the body universe and in the external universe. Such vision is possible only through *jñana chakshu,* the eye of knowledge, and *yoga chakshu*, the eye of yogic perfection. The Isha Upanishad (Mantra 1) says, *īśa vāsyam idam sarvam:* "God is infinite and omnipresent; His glory is everywhere," and *yat kim ca jagatyām jagat:* "However insignificant something may be, God exists within it."

A big banyan tree is the manifestation of a tiny seed. In the tree are millions of fruits, and in each fruit are countless seeds. So it is with God's infinite glory.

Sarvam brahma mayam jagat: "The entire universe is divine, it is the presence of the almighty Lord." In the *Purushasuka,* a prominent Vedic prayer, it says:

om sahasra sirśā puruṣaḥ
sahasrākṣa sahasrapāt
sabhumi viśvatyavritya
atyat tiṣṭha dasāngulam:

"That supreme Self, Purusha, has thousands of heads, thousands of eyes, and thousands of legs. He pervades the earth and the universe. Still, He is also in the place of ten fingers" (which is symbolically from the midpoint of the eyebrows to the fontanel.)

In spiritual life, when a person meditates sincerely, he is able to perceive God's presence within himself, as well as outside of himself. Every form is the form of God, although He is formless. He is in everything, even in grass, insects, and everywhere. At the same time, they are all in God. God alone exists, God is *sat*, existence, truth; *chit*, consciousness, wisdom; and *ananda*, bliss, supreme joy. God is *satchidananda.* God exists all the time. God is Mahakala, the supreme time. Time cannot measure God, for God has no beginning and no end. God is all time and infinite, and the infinite has no end. Thus, by the sincere effort of meditation and the grace of the loving Lord, Arjuna perceives the universal form of God.

Verse 17

kirīṣinam gadinam cakriṇam ca
tejorāśim sarvato dīptimantam
paśyāmi tvām durnirīkṣyam samantād
dīptānalārkadyutim aprameyam

Translation

Crowned, armed with a mace and a discus, a mass of effulgence, glowing everywhere, with the immeasurable radiance of the suns blazing fire, I see You, who are difficult to behold.

Metaphorical Interpretation

When a person meditates daily, deeply, and devotedly, he enters into the inner sky of God consciousness. This sky is inside the cranium. In this state, one perceives beautiful, colorful, brilliant, divine illumination. The crown is on the top of the head, studded with gems, precious stones, and diamonds that reflect and radiate light.

In this verse, there is a symbolic description of *kutastha*, the place of inner awareness. Each spiritual seeker, through deep meditation, must enter into *kutastha*, the *ajña* chakra. From there, he must proceed up to the *sahasrara* for realization. In such a state, one perceives a crown of light. As a mace can be used to protect oneself in all directions, the all-pervading light coming from the crown is also a protection. After more concentration, the light becomes a circular, golden-colored ring, and in the center there is a deep blue color and a star. This is the "discus." It is like being able to see millions of suns, moons, and brilliant fires simultaneously. This is the divine illumination perceived in meditation. Through such perception, the sense of attachment diminishes. In reality, this cannot be expressed with words. Arjuna perceives firsthand what he has heard about—the formless, all-pervading, brilliant, divine illumination—which makes him realize the greatness of the Lord.

Verse 18

tvam akṣaram paramam veditavyam
tvam asya viśvasya param nidhānam
tvam avyayaḥ śāśvatadharmagoptā
sanātanas tvam puruṣo mato me

Translation

You are the Imperishable, the Supreme, to be realized. You are the ultimate refuge of the universe. You are the protector, the imperishable, eternal *dharma*. You are the eternal spirit. I realize it.

Metaphorical Interpretation

Arjuna says, *Tvam akshara*: "O Lord! You are *akshara*, the imperishable one." People are consumed by body consciousness, but the imperishable soul resides in the perishable body. The seat of the imperishable soul is in the pituitary or *ajña* chakra. In the Bhagavad Gita (8:3), it is explained in detail. *Kutastha* is also called *akshara.* God is the Supreme; He is to be realized. God alone is knowable. To perceive the presence of God in everything and to know God is true spiritual life. This state can be acheived if one fixes his attention in the cranium and watches the imperishable soul breathe in and out.

The entire universe is created by God, from Himself. The universe is remaining in Him and ultimately merges in Him alone.

Just as waves are born in the ocean, live for awhile in the ocean, and ultimately merge with the ocean; God is the refuge for everything. A seeker, through his prayer and meditation, seeks refuge in God. God is the protector of the imperishable *dharma*.

Dharma is ordinarily translated as religion, but the word *dharma* is derived from the root word *dhru*, which means to uphold. Life is held in the body by the breath. This *dharma* or breath is flowing through the nostrils by the living power of God. One must love and watch God in every breath. God is hiding in everyone; behind every form, the formless God is hiding. To perceive Him is self-discovery. God is eternal. He is beyond everything. He is *purusha*, remaining in everybody, *deha pura* (city of the body). The body is called *prakriti*, mother nature, and the soul or God is *purusha*, the father. Creation is possible due to contact between *purusha* and *prakriti*.

Verse 19

anādimadhyāntam anantavīryam
anantabāhum śaśisūryanetram
paśyāmi tvām dīptahutāśavaktram
svatejasā viśvam idam tapantam

Translation

With infinite power, without beginning, middle, or end, with numberless arms, the moon and the sun as Your eyes, I see You, the blazing fire as Your mouth, scorching this universe with Your radiance.

Metaphorical Interpretation

A wave wanted to see the beginning and end of the ocean. Is this possible? In Arjuna's case, the created wanted to see the Creator—His beginning, middle, and end. Its similar to a statue of salt wanting to see and to measure the depth of the ocean. God is infinite, formless, beyond all human measurement and approach. God can be perceived only in the transcendental state because the glory, the beauty, strength, and vitality of God are unlimited and infinite. Therefore, with the limited capacity of the mind and senses, one cannot behold the infinite.

Ananta bahu: "Unlimited hands." A hand is the symbol of activity. God is working through all creatures through unlimited hands. This is *kri*, action, and *ya,* the soul, which is God. *Bahu* is from the root word *bah,* which means to carry the load. God, through the breath, is carrying the load of body and mind. If there is no breath, there is no life and others have to carry the load of the dead body.

Shashi-surya netra: "The moon and the sun as Your eyes." The moon and the sun are symbols of light. Without light, people cannot see. Light is the medium of perception. Light is also knowledge and strength. The power of the moon is in the left eye and the power of the sun is in the right eye. When one practices Kriya and introverts his gaze, the illumination of the sun and moon is perceived.

Dipta hutasha vaktra: "The blazing fire as Your mouth." Fire burns everything. It is in the body and the entire system, but fire manifests in two major aspects: digesting food and uttering speech. In the Vedas, it is described as *vak vai agni:* "Speech is fire." Two activities, taking food and talking, are performed with the mouth, and they are compared with fire. Fire, *hutasahan*, is split into two parts. *Huta* and *asha* meaning dissolution of all desires. Fire is all-purifying and burns everything; so as a person gradually becomes free from desires, dispositions, and ambitions, he becomes pure, like fire.

Svatejasa vishvam idam tapantam: "By Your radiance, the entire universe is scorched." When one meditates, he perceives intense energy and heat in the body. In the beginning stage of yoga and meditation, his body even perspires. Thus, Arjuna perceives the infinite glory of the Lord by the power of meditation and the grace of God and guru. (See the Mundaka Upanishad 2:1:4)

Verse 20

dyāvāpṛthivyor idam antaram hi
vyāptam tvayai kena diśaś ca sarvāḥ
dṛṣṭvā dbhutam rūpam ugram tave dam
lokatrayam pravyathitam mahātman

Translation

The space between heaven and earth is pervaded by You alone in every direction. Seeing this marvelous and dreadful form of Yours, O Supreme Soul, the three worlds tremble.

Metaphorical Interpretation

God is all-pervading in the entire universe as well as in this little human body, the micro-universe. The universe is the macrocosm and the body is the microcosm. Each human body is a little world. As in the universe, there is heaven and earth, so too in the body. Heaven is really inside. From the *muladhara* up to the *sahasrara,* the seven *lokas* (*bhuh*, *bhuvah*, *svah*, *mahah*, *janah*, *tapah,* and *satyam)* and the *muladhara* (*prithivi* or earth), the neck (sky), and the cranium (heaven) exist. Through meditation, one perceives that God is present in all these *lokas* and that He activates all the centers. Ordinary people cannot perceive and experience this because it is realized only through deep meditation. The space between heaven and earth is the space between the *sahasrara* and the *muladhara.* To come down from the *sahasrara* to the *muladhara* is descension, to go up, is ascension.

Similarly, in the Bible it says that "The heaven is My throne and the earth is My footstool" (Isaiah 66:1, repeated in Acts 7:49). God is all-pervading. He is everywhere in every direction. Each human being is nothing but soul, but God is the supreme soul (Mahatma). That is why Arjuna addresses the Lord as the supreme Self. "Seeing this marvelous and dreadful form of Yours, the three worlds tremble," Arjuna says.

The three worlds are hell, earth, and heaven; or the gross, astral, and causal bodies; or even the creative, the sustaining, and the destructive knots, and so on. When one meditates, he slowly progresses by perceiving different experiences. All these experiences are extremely marvelous, but when one meditates a little more deeply, sometimes he may experience a little fear, the fear of losing his body sense. This fear of losing one's own identity (body consciousness) is really an obstacle in meditation. Because of this fear, many cannot really progress and reach the goal. For this reason, Arjuna says: "O Lord, Your form is marvelous, beautiful, and enchanting, but at the same time, dreadful." But when one gets the guidance of the guru preceptor regularly, the fear in meditation disappears. In meditation one does not lose anything, rather, one gains the marvelous power of God.

Verse 21

amī hi tvām surasamghā viśanti
kecid bhītāḥ prāñjalayo gṛṇanti
svastī ty uktvā maharṣiddhasamghāḥ
stuvanti tvām stutibhiḥ puṣkalābhiḥ

Translation

The hosts of gods, indeed, enter You. Some, in fear and with reverence, look and praise You with folded hands. A multitude of *maharshis* (great seers), *siddhas* (perfected ones), say, "Let there be peace." They adore You with hymns and abundant praise.

Metaphorical Interpretation

The power of God activates every human body, including every part of the body and every sense organ. The sun and the moon are in the eyes, Indra is in the hands, Shiva is in the ears, Vishnu is in the skin, Ganesha is in the nose, and so forth. All of them get their strength, vitality, and agility through the breath, from God alone. These gods of the body senses know their own limitations and power. So when it is said in this verse that they "enter into God", this means that through meditation all the sense organs are introverted and one goes into the cave of the cranium. When one meditates sincerely, he offers all his activities to the fontanel with every breath.

Arjuna says, "They praise you with folded hands." The perception of the *aum* sound, the eternal divine sound in meditation, is really a prayer to God. In this state, one is free from all external activity, indicated by the folded hands of the gods, the presiding deities of the sense organs.

Maharshis are great seers. When someone comes up to the fontanel and becomes established there, he becomes a *maharshi.* This is a state of spiritual perfection. *Siddhas* are perfected ones. *Siddhis* means acquiring supernatural and spiritual powers. Ultimately, *siddhi* means perfection, namely, attaining the state of *nirvikalpa samadhi*, becoming merged in God and God consciousness.

"People want peace. For that, peace invocations are being chanted." In the Vedic prayers, there are many peace invocations. Peace cannot really be achieved by prayer sung by the mouth alone, rather it is achieved by sincere effort and meditation. Peace is attained through spiritual practice and is the result of tranquility of mind and serenity of the senses.

Verse 22

rudrādityā vasavo ye ca sādhyā
viśve śvinau marutaś co śmapāś ca

gandharvayakṣāsurasiddhasamghā
vīkṣante tvām vismitāś cai va sarve

Translation

The Rudras, the Adityas, the Vasus, the Sadhyas, the Vishva Devas, the twin Ashvins, the Marutas, the Ushmapas, the multitude of Gandharvas, Yakshas, Asuras, and Siddhas all look at You with awe.

Metaphorical Interpretation

Ekadasharudra: the eleven Rudras (See the Bhagavad Gita 10:23)

Dvadashaditya: the twelve Adityas (See the Bhagavad Gita 10:21)

Ashtavasus: the eight Vasus (See the Bhagavad Gita 10:23)

Dvadashasadhyas: the twelve Sadhyas—Manah, Manta, Prana, Sara, Pana, Viryavan, Vinirbhaya, Laya, Damsa, Narayana, Vrisha, and Prabhu

Dashavishvadevas: the ten Vishva Devas—Vasu, Satya, Kratu, Raksha, Kala, Kama, Dhriti, Kuru, Pururava, and Madrava

Asvinikumaradvaya: the Ashvinikumar twins (See the Bhagavad Gita 11:6)

Panchasamarutas: the fifty types of air

Saptoshmapas: the seven Ushmapas—Agnisvatta, Saumyah, Harishvantah, Ushmapah, Saukalinah, Varhidah, and Ajyapah

Gandharvas—Haha, Huhu, and so on.

Yakshas—Kubera, and so on.

Asuras—Bali, Virocana, and so on.

Siddhas—Kapila, and so on.

In the human body all these are present in the form of vital airs, divine qualities, and good dispositions. During meditation, they help one proceed inward. When one attains good concentration in the *ajña* and *sahasrara* chakras, one is given all these good qualities, which are looking at the divine glory of God with awe. In this state of deep concentration, the seer, the seen, and the sight (*drashta*, *drishya,* and *darshan*) become one. The breath becomes very tranquil, the gaze is transfixed. One slowly becomes free from external awareness and body consciousness.

Verse 23

rūpam mahat te bahuvaktranetram
mahābāho bahubāhūrupādam
bahūdaram bahudamṣṣrākarālam
dṛṣṭvā lokāḥ pravyathitās tathā ham

Translation

Having seen Your great form, with many mouths and eyes, O mighty-armed Mahabahu (Lord), Your many arms, thighs, and feet, Your many bellies and dreadful teeth, the worlds tremble and so too, do I.

Metaphorical Interpretation

The Lord is addressed by Arjuna as Mahabahu, which is also what the Lord called Arjuna several times. Man and God are one, just like the waves and the ocean are one, and ornaments and gold are one. Mahabahu comes from *maha*, great or mighty, and *bahu*, armed or arms that carry. God carries the entire universe. God is great. His hand is everywhere to help people in need and distress. The hand of God can approach everywhere, irrespective of distance. Arjuna is saying, "O Mahabahu! I perceive Your great form. I thought You to be like Me, but You are so great and big, there is no limit to Your form. You are *ananta* (infinite). Any ordinary form has a beginning and an end, but You are beyond all limitations. You envelop everything—all hands, legs, mouths, and eyes are Yours only."

Symbolically the mouth and eyes imply every point in the body. They are limbs of the body. We perceive the universe through every part of the body. Therefore, to perceive God's vastness and greatness through meditation, to perceive His presence everywhere and even in every part of the body, is the true spiritual life. Arjuna has attained that state of divine perception. God is very beautiful as well as dreadful—He is beautiful to the good and dreadful to the bad. The paragon of the beauty of God is beyond expression. The fearful form of God is also very dreadful. When one perceives the dissolved state of the universe in God, this is the cause of fear and tremors. In the beginning of spiritual experience one may have such fears, but with the help of the realized master, one can easily overcome all fear and achieve the state of complete fearlessness.

Verse 24

nabhaḥspṛśam dīptam anekavarṇam
vyāttānanam dīptaviśālanetram
dṛṣṭvā hi tvām pravyahitāntarātmā
dhṛitim na vindāmi śamam ca viṣṇo

Translation

Having seen You touching the sky, effulgent, multicolored, Your mouth wide open and Your large eyes glowing, My innermost soul trembles in fear. I find neither self-control nor peace, O Vishnu!

Metaphorical Interpretation

Vishnu is another name for God, meaning all-pervading one. *Vishnati pravishyati iti*: "One who penetrates everywhere is Vishnu." Vishnu is the Lord who maintains and sustains creation. He is the protector of the entire universe. Just like the presence of butter is in every drop of milk, Vishnu is present everywhere. Arjuna perceives that the form of Vishnu is so vast that His head touches the sky. This means that when Arjuna penetrates in *chidakasha*, he is able to perceive the infinite form of the Lord. In the sky of inner awareness, he perceives the all-pervading form, Vishnu. He perceives colorful effulgence in the sky.

God is the creator, sustainer, and destroyer. He is Hari as well as Hara. Now, Arjuna perceives the dissolved form of the Lord. This is called the form of Hari-Hara. He has a wide-open mouth and large, glowing eyes—a vast ring like divine light. Looking at such a great form of the Lord—creator (Brahma), the maintainer (Vishnu), and the destroyer (Shiva)—going to the state of timelessness, Arjuna becomes fearful and trembles from his innermost being. He is not able to perceive inner calmness and peace because he cannot assimilate all these visions.

Verse 25

damṣṭrākarālāni ca te mukhāni
dṛṣṭvai va kālānalasamnibhāni
diśo na jāne na labhe ca śarma
prasīda deveśa jagannivāsa

Translation

Having seen Your face (mouth) with its terrible teeth, glowing like fire at the time of universal destruction, I lose my sense of direction and do not find comfort. Have mercy, O Lord of gods, O ultimate resting place of the universe.

Metaphorical Interpretation

In this verse, Arjuna called the Lord Devesha and Jagannivasa. Devesha means Isha, the Lord, of *devas*, the gods. Each human being has divine qualities and demonic qualities. The divine qualities are called *devas*. All these divine qualities come from God. He is Devesha, the Lord of gods. Devesha also means Isha, the Lord, abiding in *div*, the vacuum. When one comes up to the vacuum from the neck center and above, he will have many kinds of experiences. The Lord is sitting inside the pituitary; Arjuna is near Him and through the third eye he is having many divine experiences.

The Lord is also Jagannivasa, the ultimate abode (*nivasa*) of the universe (*jagat*). The Lord is the creator of the universe. He has created the universe from Himself. Waves are created in the ocean, by the ocean. Waves live in the ocean and then merge in the ocean. In the same way, the universe and the Lord are related. When a person is meditating nicely and practicing Kriya, he has many divine experiences in the pituitary and fontanel. In the vacuum, with many colors and many visions, he sometimes becomes frightened. In the vacuum, in *paravastha*, he loses his sense of direction. He cannot even imagine his body mass or physical existence. Arjuna, instead of being peaceful and comfortable, experiences the fear of losing himself. When a river is extremely near the ocean, it is afraid of losing its name and form, but a river does not know that by sacrificing its little egocentric existence, it is going to become one with the vast ocean. This misunderstanding is the cause of the fear. So, Arjuna prays to the Lord to have mercy. The Lord is ever merciful and loving. His love and compassion are beyond comparison.

Verse 26

amī ca tvāmdhṛtarāṣṭrasya putrāḥ
sarve sahai vā vanipālasamghaiḥ
bhīṣmo droṇaḥ sūtaputras tathā sau
sahā smadīyair api yodhamukyaiḥ

Translation

And entering into You, all the sons of Dhritarashtra, along with a host of kings and Bhishma, Drona, and Karna, the son

of the charioteer, even the chief warriors of our side are there.

Metaphorical Interpretation

Meditation brings transformation to one's inner life. Meditation enables one to achieve thorough control of the restless senses and propensities of the mind. Meditation is the bestower of peace, bliss, and joy. Meditation gives vision of the past and the future. One is able to see incidents which are yet to happen. In the battle of life, when Arjuna saw his friends and relatives, which are all his good and bad propensities, assembled to fight, he was full of depression and unhappiness. Dejected, he declined to fight. But the able guru and guide encouraged and inspired him to be truly strong and steady. (See the *Bhagavad Gita in the Light of Kriya Yoga,* Book One.) Such is the case for every spiritual practitioner; he starts his spiritual life with enthusiasm and interest, but after awhile, he thinks that by controlling and even killing the desires of the mind, it will be difficult to live. His spiritual endeavor becomes slow and slothful, but the master, the guru preceptor, with infinite compassion, encourages the disciple to get out of this slumber. Then he meditates and has many spiritual experiences. Arjuna, in this verse, gets a glimpse of the future. In the sky of inner awareness he perceives all the sons of King Dhritarashtra, the Kauravas, with all the kings, Bhishma, Drona, and Karna, entering into the Lord.

Dhritarashtra is the blind king—symbolizing a mind with no discrimination or rationality, a mind with constant restlessness and desire. One who entertains the mind is really heading toward destruction. The sons of Dhritarashtra are the hundred Kauravas who represent lifes evil propensities. In the sky of spiritual awareness, when one comes up to the pituitary and the fontanel, the lower propensities lose their power and strength.

Bhishma, the grandsire of the Kauravas and the Pandavas,

is the false sense of vanity and determination. Drona is restlessness and fickleness. Karna is the ego arising out of hearing (*karna* in Sanskrit means ear). All of them, along with their companions, are entering into the flame of destruction—the mouth of the Lord. In the battle of life and in the battle of spirituality, one must sacrifice even one's good qualities. If one wishes to enter into the state of realization, one must give up both the good and the bad. So, Arjuna sees that the chief warriors of the Pandavas are also entering into the mouth of the Lord. In the Kularnava Tantra Verse 109, it says:

pāpa punyan paśum hat vā
jñāna khadgena yoga vīt:

"The knower of yoga, the yogi, slays the animals of *papa* (vices) and *punya* (virtues) with the sword of knowledge." In the beginning of spiritual life, good qualities and self-discipline are essential. But, while one is preparing himself to enter the highest realm of realization, one is to be free from all dualities of good and bad. That is why the Kauravas and even the warriors of the Pandava clan are all entering into the mouth of the Lord, meeting destruction.

One must be free from all dualities to reach the highest spiritual state.

Verse 27

vaktrāṇi te tvaramāṇā viśanti
damṣṭrākarālāni bhayānakāni
kecid vilagnā daśanāntareṣu
samdṛśyante cūrṇitair uttamāṅgaiḥ

Translation

They quickly enter Your fearful mouths, which look all the more terrible on account of the teeth; some are seen with crushed heads clinging between Your teeth.

Metaphorical Interpretation

Ordinary people are full of anger, ego, pride, jealousy, and many vices. Those who are trying to walk and progress along the spiritual path must make a sincere effort to be free from all these negative qualities. The negative qualities are the Kauravas. The positive qualities are the armies and the chiefs of the Pandavas: self-restraint, dispassion, detachment, determination, dutifulness, discipline, devotion, dedication, and so on. Positive qualities are essential as long as negative qualities are present. Just as soap is needed when clothes are dirty, but soap is unnecessary when the clothes are clean, when one gains complete control over the negative qualities, there is no need for the positive qualities. When the doubts of ignorance disappear, one is well established in truth. In such a situation, one enjoys constant peace, bliss, and joy.

The head is the place of knowledge and devotion, but those with ego are devoid of humility and therefore face destruction. A humble person is always meek. An egotistical man is bold and he never bends. Time devours all the negative qualities, and even the minor virtuous qualities, but truth is eternal. Truth, love, devotion, and so on are the eternal values. People think and plan for the future, but they do not know or understand how swiftly time passes. They do not realize that time is a continuous flow, devoid of distinction and the division of past, present, and future. The teeth of time crush everything to pieces, but those who honor time are really free from the shortcomings of life and become realized. They reach the state of timelessness.

Verse 28

yathā nadīnām bahavo mbuvegāḥ
samudram evā bhimukhā dravanti
tathā tavā mī naralokavīrā
viśanti vakytrāṇy abhivijvalanti

Translation

As many rushing streams race toward the sea alone, so do these warriors of the mortal world enter Your flaming mouth.

Metaphorical Interpretation

In Sanskrit, time is *kala* and God is Mahakala. Time (*kala*) flows to meet the state of Mahakala—God. A river flows but the ocean does not flow; it accepts and assimilates the river into itself. When the river and ocean meet, they become one. Similarly, knowingly or unknowingly, everyone is proceeding toward the goal of self-unfoldment and God-realization. This is the ultimate goal of life. Today or tomorrow one is to start his spiritual life. Those who start it early find that life is easier and more beautiful. Warriors are those who fight. Some people fight for their spiritual qualities; they fight against their negative qualities. They want to come up from the lower centers to the higher centers. There are also some people who try to remain absorbed in the lower propensities of life; they are engrossed in the lower centers. In each individual, there is a constant struggle and friction between the lower and higher natures.

In the battle of life, all the warriors who are fighting to establish their dominion—animality versus rationality—are heading toward the ocean of God consciousness, or Mahakala. The river and the ocean coming together is *advaita*, oneness. Although many rivers converge in the ocean, one cannot distinguish the waters coming from the different rivers. This is the state of perfect unity or *so'ham*: "I and He are one and always have been one." In the flame of God consciousness, the seeds of delusion are burned.

Verse 29

yathā pradīptam jvalanam pataṅgā
viśanti nāśāya samṛddhavegāḥ

tathai va nāśāya viśanti lokās
tavā pi vaktrāṇi samṛddhavegāḥ

Translation

As moths rush to enter a blazing flame, only to reach their extinction; thus, people rush into Your mouth with great speed for their destruction.

Metaphorical Interpretation

The river and ocean are nothing but water. The river flows, but the ocean is constant. Man and God are not different, both are one and essentially inseparable, but people who are extrovert and restless cannot realize this unity. Those who do not realize it are compared with insects in this verse. Insects have some extremely strong senses, like sight, smell, and even taste. The color and smell of the flower and the taste of honey make them extremely restless and fickle. In the night, looking at the brilliant flame of the fire, they think it is a very attractive flower and they rush to enjoy it. They do not know that it is fire and will cause their destruction.

Similarly, deluded people attached to the senses cannot judge what is right and what is wrong. They are so infatuated that they are not able to think of the outcome of their effort. Madness for sense gratification is the cause of destruction and death. In the *kutastha*, in the flame of God consciousness and divine illumination, all the insects of restlessness are burned. Meditation brings calmness.

Verse 30

lelihyase grasamānaḥ samantāl
lokān samagrān vadanair jvaladbhiḥ
tejobhir āpūrya jagat samagram
bhāsas tavo grāḥ pratapanti viṣṇo

Translation

You lick and swallow up all sides of the world with Your blazing tongue. O Lord! Your terrible splendors are burning the entire universe, filling it with radiance.

Metaphorical Interpretation

Kala is time galloping ahead, just like a blazing flame tearing into dry wood. God is Mahakala, the supreme knowledge, where ignorance cannot be sustained. Ignorance is darkness and the cause of all suffering. Due to ignorance, people do not perceive their divine nature. With the light of knowledge, the darkness of ignorance cannot be sustained. In such a state, one achieves true spiritual enlightenment. The mouth of God symbolizes the *kutastha*, in the pituitary. When one meditates deeply, one perceives brilliant light and divine illumination. In such divine light, there is no ignorance or darkness; delusion is swallowed up. Through the practice of Kriya and the perception of divine light, one is freed from sins and suffering. Desires and passions are destroyed. With knowledge of the Self, the net of delusion disappears. In the sky of inner consciousness (*chidakasha*), the seeker reaches this vision of divine illumination and enlightenment.

Verse 31

ākhyāhi me ko bhavān ugrarūpo
namo stu te devavara prasīda
vijñātum icchāmi bhavantam ādyam
na hi prajānāmi tava pravṛttim

Translation

Tell me, who You are with a form so terrible? Salutations to

You, O Great Lord! Have mercy! I wish to know You, the primal being, in particular, for I know not what You are doing.

Metaphorical Interpretation

At first when the seeker introverts his sense organs and enters into the pituitary (*kutastha*), he perceives very beautiful, brilliant, and soothing light. This golden, bluish, formless light gives tremendous joy and happiness, which are enchanting. However, the divine illumination changes. From such brilliant and beautiful light, it changes into very strong, fiery, and terrifying light. The seeker is slightly disturbed by this. This light seems to be swallowing everything. It is like a strong fire, burning everything. He is surprised and at the same time fearful because he thought the light was the soul and had reveled in its peace, joy, and happiness. Now, this light has become dreadful and it seems like the state of dissolution. So, the seeker asks: "O ferocious form! Who are You? Why is there a change in Your nature? A moment ago there was tremendous beauty, now it is so dreadful! I cannot understand such change. Are You really my friend, my heart, my soul?" The seeker surrenders to the Lord. He expresses his desire to achieve His supreme knowledge. If the Lord is not pleased, one cannot have such divine wisdom.

Arjuna therefore prays: "Devavara! Great Lord! You are omnipotent. Have mercy on Me. Through Your grace, I am able to have this experience, but still, I am confused. I am afraid. I know that You have created everything and You maintain and sustain everything, but now, looking at this dreadful state, I am not able to know what You are doing and who You are! Please reveal Thyself. Let me be realized by Your grace."

Verse 32

śrībagavān uvāca
kālo smi lokakṣayakṛt pravṛddho
lokān samāhartum iha pravṛttaḥ

ṛte pi tvām na bhaviṣyanti sarve
ye vasthitāḥ pratyanīkeṣu yodhāḥ

Translation

The Lord said:

I am Kala, the eternal time spirit, the mighty cause of the world's destruction. I am out to annihilate the worlds. Even without any action of yours, all these warriors who are arrayed in the enemys camp, or in both camps, shall cease to exist.

Metaphorical Interpretation

The one soul plays the dual role of the disciple and the master, the guru preceptor. Each individual seeks progress. The soul is the real master who helps the seeker to progress. On one side, one has doubt and therefore questions. On the other side, the soul, being the guru and guide, answers. The scriptures say: *atmaiva gurur ekam*: "The soul alone is the guru." When the seeker comes up to the pituitary, through meditation, he has different spiritual experiences. At that time, he will get the answer to all his inner questions: "Who are You? What are You doing? I thought You to be very beautiful. Why are You so dreadful? Please reveal Thyself."

The Lord, the inner self, is saying, "I am eternal time. Everything is created in time. Everything meets their end in time. I am here to annihilate all the worlds, the *lokas*." There are seven *lokas* in the seven centers: *bhuh, bhuvah, svah, mahah, janah, tapah,* and *satyam*. These seven *lokas* lose their separate existence and become one through meditation. In this way one becomes free from the sense of body and world. The Lord says, "I am eternal time, Kala, the mighty cause of the world's destruction."

The time or lifespan of each person is measured by the breath. An ordinary person breathes 21,600 times a day during normal human activity. In every breath, the lifespan of the person is slowly decreased, but no one takes notice. Restless breath is death. Therefore people with anger, ego, passion, and emotion lose their lifespan quickly. Through meditation and breath control, one can be free from restlessness, be realized, and have eternal life.

Pratyanikeshu yodhah refers to the warriors arrayed in the enemys camp, or even in both camps. The Lord is the destroyer of the warriors on both sides. In the previous verses, Arjuna saw the Kauravas including Bhishma, Drona, and Karna, along with the warriors of the Pandavas entering into the mouth of the Lord. Here, the Lord says a similar thing: "Arjuna! You are My dear disciple. You have a deep desire for soul culture, spiritual evolution, and realization. You are constantly seeking My help. I am the creator, sustainer, and destroyer. I am the cause of birth, life, and death. I also breathe through your nostrils since you are my follower. I maintain good qualities in you and destroy the bad qualities in you. When you have come up to the pituitary and the fontanel, you are free from good and bad. You are established in truth, in your real self. This is the state of perfect unity. When a rusty wire is plugged into electricity, it is completely charged. So, when you come up to the fontanel, you and I are one again."

Verse 33

tasmāt tvam uttiṣṭha yaśo labhasva
jitvā śatrūn bhuṅkṣva rājyam samṛddham
mayai vai te nihatāḥ pūrvam eva
nimittamātram bhava savyasācin

Translation

Therefore, stand up and attain glory! Having conquered the enemies, enjoy the affluent kingdom. These warriors, standing here, are already slain by Me. O Arjuna (Savyasachi)! Be only an instrument.

Metaphorical Interpretation

This verse is the essence of all the advice of the Lord to every seeker on the path of spiritual life. How a person should lead his life is clearly and systematically explained in the inimitable style of the divine master.

The Lord says,

Tasmat tvam uttishtha: "Therefore, stand up." *Uttishtha* is a beautiful word in Sanskrit, it means to get up from sleep, to be awakened. Each individual, engrossed in the material world and forgetting the indwelling self, is sleeping. When one gets up from such a slumber, the duality of the material and spiritual life is forgotten. Every task, thought, and word becomes only an expression of spirituality.

Another meaning of *uttishtha* is to stand firm on the path of spirituality. The path of spirituality is extremely slippery. On this path, one must be very careful. People who cannot stand firm may fall down. During meditation, keeping the spine straight is also *uttishtha*.

Uttishtha also comes from the root *ut*, above, and *tishtha*, to be established, so it means to be established above the pituitary and in the fontanel. The human mind is restless in the lower centers. When one is able to fix his attention on the top, that is the state of *uttishtha*.

In the Katha Upanishad, this word is used beautifully in verse 1:3:14: *uttiṣṭhata jāgrata prāpya varān nibodhata:* "Arise (sit in the fontanel), awake, strive sincerely to reach the divine goal." In the Bhagavad Gita (4:42), the Lord directs Arjuna, *uttishtha*: "Wake up, stand firm, keep the spine straight, remain on top"—all these are different meanings of the same word. The Lord is saying, "O Arjuna! Be free from slumber, laziness, drowsiness, and soul-forgetfulness. Please keep your inner attention on the top, from where the breath is pulled in and out."

Yashah labhashva means to attain glory. What is glory? In the Shri Shri Chandi (otherwise known as the Durga Saptasati, a holy scripture), we find the prayer:
rūpam dehi jayam dehi
yaśo dehi dviśo jahi:
"O Mother Divine, give me beauty, inner beauty of the soul, give me victory, victory over the enemies of spiritual life, give me glory, to be the glory of perfection." *Dvisho jahi* means "make me free from all weaknesses."
In the Yoga Sutras of Patañjali, *yasha* (glory) is described as *vivekakhyati*, the glory of discrimination. The Lord is saying, "Arjuna! If you really follow what I teach, then you will be established in the state of perfection. Self knowledge will dawn upon you. You will constantly perceive your indwelling self."

Jitva shatrun means to conquer the enemy. One's true enemies are not outside, but inside: *kama* (passion), *krodha* (anger), *lobha* (greed), *moha* (infatuation), *mada* (vanity), and *ahamkara* (ego) are called the sixfold enemies. Doubts are also the enemy (See the Bhagavad Gita 4:42). In the Bhagavad Gita (3:43), the Lord said:

jahi śatrum mahābāho
kāma rūpam durāsadam:

"O mighty-armed Arjuna! Please destroy the strong passion that is your enemy."
All enemies can be killed, destroyed with the arrow of breath control. Breath control is the key to self-control and self-realization. This state will be achieved through the regular practice of meditation.

Bhunkshva rajyam samriddham: "Enjoy the affluent kingdom." The Lord is saying, "Arjuna! You have lost the rulership of this body kingdom, your life. You were exiled. But remember, you are the son of knowledge. You have not been able to reach the state of the kingdom of knowledge until now. Knowledge is imperishable and ever affluent. Self knowledge is the highest attainment. I am Mahakala. I swallow up everything. All these mighty opponents, the enemies that you see, are really nothing. You have love for Me, therefore I have already killed them. They are powerless, devoid of all strength. You are strong with My strength."

Nimitta matram bhava savyasachin: "O Savyasachi! Be only an instrument." In this verse, the Lord addresses Arjuna as Savyasachi. This name has many implications. It means one who can use both hands with equal efficiency, and one who gains thorough control over the left and right (*ida* and *pingala*) spinal channels. It is also one who is well established in *karma* (action) and *jñana* (knowledge). "O Arjuna! You are Savyasachi and a great warrior. You know the art of breath control and self-mastery. Be an instrument; it is not you who are working. I am working through you. I am the sole doer. If you think that you are working, that is your ego. Perceive that I am working through you and your ego will dissolve and disappear. You are strong with My strength. You are rich with My wealth. You are beautiful with My beauty. You and I are one inseparable soul."

Verse 34

droṇam ca bhīṣmam ca jayadratham ca
karṇam tathā nyān api yodhavīrān
mayā hatāṃs tvam jahi mā vyathiṣṭhā
yudhyasva jetāsi raṇe sapatnān

Translation

Drona, Bhishma, Jayadratha, and Karna as well as other warriors and heroes have already been killed by Me. Do not

hesitate! Kill! Fight! You shall conquer the enemy in the battle.

Metaphorical Interpretation

All these warriors were commanders-in-chief in the battle of the Mahabharata. (The metaphorical meaning of their names is explained in *The Bhagavad Gita in the Light of Kriya Yoga,* Book One.) The Lord is saying, "Arjuna! You are strong. Be neither attached to them out of affection, nor be afraid of them out of apprehension of their strength. I am with you, giving you immense strength. All these so-called great warriors are insignificant. Drona, restlessness, Bhishma, the ego, and the others are obstacles on the path of your spiritual progress. Be fearless. Seeing your determination, devotion, and dedication to your meditation and spiritual life, they seem to be pale and dying from fear.

Please practice Kriya sincerely. Kriya is the key to success and the path to perfection. Through the practice of Kriya, the breath will be tranquil and the mind will be still. Through Kriya you will be realized. In the battle of spiritual life, regular, sincere, and devoted practice is essential. Slackness in spiritual life will bring a downfall. To stand steady, one must be inwardly strong. Arjuna! Do not feel fear or pain upon killing them. Do not hesitate. Although your mind thinks them to be your close relatives, and kin, they are your real enemies. Fight them. Kill them ruthlessly. I assure you, victory is at your hand. Do not think of the fruits. You are going to be crowned with victory."

Verse 35

saṁjaya uvāca
etac chrutvā vacanam keśavasya
kṛtāñjalir vepamānaḥ kirīṭī
namaskṛtvā bhūya evā ha kṛṣṇam
sagadgadam bhītabhītaḥ praṇamya

Translation

Samjaya spoke:

Having heard these words of Keshava (Krishna), Arjuna, with folded hands, trembling, prostrating himself with extreme terror, bowing down, thus spoke with a choked voice to Krishna.

Metaphorical Interpretation

Samjaya is a state of meditation. When one practices meditation and lives a spiritual life, the mind and thoughts become silent. This is the state of *samjaya,* the power to hear and see inwardly.

In this verse, Samjaya addressed Arjuna by the name Kiriti. *Kirita* means a golden, diamond-studded crown, or one who has a crown on the top of the head. Usually, kings and great warriors wore crowns. Arjuna, through his meditation, has not only been in the divine company of the soul Krishna, but has also been able to come up to the fontanel, to the crown of the head. His head is decorated with the beauty of the *sahasrara* chakra, the lotus of a thousand petals, the crown. So Arjuna is Kiriti, because he is trying to fix his awareness in the top.

When one comes up to the pituitary and the fontanel, one perceives many colors and is able to hear the beautiful, divine sound, the talk of God. Keshava comes from *ka* (in the head), Isha (the Lord), and *va* (abode). In the head, inside the cave of the cranium, is the abode of the Lord. He is Keshava. Arjuna is able to hear and understand the speech of the formless Lord. The inaudible speech becomes audible by the power of meditation and the grace of the Lord. The invisible form of the Lord is perceived by Arjuna, so his body is trembling with some fear, some joy, and with divine romance.

Kritanjali means with folded hands, from *krita,* who made, and *anjali,* hands folded in a gesture of reverence. *Anjali* comes from the root *anj,* to get illumination. Arjuna, through his meditation, perceives extreme, divine illumination inside the cranium through his meditation. Prostrating oneself implies a state of humility and egolessness, a divine quality achieved through meditation. When Arjuna speaks to Krishna in a choked voice, this means he speaks with extreme gratitude.

Krishna is the indwelling self. To speak to Krishna means to enter into extreme silence. In silence, free from thought, one can hear the voice of God and one can talk to God. This is speechless speech, or talking with silence.

Verse 36

arjuna uvāca
sthāne hṛṣīkeśa tava prakīrtyā
jagat prahṛṣyaty anurajyate ca
rakṣāmsi bhītāni diśo dravanti
sarve namasyanti ca siddhasamghāḥ

Translation

Arjuna said:

O Hrishikesha, this universe rightly rejoices and delights in glorifying You. The demons, being terrified, flee in all directions. And a host of *siddhas* (perfected ones) bow down before You.

Metaphorical Interpretation

Arjuna addressed the Lord as Hrishikesha, the Lord of the senses. The Lord is the real conductor and energizer of all the senses. The sense organs function by the breath and the soul. Without the soul and the breath, the senses and the mind are inert, dead, and functionless. An ordinary person is engrossed in the senses and their objects, but a true seeker like Arjuna perceives the power of the soul, the Lord of the senses. In this condition, the sense organs do not create any trouble or difficulty. Through extreme calmness, one perceives the light of the soul that illuminates the senses and the world.

Arjuna perceives God's presence in every atom of the universe. Every object of the universe sings the glory of God. In the stars, planets, five gross elements, flowers, fruit, trees, plants, animals, and humans everywhere, Arjuna perceives God's presence and sees that everything is His manifestation and His beauty. Even in every cell of his body, Arjuna realizes God's strength and beauty. Now Arjuna has no fear; he is full of delight and joy.

Arjuna is saying, "O Lord of my senses! When I perceive Your divine glory and manifestation in the whole body, I am really full of calmness and love. I realize this calmness as divinity. In this state, the mind is free from restlessness and negative attitudes. The demons are the negative qualities in the body, mind, and thoughts. They attempt to persuade me to do evil, but when I remain in Your divine presence, the mind is so pure, there is no trace of demonic qualities—as if all the demons, terrified, flee in all directions.

"O Lord! When I am in Your presence, I feel full of love. I perceive my divine nature." To perceive one's own divine nature is really perfection. This perfection is already in man, but no one realizes it. Spirituality is the perception of the perfection already there. "O Lord! I do not know how to offer my love. I bow to You within myself. I bow to You everywhere."

Verse 37

kasmāc ca te na nameran mahātman
garīyase brahmaṇo py ādikartre
ananta deveśa jagannivāsa
tvam akṣaram sad asat tatparam yat

Translation

O supreme soul! Why should they not bow to You, who are greater than Brahma, the original creator? O infinite being! Lord of gods! Abode of the universe, You are the

imperishable, You are *sat* (existence), *asat* (non-existence), and that which is beyond both.

Metaphorical Interpretation

"O Lord," Arjuna said, "You are the indwelling Self. You are also the supreme Self. You are the controller of the three qualities—creation, sustenance, and destruction. O God! You are greater than anything else. Brahma is considered the creator of the worlds, but You alone are Brahma's creator. You are the creator of the creator."

In each human being, the mind creates many thoughts, dispositions, and states, but this mind is given its power by the soul. The soul is the supreme soul. People with limited knowledge do not perceive the infinite power hidden and dormant in themselves, but those who meditate and go inside, find the source of infinite energy. "O Lord! You are infinite. Your strength is boundless. Only one who comes near You through meditation is able to perceive this. You are the Lord of gods. The gods represent the divine qualities. All the divine qualities propagate from the top, from Your presence. O Lord! You are the abode of the universe. Like the waves abiding in the ocean, the entire universe is within You alone. Without You, there is nothing." Each human body is also a little universe. This body universe is maintained and sustained by God alone, through the breath.

"O Lord! You are *akshara*—the imperishable. This universe is perishable, changing, and impermanent, but You are imperishable, immutable, and changeless. O God! You are the supreme. You are Truth. You are also *asat*—non-existence. You are unknowable. You are real and unreal, you are everything and beyond everything. *Sat* also is that which man can perceive. *Asat* is that which man cannot know, that which is beyond perception. O Lord! You are beyond these. You are inexpressible. You are transcendental."

Verse 38

tvam ādidevaḥ puruṣaḥ purāṇas
tvam asya viśvasya param nidhānam
vettā si vedyam ca param ca dhāma
tvayā tatam viśvam anantarūpa

Translation

You are the first of the gods, the ancient spirit. You are the ultimate abode of this universe. You are both knower and knowable, and the supreme goal. This entire universe is pervaded by You, O Vishvarupa!

Metaphorical Interpretation

"O Lord! You are hiding in the universe, as well as in this body universe. You are the cause of all the other gods. Because of You and through Your breath, the gods exist in parts of the body, in different sense organs, and in all the chakras. Without You, they have no existence. So You are Adideva, the first of the gods. You are *purana purusha*, the ancient spirit. You existed before creation and You will exist after dissolution. You are beyond all change and modification. You are incomparable. As the soul lives in this body house, You live in the entire universe. You can live without the universe, but the universe cannot exist without You.

"You are the ultimate refuge of the entire universe. Like bubbles dissolve in water, everything is created from You, and everything lives and dissolves in You. One who knows You as the ultimate refuge, remaining in the cave of the cranium, is truly free from all dualities and difficulties. You are the knower, you know Yourself. No one can know You without Your grace. You reveal Yourself through Your love and compassion. You revealed Your divine form to me. You are knowable. In every name and form, in every object, only You are present. You are knowledge. Through Your infinite love, people can have a little perception of Your divine nature.

"You are the supreme goal. When the mind is attracted to You, there is no restlessness or distraction; there is complete tranquility. In *paravastha* (after Kriya, the state of super- consciousness), one can really perceive this. You are formless, yet every form is Your form. As every wave is made of water, similarly, every object reflects You. O God! You are Vishvarupa, the infinite, formless form. You manifest and permeate everywhere."

Verse 39

vāyur yamo gnir varuṇaḥ śaśāṅkaḥ
prajāpatis tvam prapitāmahaś ca
namo namas te stu sahasrakṛtvaḥ
punaś ca bhūyo pi namo namas te

Translation

You are Vayu (breath), Yama (death), Agni (fire), Varuna (water), the moon, the Lord of creatures, and the great-grandfather! Salutations to You, a thousand times!

Metaphorical Interpretation

"O Lord! You are *vayu*, the air outside. You are the breath in every living being." Several Upanishads start with the following *shantipatha* (invocation of peace):

namo brahmane
namaste vayu
tvameva pratyaksham brahmasi:

"O God, the absolute, I bow to thee, thou art Vayu, the living manifestation of Brahman."

Vayu is present in the entire body universe and at the same time, in the heart center.

"O Lord! You are Yama—the lord of death." *Yama* also means thorough control. (Please see the Yoga Sutras of Patañjali.) Those who lead a life of self-control perceive constant immortality, peace, bliss, and joy. This state is achieved through meditation. The scripture also says that *yama* is present in the coccyx, the base of the spine.

"O Lord! You are Agni—the lord of fire." Fire gives off heat, light, and energy. One soul fire is present in the whole body, maintaining body temperature. At the same time, fire manifest in the navel center. This is the Lord's presence.

"O Lord! You are Varuna—the lord of water." Three fourths of the earth is water. In the body, water exists in the form of blood and plasma. Varuna is in the second (sacral) center.

"O Lord! You are Shashanka—the moon." Just as the moon rises in the sky; symbolically, the moon is the lord of the mind. The Lord is present in the vacuum center (throat) and above (in the sky or fontanel).

"O Lord! You are Prajapati—the lord of creation." Many thoughts, ideas, and activities are created in each living being. This is the Lord's play and His manifestation. He is in the pituitary.

"O Lord! You are Prapitamahas—the great-grandfather." This means that You are the root of all creation, present in the *sahasrara*, the formless one.

"O Lord! You are present in the whole universe. You are in the entire body. I bow to You again and again."

As God is all-pervading, present everywhere, in every thought, word, and action, one must love the indwelling spirit. This is bowing to the Lord. At the same time, when one practices Kriya and enters into extreme tranquility, this is also bowing to God. To bow means to be without ego and to be one with the Lord.

Verse 40

namaḥ purustād atha pṛṣṭhatas te
namo stu te sarvata eva sarva
anantavīryāmitavikramas tvam
sarvam samāpnoṣi tato si sarvaḥ

Translation

Salutations to You from the front and from the back. Salutations to You from all sides. O everything! You are of infinite glory and boundless strength. You are all-pervading, therefore, You are everything.

Metaphorical Interpretation

In the Chhandogya Upanishad (7:25:2), it says,

ātmaiva adhastāt, ātmopariṣṭāt,
ātmā paścāt, ātmā purastāt,
ātmā dakṣiṇataḥ, ātmottarataḥ
ātmaivedam sarvam iti:

"*Atma*, the soul, is below and above; *atma* is in the back as well as in the front. It is also on the left and on the right. *Atma*, indeed, is everything."

Arjuna perceives this upanishadic truth, that the soul is all-pervading: inside, outside, and everywhere. So Arjuna says: "O Lord! People try to search for You everywhere, but You are to be realized everywhere. With eyes open, in the practice of *shambhavi mudra* (a meditation technique learned from the master), I perceive only You, everywhere, in the front, back, right, left, above and below, even inside and outside. I bow to You everywhere. You are everything. You are in everything. There is no discrimination or differentiation. O Lord! You are infinite. Your glory is infinite. Your strength is boundless. No human mind with extreme intelligence can comprehend this. Just as gold is inside and outside a gold ornament, so are You present everywhere."

In meditation, when one comes up to the *kutastha*, the infinite state is perceived. Free from body consciousness, one becomes aware of the formless, vast, infinite, and unbounded state of the soul.

Verse 41

sakhe ti matvā prasabham yad uktam
he kṛṣṇa he yādava he sakhe ti
ajānatā mahimānam tave dam
mayā pramādāt praṇayena vā pi

Translation

Whatever impertinent thing I have said, as if in ordinary intimacy, O Krishna, O Yadava, O comrade, in ignorance of Your majesty, through negligence or even through extreme affection.

Metaphorical Interpretation

Man is not the body. Man is the soul, the spirit. Those who are not really aware of their indwelling self consider themselves to be the body. With a little comfort or luxury for the body, they feel happy; with a little trouble from the body, they feel miserable. But when a person is touched by the realized master, he perceives the indwelling self, and through meditation, he realizes that he is not a limited egocentric body, rather, he is the soul, immortal, infinite, and without boundary. Then his approach to life and to the world changes entirely. He perceives the soul everywhere. This is inner transformation. Meditation brings inner change. Such a state has come into the life of Arjuna. The universe is in God and the soul is in the body universe. This is beyond the comprehension of the mind.

In the Kena Upanishad, it says: "What speech cannot reveal, but who reveals the speech, know that alone is God, not that which people worship here. What mind cannot comprehend, but who cognizes the mind, know that alone is God, not that which people worship here. What eyes cannot perceive, but who allows the eyes to visualize, know that alone is God, not that which people worship here."

God cannot be realized through limited senses and inner instruments. The Bhagavad Gita (7:15) tells us, *sukshmatvat tad avijneya*: "Being extremely subtle, He is beyond mental comprehension." Arjuna says, "O Lord! I was extremely body conscious. I was also thinking You were a human being and that You had a body. So, I addressed You with many names. I thought that You were limited. All my thoughts and imagination were full of flaws. O Lord! I was ignorant. You are My real guide. You lead me from body consciousness to God consciousness, from the limited world to the unlimited, infinite state. O Lord! Before I heard and understood a little about You, but now by Your infinite grace and love I realize what You are, what I am. I ignored You previously. My devotion before was not mature or ripe. Now, my third eye is open. I am able to realize my follies and errors."

People who worship God in holy places, who address God in many names and with many attributes, think of themselves as highly advanced. However, when they attain the state of inner perception, they realize their previous approach was ignorant and wrong.

Verse 42

yac cā vahāsārtham asatkṛto si
vihāraśayyāsanabhojaneṣu
eko thavā py acyuta tatsamakṣam
tat kṣāmaye tvām aham aprameyam

Translation

And if, with humorous purpose, You were treated with disrespect, while playing, resting, seated, or dining, when alone or in the presence of another, O Achyuta! (unshaken one) for that I ask Your forgiveness, O Immeasurable One!

Metaphorical Interpretation

Through meditation and living a spiritual life, outlook, understanding, and perception change. God is all-pervading, beyond deviation, inseparable. God is the eternal companion, the help in every situation. He is the Lord, the God of the whole universe. In this verse, Arjuna is able to realize his past mistakes.

Without Achyuta (God, soul), Arjuna has no existence, or activity, or even mistakes. The world has no existence without Achyuta, for Achyuta is in every thought, action, and knowledge. There is only Achyuta; God is everywhere. Human activity can be divided into four categories: *ahara*, eating and drinking, sense perception; *vihara*, sense-enjoyment, relaxation, and resting; *sayya,* sleeping; and *asana*, sitting or working. In every activity, there is *kri* and *ya*. Without God, without breath, there is no work. Previously, Arjuna thought it was he who was doing activities, but he was perceiving duality. Now, due to his inner vision and realization, he is able to perceive unity. Now Arjuna says, "O Lord! You are formless and changeless. You have no deviation. Whatever name I call You, You are the supreme. Please forgive me for all my ignorant behavior. O God! You are beyond everything. You are immeasurable."

In this verse, Arjuna realizes his past wrong misunderstanding and therefore asks forgiveness for his mistakes.

Verse 43

pitā si lokasya carācarasya
tvam asya pūjyaś ca gurur garīyān

na tvatsamo sty abhyadhikaḥ kuto nyo
lokatraye py apratimaprabhāva

Translation

You are the Father of the world, of all things, moving and immovable. You are worthy of adoration by the world. You are the most venerable guru. There is nothing like You in these three worlds. How can there be anything else or another greater than You, O You of incomparable glory?

Metaphorical Interpretation

What was Arjuna's mistake? Arjuna thought of the Lord as a limited human being. Arjuna thought that he himself was his body and that all his inner propensities, good and bad, were his relatives. He also thought that he could not exist without these so-called relatives.

Now Arjuna realizes his folly and his mistakes. With the eye of meditation, *yoga chakshu*, he is able to perceive that he is not his body and that God is unlimited. He says, "O Lord! Everything is Your creation. Everything has come out of You. Everything is Your manifestation: sky, air, fire, water, earth, stars, planets, plants, insects, animals, and human beings. You are the father of the world and of everything moving and unmoving. Nothing is possible without You.

"O Lord! You are worthy of adoration, *pujya*." The metaphorical meaning of *pujya* is to remain in the *kutastha*. One becomes free from all lower aspects of life by bringing the divine power up from the coccyx to the pituitary. This is *pujya*, adoration.

"O Lord! You are the most venerable guru." God alone is the guru. God manifests His divine power through the realized masters, but in essence no human being is a guru. *Atmaiva guruh ekam*—the soul, God alone, is the guru. A guru dispels the darkness of ignorance. "O Lord! You have dispelled all my ignorance, through Your divine touch and teaching. O Lord! There is no one like You."

The Upanishads declare: *ekam eva advitiya brahma*: "God is one without a second." Similarly, Arjuna says, "O Lord! You are incomparable, supreme." Comparison is possible only when there is more than one. God is one, absolute, and non-dual in these three worlds: heaven, earth, and hell. Each human body is divided into three worlds: heaven from the pituitary to the fontanel, earth from the navel to the pituitary, and hell from the navel down. God is the one indwelling self in each living being.

"O Lord! I bow to You again and again." The soul is the supreme presence of God in each human being. Through the practice of meditation and living a spiritual life, one is able to perceive one's own divinity and the glory of the soul.

Verse 44

tasmāt praṇamya praṇidhāya kāyam
prasādaye tvām aham īśam īḍyam
pite va putrasya sakhe va sakhyuḥ
priyaḥ priyāyā rhasi deva soḍhum

Translation

Therefore, prostrating my body at Your feet and bowing low, I ask forgiveness of You, O Lord, as a father to a son, a friend to a friend, a lover to a beloved. Please, O God, be merciful.

Metaphorical Interpretation

Devotion starts with self-surrender. Devotion comes out of knowledge. Arjuna, realizing the greatness of God, surrenders himself at the feet of the Lord. *Kaya* means the spine, not the whole body. The spine contains all five centers and five gross elements from the coccyx to the cervix. *Praṇidhaya* means not only to bow, but also to bend the spine in the egoless state. A person with an ego cannot truly bend. Spiritual life starts with erasing the ego. To come up to the pituitary is really to bow. The feet of God are in the pituitary. In the Vedic prayers it says,

om tat viṣṇo paramapadam
sada paśyanti suraya
divi iva cakṣurātatam:

"These are the supreme feet of the Lord. Those who are holy and spiritually strong constantly perceive the all-pervading power in the vacuum center." When one comes up to the pituitary through meditation and perceives divine power, this is the state of self-surrender and bowing down.

Then Arjuna, bowing down with reverence and love prays: "O Lord! I ask Your forgiveness. Infinite is Your love and forgiveness. You are like my father, I am Your child. If the child makes a mistake, the father forgives him. O Lord, You are so forgiving. You only give and forgive. Please forgive me, I forget You many times. This is my greatest mistake. Please forgive me like a friend to a friend, a lover to a beloved. O Lord! You are my everything." In this verse, many possible relationships with the Lord are explained. One can establish the relationship with God as a child and parent, as friends, or as lover and beloved, and so forth.

Through meditation and living a spiritual life, one can receive and retain the grace of God. Devotion to God, leading life according to the instructions and injunctions of the holy scriptures and the realized master, daily meditation, and a life free from ego and vanity are highly essential for spiritual evolution. Being humble like the grass and tolerant like the trees will make one great and divine.

Verse 45

adṛṣṭapūrvam hṛṣito smi dṛṣṭvā
bhayena ca pravyathitam mano me

tad eva me darśaya deva rūpam
prasīda deveśa jagannivāsa

Translation

Having seen that which has never been seen before, I feel transported with joy. At the same time, my mind trembles with fear. Please reveal to me, O God, that divine form in which You originally appeared. Have mercy, O Lord of gods, the abode of the universe!

Metaphorical Interpretation

Deva means divine qualities. The Lord of the *devas* (gods) is the ocean of divine qualities. "O God! Ordinary people do not perceive Your divine manifestation, Your universal formless form." To reach this state of realization, one must be properly qualified through meditation and apprenticeship with the master. This is why Arjuna refers to that which no one has seen before. Through the grace of God and gurus, one is able to perceive that which has never been seen before.

God perception is the cause of inner satisfaction. Through this, one has constant peace, bliss, and joy. God is very beautiful, but the vastness and infinite aspect of God brings fear. Therefore, Arjuna is trembling with fear. The beautiful form of God brings pleasure and joy, but His ferocious aspects bring tremors. Arjuna is praying: "O Lord of gods! You are Jagannivasa, the abode of the universe. Please be kind to me and show me Your previous form again. You are *sat*, existence; *cit*, the continuous meditator, consciousness; and *ananda*, bliss." Those who are *jñani*—men of wisdom, *yogis,* and spiritual people—achieve this vision of the divine.

Verse 46

kirīṭinam gadinam cakrahastam
icchāmi tvām draṣṭum aham tathai va

tenai va rūpeṇa caturbhujena
sahasrabāho bhava viśvamūrte

Translation

I want to see You wearing a crown, armed with the mace and discus in Your two hands as before. Become that four-armed one, O Lord with a thousand arms! O universal form!

Metaphorical Interpretation

The meditation mantra of Narayana, the supreme Lord, says,

dhyatjet sadā savitur maṇḍala madhyavarti
sarasijāsana sannivista, keyura-kirīṭi dhāri
hiranmaya vapu, dhṛta sankha cakraḥ:

"Meditate in the brilliance of the sun in circular form, in the center, seated on the lotus with a golden crown, in a body with a golden complexion, holding a conch and discus in the hand."

This is the divine perception in the *kutastha*, during deep meditation. Narayana is the Lord who is the cause of all life. In its mythological aspect, Narayana has four hands holding a conch, a discus, a mace, and a lotus.

The name of the conch in the hand of Narayana is Panchajanya. The conch is the symbol of the divine sound, and when one concentrates from the *muladhara* (bottom center) up to the *vishuddha* (throat center), one hears the sound of the conch blowing. The aggregate sounds, coming up from the five centers (*pancha* chakras) are called *panchajanya*. While experiencing this, one is extremely calm and quiet. *Shankha* is the Sanskrit word for conch. *Shan* and *kha* mean that by coming up to the vacuum, through self-control, one is able to reach this state.

The discus is the circular, divinely illuminated, golden-colored ring that is constantly rotating in the pituitary. This chakra symbolizes all the centers. Chakra is also called *kala chakra*—the wheel of time.

The third weapon is the mace. It is the symbol of self-discipline, self-control, and the egoless state. The spine and the brain are also like a mace. The symbol of holding a mace in the hand means all the chakras in the spine are completely under control.

The lotus is the beautiful flower born of mud in the pond and blooming above the water. This means to come up from the lower centers and bloom in the vacuum center. The lotus is the indicator of peace. Through meditation, one perceives eternal peace, bliss, and joy. When one practices Kriya regularly, the state of *paravastha* is reached where eternal peace is prevalent. In this state, there is no hint of fear, anxiety, or tension. The lotus also refers to the many-petaled lotuses located in the centers of the spine and brain.

Arjuna prays: "O Lord! Please reveal Your divine, beautiful, crowned form to me." The crown represents multicolored, divine illumination that is perceived in meditation when concentrating on the crown of the head. Arjuna wanted to see the Lord of one thousand arms. Having four arms symbolizes thorough control, total freedom from all fear and tremors.

Verse 47

śrībhagavān uvāca
mayā prasannena tavā rjune dam
rūpam param darśitam ātmayogāt
tejomayam viśvam anantam ādyam
yan me tvadanyena na dṛṣṭapūrvam

Translation

The Lord said:

Arjuna! Pleased with you, I have shown you My supreme form through My own power of yoga. My splendid, universal, infinite, and primal form have never been seen before by anyone other than you.

Metaphorical Interpretation

The Lord is saying, "O Arjuna! Why does this form of mine scare you? I am extremely pleased with you. You are My staunch and true follower. Being pleased with you, I have shown you My divine form by yogic power. This form is unique. This is My illuminating form. I am the creator and the sustainer. All creation dissolves in Me as waves dissolve in the ocean. You have become afraid by seeing this power of dissolution!

"O Arjuna! This form, that you perceive is full of splendor and glamour. It is universal and infinite. The gross eye cannot perceive it. Those who try to perceive this with external vision are truly unfit. Through *atma yoga*, one can perceive, conceive, and realize Me."

What is *atma yoga*? It is constant union (yoga) of the body and soul (atma), which ordinary body-conscious people are not able to realize. *Atma yoga* is the foundation of Kriya practice. Regular practice of Kriya frees one from ego and vanity. When one practices Kriya with sincerity, fixing the attention in the pituitary and the fontanel, one is able to achieve such vision. In this state, there is no trace of "I" and "mine"—ego-consciousness. Through the practice of Kriya, one attains marvelous powers and can feel God's omnipresent, omnipotent, and omniscient form. Regular practice of meditation enables one to rise above the human state and to be merged in the divine state.

Verse 48

na vedayajñādhyayanair na dānair
na ca kriyābhir na tapobhir ugraiḥ
evamrūpaḥ śakya aham nṛloke
draṣṭum tvadanyena kurupravīra

Translation

O Best of Kurus (Arjuna!) Neither by the Vedas nor by sacrifice, nor by the study of scriptures, nor by charity, rituals, or austere penance, can I be seen in such a form in this mortal world by any person other than you.

Metaphorical Interpretation

The Lord addressed Arjuna as Kurupravira. One meaning of *kuru* is action or Kriya, and *pravira* means perfect, efficient, the best. One who has attained perfection in the action of meditation is *kurupravira*. Arjuna is the best follower of the Lord. Through his sincere devotion and dedication, he remains constantly near the Lord and perceives His divine presence.

The Lord expresses the rarity of Arjuna's divine vision. One cannot achieve sight of the divine form through the Vedas. The Vedas is derived from the root *vid*, which means knowledge. In the state of knowledge, there is no seer, seen, or sight. One cannot reach this state by studying the scriptures. It is good to study the holy scriptures at first; they enable the seeker to be convinced and confirmed into spiritual ways. But knowledge from books is secondhand information; it is not the same as direct perception of the divine. Charity does not bring one into the right state either. Charity is the best policy for leading a spiritual life, but it can sometimes lead to vanity and a sense of pride and ego. Practicing Kriya will prevent this when the state of *paravastha* is achieved. Penance during the practice of meditation in the form of perspiration or trembling does not bring on transcendence either. However, if one continues to practice and passes through all these states, one can be free of them.

Above all, the Lord says that to have perception or vision of the universal form is extremely rare. Ordinary people are not qualified. Extreme devotion and practice of *atma yoga,* Kriya Yoga, enables one to reach a level of spiritual fitness. As long as one is body-conscious and restless, one cannot reach such a state. When one merges in the atom point, one becomes free from mind, thought, intellect, ego, body sense, and world sense. This is the state of spiritual attainment.

When one becomes sincere like Arjuna, one is fit for realization. The Lord says, "None other than you can see Me in this form," meaning that only by the practice of meditation and being constantly absorbed in the state of *paravastha*, will one be blessed with the divine state and the vision of God's supreme manifestation.

Verse 49

mā te vyathā mā ca vimūḍhabhāvo
dṛṣṭvā rūpam ghoram īdṛn mame dam
vyapetabhīḥ prītamanāḥ punas tvam
tad eva me rūpam idam prapaśya

Translation

On seeing this dreadful form of Mine, have neither fear nor confusion. Be again free from fear and be cheerful in heart. Behold My previous form.

Metaphorical Interpretation

After having a vision or various divine experiences in the *kutastha,* or after perceiving the brilliant illumination, the mind may not remain focused, in equipoise. Excitement or fear is not good in spiritual life. One must overcome fear and confusion, for they are obstacles in the path of higher spiritual attainment. God is the creator and the destroyer. God enables one to have divine qualities and He is the destroyer of evil qualities. One should be free from doubt, confusion, and fear in order to reach a state of peace and love in the heart. One must be ever content and satisfied.

The Lord's destructive form creates fear, but His creative form, the sustainer, is loving and soothing. So the Lord shows His previous form to Arjuna. Essentially, God has no form. Every form is the form of God. Through meditation, one reaches all these levels of spiritual experience. One must practice meditation and Kriya sincerely, with love, in order to become well established in the state of constant cheerfulness, peace, bliss, and joy in the heart.

Verse 50

samjaya uvāca
ity arjunam vāsudevas tatho ktvā
svakam rūpam darśayām āsa bhūyaḥ
āśvāsayām āsa ca bhītam enam
bhūtvā punaḥ saumyavapur mahātmā

Translation

Samjaya spoke:

Having spoken, thus, to Arjuna, Vasudeva (Krishna) revealed to him His own form again. Having resumed His gentle, wonderful appearance, the great soul consoled the frightened Arjuna.

Metaphorical Interpretation

Vāsudeva is the son of Vasudeva, meaning the all-pervading supreme spirit. The name Vāsudeva is derived from two words *vasu* and *deva*. *Vasu* means jewels, like diamonds, pearls, and so forth. These jewels have the quality of radiating light, but their brillance (*deva*) is covered up. *Vāsudeva* is the divine illumination remaining covered or hidden, but it is the state of brilliant, divine illumination. In the scriptures, it is written:

jyotirabhy-antare rūpam
acintyam śyāma sundara

"When one raises one's consciousness up to the pituitary and above, one perceives beautiful gold and blue light."

This verse is a beautiful narration of the relationship between the disciple and the master. The disciple becomes interested in perceiving divinity and in having spiritual experiences. When the master, through his grace, helps him to have such visions, the disciple becomes frightened. So then, the master enables the disciple to be fearless and doubt-free. The consolation of the Lord and His gentle, beautiful, and wonderful appearance makes Arjuna free from fear, and he achieves inner peace. Slowly proceeding forward by practicing meditation, one becomes fearless and achieves inner strength for higher spiritual attainment.

Verse 51

arjuna uvāca
dṛṣṭve dam mānuṣam rūpam
tava saumyam janārdana
idānīm asmi samvṛttaḥ
sacetāḥ prakṛtim gataḥ

Translation

Arjuna said:

Seeing Your pleasant, human form, O Janardana (Krishna), now I have gained composure and my mind is restored to my normal nature.

Metaphorical Interpretation

"O Janardana! You are the creator (*janayati iti jana*) of everything, the entire universe. You are the protector, sustainer, and destroyer (*ardati iti ardana*) of everything. You are everything. You enable everyone to destroy all their negative human qualities. The name Janardana (*janayati* and *ardati* become Janardana) has been given to You in this capacity. By Your grace, I was able to have spiritual experiences.

The waves in the ocean sometimes give joy, but high waves create fear. Everyone likes to see beauty, but I became frightened when I had the vision of Your divine manifestation in the form of the destroyer. Now I am seeing Your natural form. I feel joy with Your limited, as well as Your almighty form. I came to know that You are omnipresent, omnipotent, and omniscient. I saw Your real form and I was bewildered by it. Now I see Your lofty form as I settle back into my normal nature."

Through the practice of meditation, divine experiences like these occur. Sometimes, the disciple becomes terrified because he is unable to comprehend what he is seeing. But when he comes back to his previous state, he feels quite comforted and composed.

Verse 52

śrībhagavān uvāca
sudurdarśam idam rūpam
dṛṣṭavān asi yan mama
devā apy asya rūpasya
nityam darśanakāṅkṣiṇaḥ

Translation

The Lord said:
"This form of Mine that you have just seen is extremely

difficult to perceive. Even the gods are constantly eager to behold that form."

Metaphorical Interpretation

Sudurdasham idam rupam: "This form of Mine is perceived with much difficulty." *Su* means the beautiful; *duh* means with difficulty; *darsha* means to see. One cannot see the Lord's beautiful form with the gross eyes; one must extremely introvert the mind to see it. When all the sense organs are focused inward and the mind becomes quiet from meditation and breath control, then one achieves such vision, which is extremely beautiful. This form is called *sudurdarsham rupam.*

With the greatest difficulty, one can attain the state of self-control and discipline and see the Lord's all-pervading form. No success is achieved with dreams or imagination. Everyone must try sincerely to be successful in life and to become self-realized. *Deva* means people with divine qualities, good morality, and character. They try sincerely to achieve such vision, but only those few who are truly sincere in practice and are blessed with the grace of God and gurus can have this vision. This verse explains the rarity of divine vision and experience.

Accept a realized master as guide and practice meditation sincerely.

Verse 53

nā ham vedair na tapasā
na dānena na ce jyayā
śakya evamvidho draṣṭum
dṛṣṭavān asi mām yathā

Translation

Neither through the study of the Vedas, nor by penance,

nor through charity, and not even through ritualistic sacrifices can I be seen in the form that you have seen Me.

Metaphorical Interpretation

For divine experience and God-realization, one must practice self-discipline with sincerity. In every step of life, in every breath, and in every endeavor, one must maintain this inner spiritual quality. Without this, one is unfit for divine vision. Quality in life is not attained by listening to intellectual interpretations of the holy scriptures, or even by memorizing the verses of the sacred texts. Intellectual inquiry has limitations, so one must go beyond it.

One may gain some spiritual strength by conducting ritualistic sacrifices and offering oblation to the holy fire, but that is not enough. One gains strength by developing the fire of discrimination and coming up from the lower centers to the pituitary and above, not by burning external fires. Through this practice, extreme calmness will be achieved, as well as freedom from all restlessness and duality. Negative qualities will disappear. The flame of divine illumination will be clearly perceived.

One who treads the path of spiritual practice, by following the instruction of the realized master, is able to have divine experiences like Arjuna. In this state, there is freedom from fear, doubt, and confusion. This is the state of divine manifestation.

Verse 54

bhaktyā tv ananyayā śakya
aham evamvidho rjuna
jñātum draṣṭum ca tattvena
praveṣṭum ca paramtapa

Translation

Through single-minded devotion alone, I can be known and seen truly in this form, and can even be entered into, O Arjuna, O Paramtapa.

Metaphorical Interpretation

Arjuna is Paramtapa. This name has many meanings. One meaning is one who subdues the enemies. The internal enemies are the sense organs, anger, ego, pride, vanity, and others. They can be controlled and even destroyed through breath control. Those who practice Kriya regularly are no longer troubled by these enemies. They become also Paramtapa.

The Lord is saying: "O Arjuna! You are pure. You have the quality to subdue and eliminate all the enemies and negative qualities of life. You are an efficient fighter. To know, to see, and to be is the result of spiritual practice. One can read the scriptures or hear them from the mouth of the master, but one must hear with love. Through this kind of hearing, one develops an extreme desire to know. To know, one must practice the techniques of meditation until the ability to see and experience the triple divine qualities develops. One can become merged in extreme God consciousness through deep meditation. Unflinching, single-minded devotion (*bhakti*) is an essential part of spiritual practice. *Bhakti* is implicit faith, love, and loyalty to God. *Bhakti,* or devotion, must be God-oriented."

When one churns milk to get butter and heats butter, one gets ghee (clarified butter). Similarly, by action (*karma*), one attains knowledge (*jñana*), and by knowledge, one is endowed with devotion (*bhakti*). Pure devotion is the primary quality necessary for God-realization.

Through the practice of Kriya Yoga, one will attain knowledge, consciousness, super consciousness and cosmic consciousness. These states cannot be achieved through external activities like reading, chanting, or offering oblation. By becoming deeply devoted and practicing Kriya, one can reach a state of extreme calmness and godliness. In this calm state, one can penetrate the domain of the five gross elements (*pancha tattva*), and through these one can perceive God's presence, *atma tattva*. This is spiritual evolution.

The theory of evolution is based on heredity, environment, and culture. The heredity of each human being is divinity. Every human being is the multiplicity of the divine being: God in human form, and the human being in God form. Environment refers to the company of the realized master, who teaches practical spirituality. Even in formal education, teachers in school and college teach both theory and practice. The science of spirituality is taught directly by the realized master to his worthy disciples. He will lead the student to progress in the path of divinity. Real *bhakti* or devotion dawns in the *samadhi* stage. This is the state of liberation. Devotion is divine emancipation.

Verse 55

matkarmakṛn matparamo
madbhaktaḥ saṅgavarjitaḥ
nirvairaḥ sarvabhūteṣu
yaḥ sa mām eti pāṇḍava

Translation

O Pandava! He who does all his work for My sake, considers Me as the supreme, is devoted to Me, has no attachment, and is free from malice towards other beings, reaches Me.

Metaphorical Interpretation

This verse concludes this chapter. In this verse, the Lord explains the qualities necessary for self-realization. Although people consider *karma* (action), *jñana* (knowledge), and *bhakti* (devotion) to be different and distinct, they are essentially the same. The unity of these three is established in this verse. This is the basic requirement for the practice of Kriya Yoga, which ultimately bestows God-realization.

Mat karmakrit: "Work in the world, keeping your mind on Me. This is *karma* (action)."

Mat paramo: "I am the supreme." Know God as the supreme, for without God there is nothing—this is knowledge. God is Purushottama and Paramakrishna. God is the cause of everything. To know this is knowledge, *jñana*.

Madbhaktah: "Be devoted to Me (the Lord)." The practice of Kriya in meditation and daily life enables a person to have real devotion. *Bhakti-paranuraktih ishvare*—devotion is the state of attachment to the Lord. This is supreme love.

Kriya Yoga is the combination of *karma* (action), *jñana* (knowledge), and *bhakti* (devotion). By the combined practice of the scientific technique of Kriya Yoga, one reaches the state of inner detachment, *sanga varjita*. Ordinary people are attached to the lower five centers, five elements, and five sense organs. But those who practice meditation perceive inner detachment. To remain compassionately detached and be attached to the Lord is the result of Kriya practice.

Only then will one be free from attachment and hatred, *raga* and *dvesha*. Attachment to the senses and their objects is the cause of many vices, one of which is enmity. One who meditates deeply has no enemies, is full of divine love, and becomes well established in the cave of the cranium, in extreme God consciousness. By this, one reaches God-realization.

The Lord says: "Arjuna! You are Pandava! You have all the qualities born of knowledge (*panda*). You have the inner strength to come up from the lower centers to the pituitary and the fontanel; thus, you can become realized. He who has hatred, quarrels, and ego is far from this state. He who perceives My presence everywhere and loves everyone as My form, enters into Me. He is My real devotee. He is free from all evils. Any person who meditates and leads such a life will surely attain Me. He will become liberated and realized, there is no doubt about it."

Summary

There are two steps in spiritual experience. At first, the seeker tries to see God in all; then, the next step is to see all in God. The first step is the micro-experience, and the second is the macro-experience. Chapter 11 reveals how to see God in all: being freed from ego and inner narrowness, one a must try to be worthy in order to be blessed and graced with the experience of the divine glory.

This chapter is called *Vishvarupa darshana yoga*—The Yoga of the Cosmic Form Revealed. Arjuna prays to the Lord, "Please reveal Thy divine form to me, O Lord!" Seekers thirsting for divine experience remain unsatisfied until they merge in the supreme, in cosmic awareness. Every prayer is answered, but only to the degree of the intensity and sincerity of the prayer. Arjuna's efficiency and deep desire moved the Lord to bestow upon him the vision of the divine. This vision is possible through the divine eye, the third eye, also known as the eye of wisdom.

The glory of the Lord is endless, infinite, and eternal. The universe is small, and the Lord, God, is beyond comprehension. The realization of the absolute is only feasible when we sincerely strive and get the grace (*kripa*) of God. *Kripa* comes from *kri*, to do, and *pa*, to get. Spiritual experience is not daydreaming; on the contrary, it is hard-earned through deep meditation and a spiritual life.

Among the 55 verses of this chapter, only 14 are attributed to the Lord, 8 to Samjaya and 33 to Arjuna. This is the first place since Chapter 1 where Arjuna speaks to a great extent: Arjuna's talk here is not talk of ignorance as with the first chapter. Rather, it is out of inner fulfillment, love and devotion to the Lord, because of his experience.

Verses 1 to 4: Arjuna requests to behold the universal form of the Lord.
Verses 5 to 8: The Lord blesses Arjuna with the divine eye.
Verses 9 to 14: Samjaya describes the universal form of the Lord.
Verses 15 to 31: Arjuna describes the cosmic vision and his experience of the past, present, and future. Arjuna is overwhelmed by the experience and asks, "Who are You?"
Verses 32 to 34: The beautiful reply of the Lord is, "I am Time," and He advises Arjuna to be His instrument.
Verse 35: Samjaya's description of Arjuna's state.
Verses 36 to 46: Arjuna's heart-touching prayer to the divine, asking the Lord to withdraw His cosmic form so he can behold the pleasing form once again.
Verses 47 to 49: The Lord's declaration of the rarity of such vision.
Verse 50: Samjaya again describes Arjuna's fear.
Verse 51: Arjuna returns to normal consciousness.
Verses 52 to 55: The essence of the Bhagavad Gita—a description of the superiority of divine love.

God and man are alike in that each human body is a little universe, a miniature form of the vast cosmos. The all-pervading God is manifest in each human body, but man with his restless mind and extrovert senses is not able to realize the presence of the Lord in his own self.

Soul culture, deep meditation, and the company of good people enables one to achieve this experience. This chapter ends with a narration of devotion and divine love. Arjuna, through his deep devotion and self-surrender was qualified to have divine experiences. Through the practice of concentration and meditation, as described in Chapter 6, divine manifestation is possible for all true seekers.

Chapter 12

Bhakti yoga

The Yoga of Divine Love

Introduction

Right action with God awareness brings experience and expertise. If every activity is directed towards God, if everything is done in God consciousness, then the life flower blooms with its inner beauty, joy, and purity.

In the concluding verse of the previous chapter, the Lord emphasized the essence of His teaching:

Work for Me,
Accept Me as the supreme goal,
Be devoted to Me,
Be free from attachment and enmity toward others.

Everyone is born to work, but work should be done with devotion, as a worship of God. As explained in the previous chapter, one can have divine experience when the eye of spiritual awakening is bestowed by the grace of the Lord. But the Lord also tells Arjuna that after theoretically understanding spiritual life, you must apply this knowledge in daily life through work. Moreover, you must be careful about your spiritual attainment; you must have devotion—divine love.

This chapter is called *bhakti yoga*, the yoga of divine love. From action (*karma yoga*) one obtains knowledge (*jñana yoga*), which then leads to divine love (*bhakti yoga*). Love is the way and love is the goal. You must work with love, grow with love, and acquire your own spiritual experience. Love brings fulfillment. Love is pure and perfect. Love is divine. Love is eternal. Love itself is liberation.

In this chapter, the Lord explains the conclusive teaching of the middle six chapters, helping Arjuna become more spiritual and divine. The love of God should be reflected in a person's every action; thus, one will proceed to reach the state of liberation.

Verse 1

arjuna uvāca
evam satatayuktā ye
bhaktās tvām paryupāsate
ye cā 'py akṣaram avyaktam
teṣam ke yogavittamāḥ

Translation

Arjuna said:
Of those devotees who constantly fix their minds on You, who worship You with devotion, and those who worship the eternal unmanifest, which of these have the greater knowledge of yoga?

Metaphorical Interpretation

God is supreme. He is present in all states such as *kshara* (perishable), and *akshara* (imperishable). He is Parameshvara, the supreme Lord. He has *sakara* (form), He is *nirakara* (formless); He is *vyakta* (manifest), as well as *avyakta* (unmanifest); He is everything and beyond everything. Now the devotee has doubts about which way he should worship the Lord.

Arjuna is asking, "O Lord! I am confused. In the previous instruction, You told me to be constantly attached to You. Should I be attached to the form or the formless? Out of these two, which is better? O Lord! I have understood two ways.

One way is to worship You as manifested in the body through *pranakarma*, as the breath goes in and out. This is done by practicing Kriya breathing. Breath is manifested in the body; breath is life. *Prana* is activating all of the body's centers and states of consciousness. Your presence can be perceived in the flow of *prana*, the vital breath. This state can be achieved by remaining in and above the *ajña chakra*. By watching the breath, which is the *prana*, one can keep constant awareness on You, O Lord.

This *prana* is *kshara* (perishable). In each moment, *prana* (life) is destroyed."

The other way to worship is to go to the state of *avyakta*, the unmanifest, and *akshara*, the imperishable. (See the Bhagavad Gita 15:16). *Avyakta-upasana* means to worship the eternal unmanifest during the practice of *jyoti mudra* in Kriya Yoga. By doing this one can reach the state of transcendental reality in which all the sense organs are introvert. From the outside, with sense organs active and extrovert, one cannot really perceive divine light, divine sound, and divine vibration. But by going inside, one can perceive the flow of *prana* because it is manifest as form, on the outside. This internal state is *avyakta akshara*. In the Mundaka Upanishad (2:2:10), it says,

hiraṇmaye pare kośe virajam brahma niṣkalam
tac chubhram jyotiṣām jyotiḥ tad yad ātma-vido viduḥ:

"Being free from the restless extrovert state, *rajoguna*, Brahma abides in brilliant illumination, the light of lights. Only one who knows the self can experience this."

The divine illumination of the almighty Brahman is hiding as *akshara*, the imperishable, and as Purushottama, the supreme spirit, the almighty father. The worship of the manifest, *vyakta*, God, is possible through the senses, but the worship of the unmanifest, *avyakta*, God, cannot be done with the senses or the mind. So Arjuna asks, "Please tell me, O Lord! Of the two, which is better?" The Lord answers this question in the following verse.

Verse 2

śrībhagavān uvāca
mayy āveśya mano ye mām
nityayuktā upāsate
śraddhayā parayo 'petās
te me yuktatamā matāḥ

Translation

The Lord said:

I consider those to be the most devoted to Me (the best of the yogis), who fix their mind on Me, who are eternally united with Me and are endowed with supreme faith.

Metaphorical Interpretation

People who rely only on their intellectual faculties argue among themselves, discussing whether God should be worshipped with attributes and form, or without attributes as formless. In the Upanishads, it says, *yato vāco nivartante aprāpya manasā saha, ānandam brahmaṇo vidvān na bibheti kadācana*: "Both speech and mind come from God, even when He is not perceived; God is supreme bliss, know this and do not be afraid of anything."

The Lord is saying,

> *Mayy aveshya mano ye mam*: "Fix the mind on Me." The mind is restless by nature. The flow of thoughts is natural to the mind. The ordinary mind cannot remain on a particular point for very long, thus it is the cause of many troubles in life. To make the mind calm and quiet, one must know the easiest technique of breath control. Breath control is self-control; breath mastery is self-mastery; breathlessness is deathlessness. Those who practice Kriya sincerely know that through daily practice, they can gradually gain control over the mind. Practicing Kriya Yoga is the easiest way to regulate the mind.
>
> *Nityayukta upasate*: "Be eternally united with Me." The formless is manifest in different names and forms, so every spiritual seeker must train the mind to feel the presence of God in all. This is the art of living in the presence of God. One must perceive the living presence of God in the family, in friends,

at work, in flowers, fruit, and trees, in every object and every element. As the waves and the ocean are one, the world and God are one. One can see this by watching the breath and by perceiving the manifestation of God in everything. There is a proverb, "If you cannot see God in all, you cannot see God at all."

Shraddhaya parayo 'petas: "Maintain deep faith." Faith (*shraddha* in Sanskrit) is the foundation of spiritual life. *Guru-vedanta-vakyeshu shraddha*: "Maintain implicit love in the words of the master and the scriptures, i.e. faith." When one practices Kriya, the practical side of the teachings and spiritual life is perceived. When one hears the divine sound day and night, one is free from all negative qualities; faith becomes stronger. A person with faith can overcome obstacles on the path very easily. Then with every breath, one should see the flow of divine energy rotating in the spine.

The Lord is saying, "O Arjuna! Those who practice these things are, in My view, the supreme among the yogis. A yogi is one who perceives constant unity with Me. One who perceives eternal unity is the best of the yogis."

Verses 3-4

ye tv akṣaram anirdeśyam
avyaktam paryupāsate
sarvatragam acintyam ca
kūṭastham acalam dhruvam

samniyamye 'ndriyagrāmam
sarvatra samabuddhayaḥ
te prāpnuvanti mām eva
sarvabhūtahite ratāḥ

Translation

But those who worship the imperishable, the indefinable, the unmanifest, the omnipresent, the unthinkable, the unchanging, the immovable, the eternal,

By controlling all the senses, maintaining even-mindedness towards everything, and rejoicing in the welfare of all creatures, will surely attain Me.

Metaphorical Interpretation

The formless God is hiding in the form of each living being. He is the indwelling self. Because of the presence of the formless, the body form can be active and energetic. Without the formless, the body form is useless.

God is manifested in each human being, but He is also unmanifest. God is manifest from the *ajña* chakra downward. In this form He is called *saguna* (with attributes), *avyakta* (manifested), and *kshara* (changing). From the *ajña* chakra upward, he is called *nirguna* (without attributes), *avyakta* (unmanifest), *akshara* (imperishable), *kutastha* (immutable), and *achala* (immovable), and so on. The formless is static above the *ajña* chakra, and dynamic in the lower centers. The ocean is calm and quiet beneath the restless waves.

Those who worship *vyakta* (*kshara*) perceive the power of God in daily life, in all activities, and in every breath. Those who meditate and bring their consciousness up from the lower centers become free from restlessness. The restless world is below the eyebrows. *Akshara*, the imperishable Brahman, is above the eyebrows. It is known as Purushottama, the supreme indwelling spirit. The vital breath is *sthira-prana*, imperishable, above the eyebrows.

Anirdeshyam means indefinable. God, the absolute, is beyond all definition. No one can express God through words; God is transcendental. *Avyaktam* means unmanifest, beyond the reach of name or form. The Lord is beyond the reach of the word. *Sarvatragam* means omnipresent. The Lord is *vindu*, as small as an atom, and *sindhu*, even greater than the ocean; he is all-pervading. *Achintyam* means unthinkable. The mind can comprehend and cognize names and forms, material objects and ideas, but God is unthinkable because He is not in the world. He is beyond everything; He is everything; He is beyond the reach of the mind and thought. *Kutastha* is the unchangeable, immutable, beyond all modification and transformation. God is the supreme and changeless. *Achalam* is the immovable. God is all-pervading, He cannot move. Movement is possible from one place or state to another. God is beyond that. *Dhruvam* means eternal; God is present in all periods of time: past, present, and future.

Having explained that He is formless, *avyakta*, the Lord now tells us how one can try to realize Him.

> *Samniyamya indriya gramam*: "Control the senses." People try to worship God with the five sense organs: they sing, chant, and pray with the mouth; see statues and idols with the eyes; listen to talk and discourses with the ears, and so forth. God is everywhere, but to perceive, conceive, and realize Him, one must introvert all the sense organs. (See the Bhagavad Gita 8:12 and the Bible, Matthew 6:6).
>
> God is transcendental. After closing all the doors of the outward-directed senses and controlling these senses, one must then go above the pituitary. It is there that one will perceive the divine presence—not with the sense organs, but through inner realization.

> *Sarvatra sama-buddhaya.* Ordinarily this describes a state of equanimity toward everything—but when one is in the pituitary and above, where the senses are introverted, there is no external world, so equanimity does not exist. So the real meaning of *samabuddhi* is dissolution of the mind and intellect. This state is achieved by making the breath extremely feeble and tranquil. In daily life, one should try to help others with love,

and one should think, speak, and work for the betterment of others; this is the equanimity of the external world.

Sarvabhuta hite ratah. Ordinarily this means rejoicing in the welfare of all creatures. As with the ordinary meaning of *samabuddhi*, at first this concept seems to contradict *avyakta hita,* which means hidden or hiding. Consider however that the *bhutas* are the gross elements dissolved or hidden in the lower five centers, which are earth in the coccygeal center, water in the sacral, fire in the lumbar, air in the dorsal, and sky in the cervical; by rejoicing, one is able to reach the state of *sarva bhuta hite ratah,* which means engrossed in an extremely subtle state where there is no manifestation of these five gross elements.

Te papnuvanti mam eva: "They surely attain Me." They become realized. They become one with Me.

In summary, it can be said that in every form there is formlessness. Formlessness is beyond the perception of the senses, but in the body form, manifestation of the formless is true and evident. Those who fix their attention in the *ajña chakra* and above, the center of soul consciousness, who practice the scientific technique of Kriya Yoga and control their sense organs, will be free from the play of mind, thought, intellect, ego, body, and the world. This is the state of extreme calmness, which is formless meditation and realization of the absolute. This is the assurance of the Lord, the way to success and self-realization.

Verse 5

kleśo 'dhikataras teṣām
avyaktāsaktacetasām
avyaktā hi gatir duḥkham
dehavadbhir avāpyate

Translation

Of course, the strain is greater for those who have their mind attached to the unmanifest, for the goal of the unmanifest is attained with difficulty by those who are centered in the body.

Metaphorical Interpretation

Spiritual practice is not play. With a restless and sense-oriented mind, steady progress cannot be made in spiritual pursuit and attainment. In the material world, people are more attached to the lower centers, so they remain in delusion, illusion, and error. They are so attached to material activities that they think reaching the formless state is extremely difficult. One whose mind is engrossed in sense pleasures cannot easily come up to the pituitary and remain attached to the formless.

Most people are body-conscious, yet they want to attain self-knowledge. They must try to practice meditation sincerely. Daily, they must work toward inner calmness and concentration. Their effort is not futile, but to make progress, they must take their endeavor seriously. To raise awareness above body consciousness and sense pleasures takes some effort. But with sincere effort and regular practice, one can come up and find the ability to concentrate. The Lord uses the word *dehavadbhi,* which means body- centered, ego-centered, body-conscious, to describe people whose senses are turbulent, who do not find the practice of meditation easy. Nonetheless, by the grace of guru, if these seekers practice the scientific technique of Kriya Yoga with effort and attain the knowledge of *kutastha*, they can perceive the inner calm.

Through breath control, one can regulate the body and mind, gradually increasing concentration so one will be able to hear *aum*, the eternal voice of God. As the mind penetrates inwardly more and more, divine illumination is discovered. As the attitude of "I" and "mine" diminishes through Kriya Yoga practice, one enters into the state of *paravastha*—super consciousness. Those who are weak and sense-oriented cannot easily introvert the senses, but through Kriya, the mind and intellect are stilled. When the doors of the sense organs are closed, one can perceive *kutastha*. In the sky of inner awareness, the mind dissolves.

Worshipping the unmanifest by name is not enough. One must engage in sincere worship of the formless. To do this, one must first worship the manifest. To be in the *kutastha* is worship of the unmanifest; to do *pranakarma* or Kriya—the scientific breathing—is worship of the manifest. Kriya must be practiced with devotion and faith. Through regular practice this becomes easier, but in the beginning, it seems troublesome or difficult. In the Bhagavad Gita (9:2), it says, *susukham kartum avyayam*: "It depends upon human desire and self-effort."

With effort and by perceiving the love of God in every breath, one can easily come up from the state of *hamsa* (body and soul, ego and self), and merge in *sa* (God).

Verse 6

ye tu sarvāṇi karmāṇi
mayi samnyasya matparāḥ
ananyenai 'va yogena
mām dhyāyanta upāsate

Translation

Those who surrender all actions to Me, regard Me as the supreme, worship Me, meditate on Me with single-minded devotion (yoga),

Metaphorical Interpretation

There are two steps in spiritual practice: *avyakta sadhana* and *vyakta sadhana*. *Avyakta sadhana* is meditation on the unmanifest; it means going to the state of extreme formlessness through *paravastha* and *jyoti mudra. Vyakta sadhana* is the practice and application of Kriya in daily life.

The Lord now explains spiritual practice in daily life:

"Surrender all actions to Me." Each human body is associated with the soul. This state of union is yoga, which keeps the breath in the body. Every person is alive and active because of the breath. Whatever work one does, it is done through the breath, and ultimately, by the grace of the soul. This is *kri* and *ya* in daily life. Seeing, hearing, smelling, tasting, touching, praying, and all activities are nothing but the manifestation of the indwelling self.

Those who truly want to lead a spiritual life must dedicate all their activity to the indwelling self, the sole doer in each human body. The body is just a machine, an instrument that performs actions. Each person must love the indwelling self and dedicate every action their body performs to the Lord. Then, work becomes worship of the Lord. To surrender one's work is to surrender one's self, and all impurities of the mind and the thoughts are cleared away.

"Regard Me as the supreme." God is all-pervading. He is in the stars, planets, sky, air, fire, water, earth, forest, mountains, trees, insects, animals, birds, and human beings. Everything is created by the Lord and everything is alive because of the Lord. The Lord, God, is the supreme, without second.

"Worship Me." This is not the external worship or chanting that is done in religious rituals. The spiritual seeker must offer every breath to the Lord, who is ever present in the fontanel. The yogic scriptures declare that during normal activity every human being inhales 21,600 times a day. If one can watch this inhalation and exhalation and perceive the divine energy flowing through the spine from the top, then this is true worship, *pranopasana*, worship with breath and love.

"Meditate on Me with single-minded devotion (yoga)." When one meditates and practices Kriya, the restless mind disappears. Inner tranquillity is perceived. When the impurities of the mind are cleansed, one truly loves God. The mind becomes concentrated. Meditation is the key to purifying the mind and to soul consciousness.

Verse 7

teṣām aham samuddhartā
mṛtyusamsārasāgarāt
bhavāmi nacirāt pārtha
mayy āveśitacetasām

Translation

I will deliver very quickly from the ocean of death and the world those whose minds are fixed on Me, O Partha (Arjuna).

Metaphorical Interpretation

In the previous verse, the Lord explained in detail about worship with breath, as well as with breath control. Through the Kriya practice of breath control, one's inner life is purified, and one's mind becomes fixed on the Lord as well. In every thought, word, and action, *kri* and *ya* are perceived. The mind that is completely engrossed in God consciousness cannot perceive anything except God.

Let's say each human body is a boat, and this world is the ocean. The ocean of the world is restless, dangerous, difficult, and disturbed. The world of the ocean is also the world of death, because in the ocean there are hidden rocks, which are dangerous for sailing. The external world constantly changes, leading to decay and destruction. Each human body is like this world—

the lower centers are obstacles that must be crossed to reach the goal of the fontanel, and the body is a world of death. In every exhalation, every human being dies, and with each inhalation, they are born again.

To see the world as the world is death; to see the world as the manifestation of God is immortality. Man faces death because he thinks he is the body and cannot perceive that he is the indwelling self. In the Katha Upanishad (2:1:10), it says, *mṛtyoḥ sa mṛtyum āpnoti ya iha naneva paśyati*: "To perceive multiplicity (diversity) is death, and to perceive unity with the divine self is immortality. To forget the indwelling self is death, and to be aware of the inner self is liberation."

God in the form of the guru is the sailor, the guide who helps the lifeboat of each person across the world ocean. When the wind is strong, the waves in the ocean become large. When the mind is disturbed, the breath is restless. But by attaining a tranquil breath, one can be free from the waves of thoughts and emotions. Breath control is the foundation of spiritual life.

God is saying, "O Partha! I bless those with self knowledge who calmly concentrate on Me, fixing their attention on Me with love. Self knowledge makes one free from the door of death and the dangers of the worldly ocean. When one perceives himself as the indwelling self, he is liberated." Every person holds bondage and liberation in their own hands. When one comes to the realized master with a strong desire and practices the techniques according to his master's direction, realization is possible. The strength of desire determines one's progress. Scientific techniques such as Kriya Yoga help in quickening progress in spiritual life.

Verse 8

mayy eva mana ādhatsva
mayi buddhim niveśaya
nivasiṣyasi mayy eva
ata ūrdhvam na saṁśayaḥ

Translation

Therefore, fix your mind on Me, establish your intellect on Me alone. Thus, you shall dwell in Me thereafter. There is no doubt about it.

Metaphorical Interpretation

The human mind is ever restless and constantly preoccupied with desire. So long as the mind is loaded with desire, life is burdened and one cannot remain still and attached to God. A mind with desire is gross and God is extremely subtle. So to be united with God, the mind must be very refined and subtle. The human mind is ever roaming from center to center, up and down the spine. The ordinary mind goes down in the spine, but the spiritual mind comes up through the spine. The material mind is tempted by the objects of the senses, but the spiritual mind is always attracted toward divine dispositions, like purity, love, discipline, devotion, and so forth.

The foundation of spiritual practice rests on withdrawing the mind from sense objects and establishing it on God (See the Bhagavad Gita 6:35–36). Meditation is the means of withdrawing the mind from the extrovert state. Scientific meditation is based on control of the breath. Control of the breath does not imply that the breath is held uncomfortably; rather, it refers to the tranquillity that automatically occurs in the breath during the practice of Kriya. When the breath is extremely fine, feeble, and slow, there is no warm breath coming out of the nostrils (See the Bhagavad Gita 5:27).

The breath and mind are causally connected. When the mind is restless, the breath is restless. Breath control is the easiest way to discipline the mind and to get success in life. The Lord says,

Mayy eva mama adhatsva: "Fix your mind on Me." When the mind becomes extremely subtle and fine through breath control, it comes up from the lower centers and penetrates into the pituitary and fontanel—the seat of God, the absolute, in the *sahasrara chakra*—the atom point. When the mind is extremely calm and quiet, there is no trace of restlessness. xtreme calmness and tranquillity are divine. When the mind is absorbed in divinity, it is extremely pure, filled with only divine spiritual thoughts. Day and night, the mind can roam in this super-conscious state. Even when the eyes are open in daily life, the eyes are calm and quiet, and the face radiates serenity, peace, and love.

Mayi buddhim niveshaya: "Establish your intellect on Me." The mind and intellect are not completely different. The mind is the doubting faculty and the intellect is the deciding faculty. The mind roams everywhere; the intellect is quieter than the mind. The intellect is the rational, discriminating aspect of consciousness. During meditation, there is no play of the mind or intellect. They completely disappear. Meditation is the state of complete freedom from mind, thought, intellect, and ego.

The Lord is saying, "Rise up from the lower propensities of life. Sit in the *sahasrara* (fontanel). Be united with Me. This union is yoga—oneness. As a cold iron becomes hot and fiery when in contact with fire, in the same way, the mind and thought become divine when attached to the soul. When your mind is established in Me, this is the state of *urdhva*, the highest" (See the Bhagavad Gita 15:1–2). *Urdhva* means the top of the head, and implies the kingdom of heaven, the abode of God. To sit there constantly is to become absorbed in God consciousness.

Verse 9

atha cittam samādhātum
na śaknoṣi mayi sthiram
abhyāsayogena tato
mām icchā 'ptum dhanamjaya

Translation

Or, if you are not able to keep your mind steadily on Me, then seek to attain Me through the yoga of repeated practice (*abhyasa yoga*), O Arjuna!

Metaphorical Interpretation

To enter into the unmanifest Brahman, *avyakta*, one needs to practice Kriya, *pranakarma*, which is *avyakta sadhana*. While practicing Kriya, one should keep the attention on the top, but to fix the mind in God and to be established in intellect may not be easy in the beginning because after a while the mind will be distracted. When the mind is not fixed and engrossed in the atom point of the fontanel, then one must follow the spiritual path of *abhyasa yoga*.

Abhyasa means repeated practice. Through repeated practice, a child can learn and memorize. In spirituality, practice is essential. What does one practice? First, keep the spine straight. Then, since the restless mind cannot remain in one place or on one point, rotate your awareness from the lower centers to the top, and then down, all the while perceiving the triple divine qualities. This is the easiest way to keep the mind introverted and concentrated in each chakra. Thus, the centers will be energized and the mind will be well composed.

Patañjali's Yogas Sutras (1:13) say, *tatra sthitau yatno'bhyāsaḥ*: "To remain there, practice carefully." Practice brings perfection. Repeated practice with love brings success. Regular practice of Kriya and meditation as taught and directed by the master will enable the restless mind to be absorbed in God-consciousness. The practice of *abhyasa yoga* will help you keep your mind still and will improve concentration. Even when you are not meditating, maintain a meditative mood. Search and seek the presence of God in every thought, word, and action.

Patañjali's Yogas Sutras (1:14) further state, *sa tu dīrghakāla nairantarya satkārāsevito dṛḍha bhumiḥ*: "Spiritual practice must be continued for a long period of time, continuously, nonstop, with love and faith." One must be firm and strong in practice in order to prevent deviations and distractions. It is difficult to become realized with only a little practice. In the Bhagavad Gita (8:7) the Lord said: *tasmāt sarveṣu kāleṣu mām anusmara yudhya ca*: "To become truly divine, remember Me all the time and fight restlessness and negative qualities. Let every breath be offered to the soul fire in the cave of the cranium. This is the easiest practice, *abhyasa.*

Verse 10

abhyāse 'py asamartho 'si
matkarmaparamo bhava
madartham api karmāṇi
kurvan siddhim avāpsyasi

Translation

If you are really unable to keep such a practice, be intent on My work, you will attain perfection even by performing actions for Me.

Metaphorical Interpretation

Some people may find it difficult to reach the state of perfection through the type of practice described earlier. They do not have enough time or they are busy with other things. The Lord says, *mat karma paramo bhava*: "Be intent on My work." What is the work of the Lord? How can one be oriented toward the work of the Lord? God has created everything in the universe and maintains and sustains all of creation. He is breathing through the nostrils of every living being. Without breath, there is death. Breath is the easiest work we do; it is the work of God. Breath is described as *sahaja karma* in the Bhagavad Gita. The real meaning of *mat karma paramo bhava* is to keep your attention on the breath. God is breathing through your nostrils 21,600 times every 24-hour period. Love God in every breath. The yogic scriptures describe it,

sankoca bhava durjanāt
sangama bhaja sajjanāt
nirgame praveśe vāyoḥ
gurur lakṣam vilokayet

"Refrain from keeping bad company and its evils, and associate with good company. Keep the attention on your incoming and outgoing breath, and love God and guru."

By constantly watching the breath with love, the mind becomes pure. Breath awareness is God awareness. Only by watching the breath, can the mind become tranquil, calm, and pure. Try to make a habit of not missing one breath without loving the indwelling self and inwardly offering gratitude. This will purify the chakras, the elements, and the memory. Practice it with love, for the love of God. God sees the heart and the mind. When the mind is clean, there will be no distraction or deviation from Him.

Do every action for the satisfaction of the Lord. Do not entertain evil moods or negative attitudes. Work is worship. Work with love, not with tension or stress. Every action done in God-consciousness will bring more love and peace. Every action will be worship of the Lord. This is *kri* and *ya*, perceiving God in every action.

Verse 11

athai 'tad apy aśakto 'si
kartum madyogam āśritaḥ
sarvakarmaphalatyāgam
tataḥ kuru yatātmavān

Translation

Or, if you are unable to do even this, take recourse to the yoga of realization (disciplined action); renounce the fruits of the actions out of self-restraint.

Metaphorical Interpretation

In the previous verses, the Lord spoke of *abhyasa*, repetition of practice. Now the Lord is explaining *vairagya*, inner detachment.

The Yoga Sutras (1:12) of Patañjali say, *abhyāsa vairāgyābhyām tat nirodhaḥ*: "Tranquillity of mind is obtained by the twofold practice of *abhyasa* and *vairagya*." (Also see Bhagavad Gita 6:35). *Abhyasa*, spiritual practice, and *vairagya*, detachment, are the two legs required to make progress on the spiritual path. Without one, the other is incomplete; the seeker is lame. They are the two sides of the same coin. *Abhyasa* is repeated practice of meditation and a spiritual lifestyle. But people do many things, even meditation, without detachment, with the expectation of getting results.

In the preceding verse, the Lord explained in detail the highest state of meditation and all the spiritual practices down to the lowest state. In this verse, the Lord discusses two things: first, giving up or renouncing the fruits of actions, and second, taking recourse to the yoga of divine realization (restrained action). The result of every action follows the person who performs that action. Merely thinking, "I renounce the fruit of this action," is not real renunciation.

Who is really doing the action in each living body? Can a body function on its own? No. In James 2:26 it is said "A body without the spirit is dead, inert; faith without deed is dead." Can the soul work in the world without the body? No. The body and soul can only work in the world when they are united.

Ordinary people are body-conscious and egocentric. They think and behave as though they are the body, and thus, they cannot perceive the soul. Essentially, man is the image of God; he is the soul, the formless power of God. This formless power permeates and functions through the body. The scriptures say, *aham karta iti bhavah ahamkara*: "I am doing this. This sense of doership is the ego." But the power of God, which is present in the body, is doing all action through the breath. Therefore the soul is the sole doer. Realizing this is devotion and the egoless state. Thus even while working, one is free from the expectation of the fruit of action.

One becomes detached from the fruits of actions through the practice of meditation, living a spiritual life, perceiving the presence of the soul, and by realizing *kri* and *ya* during every action. Moreover, by perceiving the power of God, all one's activities become pure, and one becomes free from temptation and passion.

One does not renounce action to become detached from the fruits of one's actions. As long as the breath remains in the body, many kinds of work will be accomplished through activity in the different centers. It is by regular meditation, leading a spiritual life, disciplined action, avoiding useless, negative, and distracting thoughts, words and actions, and by sincere practice of Kriya with faith, that inner renunciation and detachment is achieved.

Verse 12

śreyo hi jñānam abhyāsāj
jñānād dyānam viśiṣyate
dhyānāt karmaphalatyāgas
tyāgāc chāntir anantaram

Translation

Knowledge is better than practice. Meditation on God is superior to knowledge. Renunciation of the fruits of one's actions is even superior to (and also the result of) meditation, for peace immediately results from renunciation.

Metaphorical Interpretation

In the following verses, the Lord speaks of *abhyasa* (practice), *jñana* (knowledge), *dhyana* (meditation), *tyaga* (renunciation), and *shanti* (peace).

Although the simple translation of this verse implies that one practice is superior to another, in fact, this text is revealing that all of the steps are interdependent, one leading progressively to the next, to higher and higher levels. These five steps are essential for spiritual practice, soul culture, and self-realization. One must proceed from one step to the next, otherwise progress will be stagnant. So, each step is described as being superior or higher, but in reality, the higher steps are supported and resting on the lower ones.

Abhyasa, repeated spiritual practice is the first step. This is *karma* (action) in God-consciousness. This is the foundation of spiritual practice. In the Bhagavad Gita, it is described as *abhyasa yoga*—the yoga of spiritual practice. In the previous verses, there was an elaborate discussion of *abhyasa*. It is *karma,* or the repetition of action, which gives rise to *jñana* (knowledge).

Jñana, knowledge, is the second step, and therefore a higher level. What is knowledge? In the Jñana Shankalini Tantra, it is defined as: *abheda darshana jñana*: "To perceive everything as inseparable from the Lord. God is knowledge and is all-pervading. To live in the presence of God is *jñana. Jñana* is the theoretical approach, an intellectual understanding of spiritual teachings. This knowledge must be assimilated and directly perceived.

Dhyana, meditation, is the result of *jñana* or knowledge. What one reads in the scriptures or hears from the mouth of the realized master, must be directly perceived. This direct perception of knowledge is possible through meditation. So meditation is the fruit of *jñana* or knowledge. It is the third step. In the Jñana Shankalini Tantra, meditation is described as *dhyanam nirvishayam manah*—the state of complete dissolution of the mind. In this state, one is completely free from everything.

Tyaga, renunciation, is the fourth step. It refers to renunciation of all action, but it is not an outward show. Inner detachment is possible only when one is meditating sincerely and surrendering completely to the will of God.

Shanti, peace, is the highest step of spiritual attainment. Peace, bliss, and joy are the nature of God Himself. Continuous and uninterrupted peace are attained through the four steps of spiritual practice. When one is merged in God-consciousness, one perceives inner peace, the greatest spiritual wealth. *Shanti* and *samadhi*, the supreme divine communion, are one.

Verse 13

adveṣṭā sarvabhūtānām
maitraḥ karuṇa eva ca
nirmamo nirahamkāraḥ
samaduḥkhasukhaḥ kṣamī

Translation

He who is free from malice toward all beings, friendly and compassionate, free from attachment to possessions and ego, indifferent to pain and pleasure, and patient (forgiving),

Metaphorical Interpretation

From this verse, to the last verse in this chapter, the Lord explains the qualities of a *jñani* (a man of wisdom) and a *bhakta* (man of devotion). In the practical sense, there is no distinction between these two states. One who meditates is a *jñani*, a *bhakta,* and a *yogi*. He perceives the presence of God both outside and inside. He is extremely devoted to God and remembers Him in every breath and every moment. God and the devotee are inseparable like sweetness and sweets. The truly spiritual person is endowed with the following qualities:

> *Adveshta*: "Freedom from malice." Hatred comes from duality; love comes from unity. Hatred and malice are products of the human complexity. He who practices Kriya regularly with love reaches purity of mind. He has no sense of ordinary things. He behaves like an intoxicated person. He is so engrossed in the divine mood that he is not aware of others. Even when he is with others, he is full of extreme, divine love, so he cannot have hatred or malice. His love is pure and without expectation.
>
> *Maitra*: "Friendly." After deep meditation, when he is coming back into body consciousness, he perceives the living presence of God everywhere. He perceives everyone as the child of God. His perceptions, words, and behavior are full of love. He is friendly to everyone.
>
> *Karuna:* "Compassionate." His heart is full of compassion. He perceives everyone as being his own self, no different from himself. The troubles of others give him extreme pain and he tries to help people in every possible way. He distributes his material as well as his spiritual power to everyone and gives strength to the weak. He lifts the downtrodden to the highest spiritual awareness. He gives remedy to the diseased people of the world.
>
> *Nirmama:* "Freedom from attachment." He is free from affection and attachment. External objects do not disturb his

mind. Truly attached to God, he is inwardly detached. An outward show of detachment is not true detachment. Inner transformation into God-consciousness is true detachment. This is the state of *paravastha* in which one remains compassionately detached.

Nirahamkara: "Freedom from ego." Ego is the sense of "I am doing" and individuality. Ego breeds arrogance. Without ego, one is free from body consciousness, vanity, and attachment, constantly engrossed in the soul. The soul's presence is perceived everywhere.

Sama duhkha sukha: "Indifference to pain and pleasure." *Duhkha* is suffering or pain. *Sukha* is pleasure and happiness. In these two words, there is a common word *kha*. *Kha* means the vacuum center. Those who deviate from the vacuum go down, and they experience pain. Those who are engrossed in the beauty of the vacuum remain in happiness. Pleasure and pain are the play of God. A true yogi or devotee is engrossed in God consciousness to such an extent that he is not aware of external happiness or pain.

Kshami: "Forgiving." To err is human, to forgive is divine. Even if something extremely bad is done, a truly spiritual person will forgive it, just like Jesus did when he was on the cross. The spiritual person is beyond praise or blame, always in the *kutastha*.

Verse 14

samtuṣṭaḥ satatam yogī
yatātmā dṛḍhaniścayaḥ
mayy arpitamanobuddhir
yo madbhaktaḥ sa me priyaḥ

Translation

He who is ever content and a yogi (in God communion), self-controlled, of firm determination, whose mind and intellect are fixed (offered) to Me—that devotee is dear to Me.

Metaphorical Interpretation

Samtushta satatam: "Ever content." A truly spiritual person is always content. Contentment is the best policy. Desire is born of delusion, and delusion is the cause of danger and difficulties. With expectations, one becomes discontent. People with expectations cannot remain at peace. Balance of mind and inner equipoise cause contentment.

Yogi: One who perceives constant unity with God, the indwelling spirit, is a yogi. One becomes a yogi through regular meditation and by living a life of God consciousness. The restless mind does not enable one to be well established in yoga. Yoga is the highest spiritual attainment. A yogi is the greatest spiritual person, rich with the treasure of spiritual wisdom. In the Bhagavad Gita (6:46), the Lord speaks highly of the yogi.

Yatatma: "Self-controlled." *Yatatma*, the self-controlled person, is a *mahatma*, a great soul. He has thorough control over the ten senses and four internal instruments. The ten senses are the five organs of perception (sight, hearing, smell, touch, and taste) and the five organs of actions (hands, legs, mouth, anus, and genitals). The four internal instruments are mind, thought, intellect, and ego. Through breath control and living a self-disciplined life, true self-control is achieved. those who are not self-controlled cannot be called a yogi (See the Bhagavad Gita 6:36). A yogi is a self-controlled person.

Dridha nishchayah: "A person of firm determination." His mind and intellect are always engrossed in the soul and God. He does everything with firmness and God-consciousness. He never deviates from the path of truth. He never compromises his goals or his ideals.

Mayy arpita mano buddhir: "Mind and intellect are dedicated to God." The mind and intellect of the yogi are always roaming in God-consciousness. Every thought, word, and action are God-oriented; there are no other thoughts.

All these divine qualities arise from regular Kriya practice. The Lord also says, "These devotees are dear to Me." But in the Bhagavad Gita (9:29) the Lord said, *samo 'ham sarva bhūteṣu na me dveṣyo 'sti na priyaḥ*: "Being equally present in everyone, no one is dear or far from Me." God is free from all partiality. He is everywhere. We are all His children. But the more divine qualities manifest in someone's life, the more dear this person becomes to everyone. Everyone loves such a person. Although God is in everyone, those who do not meditate cannot realize this. Those who do realize this, love God extremely and feel God's love extremely; their lives are a manifestation of divine love.

Verse 15

yasmān no 'dvijate loko
lokān no 'dvijate ca yaḥ
harṣāmarṣabhayodvegair
mukto yaḥ sa ca me priyaḥ

Translation

He who is not a source of annoyance to his fellow creatures, and who in his turn, does not feel vexed with his fellow

creatures, and who is free from delight and envy, fear, and agitation is dear to Me.

Metaphorical Interpretation

He who is not a source of annoyance to his fellow creatures perceives God's presence in everything. His eyes and heart, his words and actions are full of love. His every movement give joy and peace to everyone. Everyone derives pleasure by looking at the serene face of such a person, who considers everyone to be his family.

"He who is not a source of annoyance to his fellow creatures." He gives love in return for anger and hatred. He is always full of love and compassion.

"He is free from delight." Ordinary people are delighted when they get objects of their expectations, and disturbed when they cannot get them, but the spiritual person is absorbed in God-consciousness. He is not affected by worldly possessions.

"He is free from envy." He is neither jealous nor does he have hatred. He accepts everything as the gift of God. He has reached the state of inner detachment. Where there is divine love, there is no envy, hatred, or jealousy.

"He is free from fear." People are afraid of loss of wealth, possessions, and family because they consider these to be the source of happiness. A sense of insecurity is the cause of fear. They think that happiness increases with the increase of all these, and decreases with the loss of them. But happiness is the state of remaining in God-consciousness, the state of inner equipoise. Happiness is within.

"People are also afraid of losing their lives, of death." They think that they are the body. When the body is burned and dying, they do not perceive the immortality of the soul. A sincere devotee, however, is always established in God and is therefore free from the fear of loss. The yogi who has gained the spiritual treasure of God awareness has nothing to gain or lose; he is fearless.

"He is free from agitation." Fear is the cause of inner agitation. Through breath control and meditation, reaching the state of tranquillity and peace, one becomes free from the effects of the external environment and agitation of body and mind.

As the sun dispels darkness and gives light, so also, the guru, through distribution of divine wisdom, removes all the weaknesses of life. One becomes very strong and steady in daily life.

Verse 16

anapekṣaḥ śucir dakṣa
udāsīno gatavyathaḥ
sarvārambhaparityāgī
yo madbhaktaḥ sa me priyaḥ

Translation

He who is free from expectations, who is pure, capable, impartial, free from anxiety, who has renounced the feeling of doership in all undertakings—that devotee of Mine is dear to Me.

Metaphorical Interpretation

"He is free from expectations." People depend upon the external world, the sense objects, the sense organs, and even the breath. A true spiritual person does not depend upon anything. He has no expectations. All his work is performed as a worship to God.

"His mind, thoughts, words, and actions are pure." In the Katha Upanishad (1:3:8), it says, *yastu vijñānavān bhavati samanaskaḥ sadā śuciḥ*: "One whose mind is remaining in the *ajña* and *sahasrara*, who remains engrossed and absorbed in God-consciousness is truly pure—externally and internally.

Daksha: "He is capable." He is efficient and capable in all work. A true devotee is not idle. He gets enough energy from God. He works extremely hard with love. Efficiency leads to perfection.

Udasina: "He is impartial." The devotee shows no favoritism. The real meaning of *udasina* is *ut,* at the top, and *asina,* to be seated, therefore, one who is seated at the top in the fontanel, in extreme God-consciousness.

"He is free from pain and anxiety." He has no feelings of pain. He is beyond the domain of the duality of pleasure and pain.

Sarvarambha parityagi: "Renunciation of the feeling of doership." God is the doer. The soul is the doer. The body is merely an instrument. The devotee is always absorbed in God. He dedicates everything to God; he feels, "I am nothing, and God is everything."

Verse 17

yo na hṛṣyati na dveṣṭi
na śocati na kāṅkṣati
śubhāśubhaparityāgī
bhaktimān yaḥ sa me priyaḥ

Translation

He who neither rejoices nor hates, nor grieves nor desires, who renounces both good and evil action, and is full of devotion is dear to Me.

Metaphorical Interpretation

Na hrishyati: "He does not rejoice." People get pleasure from achieving good things or expecting things, but it is temporary. The inner tranquility achieved in meditation gives one freedom from rejoicing. Real joy is not temporary, it is eternal.

Na dveshti: "He is free from hatred." He loves everything, all people and all experiences. He does not condemn anything.

Na shochati: "He does not grieve." He is free from the grip of grief. Grief is a state of attachment and infatuation. At first, Arjuna was full of *shoka*, grief or serious dejection, due to wrong understanding and egotistical attachment (See *The Bhagavad Gita in the Light of Kriya Yoga*—Book One).

Na kankshati: "He is free from desires." People are chained to the fetters of their desires, but desire is never satisfied; on the other hand, it always multiplies. Contentment is the best policy in spiritual life.

Shubha parityaga: "He renounces good action." In the view of the true devotee, God alone is good. He spends every moment in God awareness. He is free from so-called external good or virtues.

Ashubha parityaga: "He renounces evils." He avoids and abandons all evils and inauspicious thoughts, words, and actions. His mind is always roaming in God and truth. He is beyond the duality of good and evil.

Bhaktiman: "He is full of devotion." From action to knowledge, then to devotion and beyond, meditation gives one a taste for God. Through self knowledge, one becomes devoted to God. Shri Shankaracharya said in the Viveka Chudamani (31):

mokṣakāraṇasāmagryām bhaktireva garīyasī
sva svarūpa anusandhānam bhaktiḥ iti abhidhīyate:

"Among all the things that bestow liberation, devotion alone holds the supreme place. Self knowledge is the manifestation of devotion." By perceiving his constant association with the almighty, A yogi is endowed with true devotion.

Verse 18

samaḥ śatrau ca mitre ca
tathā mānāpamānayoḥ
śitoṣṇasukhaduḥkheṣu
samaḥ saṅgavivarjitaḥ

Translation

He who is alike to foe and friends, who is the same in honor and disgrace, remains balanced in heat and cold, pleasure and pain. He is balanced and free from attachment (company).

Metaphorical Interpretation

Samaḥ shatrau cha mitre cha: "He is alike to friend and foe." Ever compassionate, the spiritual person treats and perceives everyone in the same way. He is free from partiality. His vision is broad. Realizing God's omnipresence, he does not discriminate against anyone.

Tatha mana apamanayoh: "He is the same in honor and disgrace." Worldly people are flattered by honor and disheartened with disgrace, but the spiritual person is untouched by either.

"He is not perturbed by heat and cold." It is the law of nature that summer and winter come in their turn. The true devotee accepts everything as the will of God.

"He is balanced in the face of pleasure and pain." He is free from all external achievements and their effects.

Sanga vivarjita: "He is free from attachment and company." His mind is detached from the senses, the world, and the body, but is attached to God. He lives a life of compassionate detachment. He never grumbles. The scriptures say:

sukhasya duḥkhasya na ko'pi dātā
paro dadāti iti kubuddhiḥ eṣa
aham karomi iti vrithābhimāna
svakarma sutraiḥ grathitohi lokāḥ:

"No one is the giver of happiness or sorrow. Thinking that

happiness or sorrow is caused by others is purely evil-minded. 'I do everything' is useless ego. Beware your every thought, word, and action." This is the attitude of a *jñani*, the person of knowledge.

Verse 19

tulyanindāstutir maunī
samtuṣṭo yena kenacit
aniketaḥ sthiramatir
bhaktimān me priyo naraḥ

Translation

He who is indifferent to blame and praise, silent, content with anything whatsoever, homeless, firm in mind, and full of devotion is dear to Me.

Metaphorical Interpretation

"He is indifferent to blame and praise." A *sadhaka*, the seeker, does not feel pain or discomfort when he is blamed and does not become excited by praise. He who has ambition and expectations is affected by blame and praise, but the mind of the spiritual person is merged in the ocean of peace, so he is not affected by the dualities of mundane life.

Mauna samlina manasah: "He is *mauni*, silent. He whose mind is always absorbed in God is truly silent." External silence, or not talking, is extremely minor. Real silence is to be free from thought, which is possible during meditation.

Samtushto yena kenachit: "He is content with anything, regardless of circumstances." A real yogi is content and satisfied. He always remains with God. Godhood is his satisfaction.

Aniketah: "He is without home (detached from the material world)." He is a renunciant monk. The real meaning of "without home" is to be free from body consciousness. The body is the home where the soul lives. In deep meditation, there is no sense of the body; this is the state of homelessness. The real home is with God, in heaven, the divine kingdom, the fontanel.

Sthiramati: "He is firm in mind and free from restlessness." This state is obtained through breath control. As one practices Kriya, breath control brings tranquility of mind; then, one slowly enters into the state of *paravastha*; here, complete freedom is tasted; there is no sense of the body, mind, intellect, ego, or world.

Verse 20

ye tu dharmyāmṛtam idam
yathoktam paryupāsate
śraddhadhānā matparamā
bhaktās te 'tīva me priyāḥ

Translation

Those who honor this immortal law (the nectar of wisdom), with faith and devotion, and who are intent on Me as the supreme, are dear to Me.

Metaphorical Interpretation

The nectar is a mythological drink that makes one immortal. The nectar of wisdom establishes one in the soul and in God. Every person is the image of God, but due to delusion, illusion, and error, they do not perceive their immortal nature and they suffer in body consciousness and the material world. But those who come to receive the touch of the divine master, who truly learn and practice the essence of spirituality, and who are free from all negatives drink the nectar of immortality. Such divine wisdom cannot be perceived or realized by the senses, but only through deep meditation, when one is able to enter into the cave of the cranium and drink the nectar of wisdom.

The Lord spoke of this nectar-like divine wisdom in Verses 13 to 19. In the *Goraksha Samhita*, it says,

brahma randhre mano dattvā
kṣanārdham api tiṣṭhati
sarvapāpavinirmuktvā
sa yāti paramagatim:

"If anyone can penetrate into the fontanel, the *brahma randhra*, and stay a little while, he becomes free from all evils and attains the supreme state. The yogi whose mind is free from defects, delusions, and doubts is truly great." Meditation is real *dharma*, righteous living in breath consciousness. Meditation grants immortality, *amrita,* the nectar. It is taught by the Lord.

One who follows the Lord's instruction and translates it into practical life is dear to the Lord.

Summary

Among the chapters of the Bhagavad Gita, this chapter and Chapter 15 are the smallest, each consisting of only twenty verses. In this chapter, one verse is attributed to Arjuna and nineteen verses to the Lord.

From knowledge, one develops the state of divine love. Although this chapter is called the Yoga of Divine Love (*bhakti yoga*), it is also the concluding chapter of the second *sataka* (set of six chapters), which is dedicated to the steps of knowledge. Knowledge and theoretical understanding without practice are the roots of ego, but when they are applied to daily life, the tree of knowledge blossoms with love and devotion, bringing the fruit of self-realization and liberation.

Through the experience of the cosmic vision of the Lord, Arjuna's heart and mind will be flooded with waves of devotion. So this chapter is not the conclusion of divine knowledge, rather, it is the stepping stone to divine love.

When the Lord praised devotion in the last two verses of the previous chapter, Arjuna asked Him, "What is the real way to love." Nineteen verses of this chapter answer that question and may be summarized as follows:

Verse 1: Arjuna asks how to discriminate between worshiping the divine form and loving the formless eternal spirit, which appears to be contradictory.

Verses 2 to 8: The Lord replies, explaining the steps on the spiritual ladder.

Verses 9 to 12: The Lord elucidates different means of devotion and the greatness of action combined with devotion (*kri + ya*).

Verses 13 to 19: The Lord describes the qualities of a true devotee (a *yogi*) who is really dear to the Lord.

Verse 20: The Lord explains that one who follows and practices these doctrines is the best.

Do not be free from action, be free from attachment. Have equal vision everywhere. With thorough control of the senses and by giving up the ego, one will be able to manifest love for all. One will be free from bursting with joy over tiny gains, or sinking into depression over some petty losses. This state of balance is achieved through deep meditation, and a true devotee becomes adorned with all the divine qualities.

Every word, action, and thought must be God-oriented. One must make both heart and soul merge in God-consciousness. This can also be achieved through concentration and meditation. Through the Yoga of Constant Practice (*abhyasa yoga*, Verse 9), one attains this divine attitude.

In this chapter, the Lord explains a beautiful quality of the yogi—constant contentment (Verse 14). Contentment and self-realization are not far from each other.

By explaining in detail the path of action and knowledge, the divine master tries to make the sincere disciple fit to experience the ecstasy of divine love and liberation, which will be described in the third *sataka,* the final six chapters of the Bhagavad Gita.

Kriya Yoga Contacts

For more information please contact the following centers:

U.S.A.

Kriya Yoga Institute
P.O. Box 924615
Homestead, FL 33092-4615
Tel: +1 305-247-1960
Fax: +1 305-248-1951
Email: institute@kriya.org
Web Site: http://www.kriya.org

INDIA

Kriya Yoga Ashram
Nimpur, P.O. Jagatpur
Cuttack 754021, Orissa
Tel/Fax: +91 671-682724

EUROPE

Kriya Yoga Centrum
Heezerweg 7
PP Sterksel 6029
THE NETHERLANDS
Tel: +31 40-2265576
Fax: +31 40-2265612

Kriya Yoga Zentrum
Diefenbachgasse 38/6
1150 Wien
AUSTRIA
Tel: +43 1-8129626
Fax: +43 1-8956712
Email: kriya.yoga.centre@aon.at

Kriya Yoga

Kriya Yoga is a direct gift from God. The modern revival of Kriya Yoga began in 1861 by Mahavatar Babaji and has been handed down to this day through the master-disciple method of teaching.

Most of us live with a conception of God as almighty, omnipotent, and omnipresent, but few are searching for God within ourselves. More so, we do not feel the living presence of God within us through our daily chores and duties. Kriya Yoga can make us feel the living presence of God through breath control and meditation. Any work, *kri* is done by *ya*, the indwelling soul.

This mission has brought ancient secret teachings within the reach of householders and families who are searching for eternal peace and happiness, and who are hungry to know God. It will provide information about initiation into the original Kriya techniques and explain how this meditation can be added to enhance one's religious and spiritual practice.

About the Author
Paramahamsa Hariharananda

Paramahamsa Hariharananda, the greatest living master in Kriya Yoga, was the head of Karar Ashram, Puri, India, founded by Swami Shriyukteshwar Giri. He is the founder of the international organization, Kriya Yoga Ashram. He began as a devoted disciple of Shriyukteshwar and learned other higher techniques of Kriya Yoga from Paramahamsa Yogananda, Swami Satyananda Giri and Shrimat Bhupendranath Sanyal.

He is widely known as a self-realized Kriya yogi in the lineage of Shri Shyama Charan Lahiri Mahasaya and Swami Shriyukteshwar Giri. He received divine instructions to come to the Western countries and teach the original Kriya Yoga.

The master saint of the scientific technique of Kriya Yoga, Swamiji occupies a very high rank among the Indian yogis of this century. He has attained the supreme yogic state of *nirvikalpa samadhi*, and has demonstrated his pulseless, breathless state many times. It is extremely rare for a saint to attain this *yogic* state.

He has attracted the attention of educated Indians and Westerners for his vast knowledge of the Vedas, Upanishads, Bhagavad Gita, other Hindu scriptures, astrology, astronomy, and palmistry, as well as a thorough knowledge of major Western scriptures. Through his proficiency in many languages, he is accessible to people of different countries.

About the Compiler Swami Prajñanananda Giri

Born in 1960 in Cuttack, district of Orissa, India, Triloki Dash was a sincere seeker of Truth since childhood. After completing his post-graduate degree in economics, he left for the Himalayas and met many saints and visited many ashrams. But his spiritual hunger remained unsatiated. Returning to Orissa, he became a professor of economics who not only taught his subject, but also guided and inspired his students spiritually.

While a student he met his master Paramahamsa Hariharanandaji at the Karar Ashram in Puri and learned the marvelous technique of Kriya Yoga under his guidance. The divine master guided, shaped, and transformed his life into a sincere follower of the Kriya Yoga path.

An accomplished orator, philosopher, scholar of scriptures, author and editor of many books, proficient in many languages, highly advanced in Kriya Yoga practice, and a truly young reflection of his master, Swami Prajñanananda is currently teaching and propagating the authentic and original Kriya Yoga in the East and West. His brain power is remarkable, and he is deeply versed in all of the world's scriptures—Vedas, Upanishads, Patanjali Sutras, Brahmasutras, Bible, Koran, and so forth. He is Paramahamsa Hariharananda's designated spiritual successor.

Current Books on Kriya Yoga:

Kriya Yoga: The Scientific Process of Soul Culture and Essence of All Religions, 5th revised edition, by Paramahamsa Hariharananda

Isha Upanishad: The Ever New Metaphorical Interpretation for Soul Culture, by Paramahamsa Hariharananda

Bhagavad Gita in the Light of Kriya Yoga—Book One (Chapters 1–6), by Paramahamsa Hariharananda

The Bible, The Torah and Kriya Yoga: Metaphorical Explanation of the Torah and the New Testament in the Light of Kriya Yoga, by Swami Prajñanananda Giri in consultation with Paramahamsa Hariharananda

Words of Wisdom: Stories and Parables of Paramahamsa Hariharananda, compiled by Swami Prajñanananda Giri

Nectar Drops: Sayings of Paramahamsa Hariharananda, compiled by Swami Prajñanananda Giri

Babaji: The Eternal Light of God, by Swami Prajñanananda Giri

---

To be Released at a Later Date:

Bhagavad Gita in the Light of Kriya Yoga—Book Three (Chapters 13–18), by Paramahamsa Hariharananda

Lahiri Mahasaya: Fountainhead of Kriya Yoga, by Swami Prajñanananda Giri

Swami Shriyukteshwar Giri: Life and Teachings (working title), by Swami Prajñanananda Giri

Jñana Shankalini Tantra in the Light of Kriya Yoga (working title), by Swami Prajñanananda Giri